MORNING LIGHT

366
DEVOTIONAL THOUGHTS
from the Old Testament Books
of the Law, History, and Prophets

PUBLISHED BY
HELP4U PUBLICATIONS
CHESTERTON, IN

HELP4U
PUBLICATIONS

Morning Light: Devotional Thoughts from the Old Testament Books of the Law, History, and Prophets
by David J. Olson
Copyright©2017 by David J. Olson

ISBN 978-1-940089-39-3

Library of Congress Control Number: 2017918585

www.help4Upublications.com

Credits: Cover Photo from Canstockphoto.com

All rights reserved. No part of this publication may be reproduced or transmitted in any form, except for brief quotation in review, without written permission from the publisher.

All Scripture quotations are from the *King James Bible*.

DEDICATION

To my wonderful wife, Lisa –
Thank you for your faithfulness, prayers, and encouragement.
I'm so glad the Lord put us together!
"Two are better than one…"

"Two are better than one; because they have a good reward for their labour" (Ecclesiastes 4:9).

PREFACE

A few years ago, the Lord led me to write *Daily Light*—a daily devotional which takes the reader through the entire New Testament and provides a practical thought from each day's reading. The response to the book by both mature Christians and new converts was overwhelming. Soon, people began requesting that I write another devotional—one through the Old Testament. Though I thought it was a good idea, I was preoccupied with other writing projects. When I began seeking the Lord's direction for my next book, He clearly led me to begin work on *Morning Light*.

With great anticipation, I began searching for helpful lessons from the Old Testament in my morning devotional time. More than ever before, I looked forward to my time in the Old Testament. I was confident that the Lord would give me a practical thought from each day's reading. I knew that even in the genealogies hidden gems were waiting to be discovered. I soon realized that this project was more for my benefit than anyone else's. It is my hope that others can glean from what the Lord has shown me.

This book is designed to provide the reader with a schedule to read through the Old Testament books of the Law, History, and Prophets in a year's time. Such a goal can be accomplished by reading the passage indicated in each day's heading. Additionally, at least one practical thought from the daily reading provides either a challenge or promise for the day.

While devotional books can provide understanding of the Scripture, they must never become a substitute for personal Bible reading. As you seek the Lord through His Word, He will teach you lessons that the pages of a book like this could never provide.

INTRODUCTION

Let's face it; there are some difficult passages in the Old Testament. Perhaps that is the reason that most Christians seem to be more familiar with the New Testament than they are with the Old Testament. It seems that some people are intimidated by books such as Leviticus, Ezekiel, and the Minor Prophets and shy away from them. However, Peter said that we should *"be mindful of the words which were spoken before by the holy prophets"* (2 Peter 3:2). In order to be mindful of their words, we must take the time to read and study them. While *Morning Light* is not a commentary per say, it does shed light on many challenging portions of Scripture.

The Old Testament should never be considered irrelevant or impractical. In fact, it sets the stage for the events in the New Testament. The better one grasps the Old Testament, the better he will understand the New Testament. Many foundational truths and practical lessons are contained in the Old Testament. To ignore them would be to shortchange one's self of God's counsel and direction. As believers, we need *"all the counsel of God"* (Acts 20:27).

Perhaps you are like many others—you want to know more about the Old Testament but need a little guidance. Well, this book is for you. My goal in writing *Morning Light* was to provide one practical thought from an assigned daily reading schedule through most of the Old Testament. Admittedly, some passages lend themselves more easily to personal application than others. However, we must not neglect the richness and fullness of God's Word. After all, Paul reminds us, *"All scripture is given by inspiration of God, and is profitable"* (2 Timothy 3:16). Therefore, we must conclude that every portion of Scripture has significance and can provide instruction. With that in mind, my hope is that you will be challenged to search for truths in portions of Scripture that you may have previously overlooked. Allow *Morning Light* to stir your interest to seek for spiritual nuggets of your own.

If you plan on reading the Bible through in a year, a convenient schedule is located in the back of this book. May the Lord bless you as you seek His guidance in your daily time with Him!

Dave Olson
December, 2017

"Unto the upright there ariseth light in the darkness" (Psalm 112:4).

GOD REVEALED

"In the beginning God created the heaven and the earth" (Genesis 1:1).

The first chapter of the Bible reveals much to us about God. Consider the *preeminence* of God—He was in *"the beginning."* Since He was first, He is supreme. Many who reject the Bible primarily do so because they refuse to submit themselves to Almighty God.

Notice also the *Person* of God. The word *God* is translated from the Hebrew word *Elohim*, which is plural. This reveals the plurality of the One true God, providing a foundation for the doctrine of the Trinity later revealed in Scripture. The use of the pronouns *us* and *our* also support this—*"And God said, Let us make man in our image, after our likeness"* (1:26). The Lord is a personal God who has revealed much about Himself to those who are willing to study His Word.

The *power* of God is also described—*"God created the heaven and the earth."* The beauty and complexity of the earth, sky, and space are all the handiwork of God. Six times in chapter one we read, *"And God said...and it was so."* What He declares always comes to pass! As we start a New Year, determine to search for and claim every available promise in the Bible. The Creator still desires to display His power to us.

THE FIRST SIN

"And the eyes of them both were opened" (Genesis 3:7).

Much can be learned from man's first sin. For starters, sin often involves *deception*. The devil is crafty—*"the serpent beguiled Eve through his subtilty"* (2 Corinthians 11:3). Since the fall, man has been deceived not only by Satan but also by his own heart—*"The heart is deceitful above all things, and desperately wicked"* (Jeremiah 17:9). Don't trust your heart! Next, notice that sin is a *decision*—*"she took of the fruit thereof, and did eat, and gave also unto her husband with her; and he did eat"* (3:6). Nobody forced Adam and Eve to disobey God. Sin is a choice.

After sin comes *disgrace*. We read, *"they knew that they were naked."* Your conscience will bother you as theirs did. Their efforts to cover their shame were unacceptable to God, teaching us not to trust self-reformation. Sin brings *dread*—they *"hid themselves from the presence of the LORD"* (3:8). Thankfully, God provided *deliverance*. He made *"coats of skins, and clothed them"* (3:21). We, too, must accept the covering that God offers for our sins through Jesus. Though Adam and Eve escaped eternal damnation, they were exiled from the Garden of Eden, proving that sin brings *discipline* and loss. Beware!

| JAN. 3 | GOD IS CONCERNED | GEN. 5-6 |

"And God looked upon the earth, and, behold, it was corrupt; for all flesh had corrupted his way upon the earth" (Genesis 6:12).

Unlike what the deist believes, God is very much involved with His creation. He is ever looking at the activities and affairs of men. What did He see in Noah's day? *"And GOD saw that the wickedness of man was great in the earth"* (6:5). We can rest assured that He sees our sins too! Nobody can escape the all-seeing eye of the Lord.

We also observe that God was disturbed by the actions of men— *"And it repented the LORD that he had made man on the earth, and it grieved him at his heart"* (6:6). Our wicked ways cause pain and grief in the heart of a loving God who longs to fellowship with us and bless us. God repented, meaning that He changed how He would deal with His creation. Instead of bestowing His goodness upon it, He decided to destroy it. Remember that your actions can change how God treats you!

Thankfully, we also notice that God extends grace. *"Noah found grace in the eyes of the LORD"* (6:8). Since God is no respecter of persons, we can find favor too. Let us follow the example of Noah who *"was a just man"* and *"walked with God"* (6:9). God still gives grace.

| JAN. 4 | SAFE IN THE ARK | GEN. 7-8 |

"And every living substance was destroyed which was upon the face of the ground...and Noah only remained alive, and they that were with him in the ark" (Genesis 7:23).

The ark provides a picture of salvation granted through Christ. Jesus offers deliverance from God's judgment upon sin as did the ark. Noah and his family were spared death and *"remained alive"* because they entered the ark. We escape eternal hell by trusting Jesus to save us.

Notice the *invitation* made to Noah—*"Come thou and all thy house into the ark"* (7:1). When Jesus called people to salvation, He spoke similar words—*"Come unto me"* (Matthew 11:28). Those who want a relationship with the Lord only need to respond to His call. Consider the *acceptance* of God's offer. The Lord said, *"Come,"* and *"Noah went in"* (7:7). Salvation is quite simple. We must repent and go to the Savior.

Once we respond to Christ's call, we are *sealed*. Noah was safe in the ark because *"the LORD shut him in"* (7:16). As Noah was sheltered from the flood, Christ protects us from eternal judgment. We have no need to fear. Jesus keeps us saved! If you have received Christ as your Savior, you have His promise—*"him that cometh to me I will in no wise cast out"* (John 6:37). Like Noah, let's warn others of coming judgment.

GEN. 9-10 — FINISH WELL — JAN. 5

"And he drank of the wine, and was drunken; and he was uncovered within his tent" (Genesis 9:21).

Noah was a great man, but one of his last recorded acts in Scripture is terribly sad. Before the flood, he had lived an exemplary life— *"Noah was a just man and perfect in his generations, and Noah walked with God"* (Genesis 6:9). Of all the inhabitants of the world, only he and his family escaped destruction. He was a man of faith (Hebrews 11:7).

Further, Noah took a stand against the wickedness of his day and was *"a preacher of righteousness"* (2 Peter 2:5). There is no doubt that he was ridiculed and mocked by his wicked generation, but he faithfully served God for one hundred years as he prepared the ark. How sad to see Noah stumble after living such a life of sacrifice and service!

What can we learn from the account of Noah's drunkenness? First, past victories do not make us invincible. Second, it does not matter how much we have previously done for God, we are still susceptible to sin. Third, serving the Lord faithfully for many years does not grant us a free pass to indulge in sin. Fourth, we cannot let our guard down until the day we die. Fifth, sin can hinder our future. Though Noah lived for another 350 years, the Bible records no further acts of service.

GEN. 11-12 — FAITH FOLLOWS — JAN. 6

"Now the LORD had said unto Abram, Get thee out of thy country, and from thy kindred, and from thy father's house, unto a land that I will shew thee…So Abram departed, as the LORD had spoken unto him" (Genesis 12:1, 4).

Following God is not always easy. Abram was instructed to leave his homeland and family. For many, leaving the comforts and security of home for "the unknown" can be one of the hardest things they could ever imagine doing. The Lord had not shown Abram where to go but simply said, *"I will shew thee."* To pack up and leave with no definite direction would be a challenge indeed! However, Abram believed God would guide him—*"By faith…he went out, not knowing whither he went"* (Hebrews 11:8).

The Lord often leads us one step at a time. Abram was not shown the next step until he had taken the first. We should learn from his example to follow God by faith *"not knowing"* what our next step will be. If we are willing to move in the direction God nudges us, we can be assured that He will reveal more of His will. As God rewarded Abram, He will reward us too. Only be careful not to demand to know the second step before you take the first. Follow by faith!

JAN. 7	STRONG CHARACTER	GEN. 13-15

"And when Abram heard that his brother was taken captive, he armed his trained servants...and pursued them" (Genesis 14:14).

Trouble often reveals much about a man's character. Those who are spiritual will handle their trials well. How do you react to problems? Let's consider how Abram responded and see how we compare.

When contention arose between the herdmen of Abram and Lot, Abram was *civil—"Let there be no strife...between me and thee"* (13:8). Instead of finding fault or arguing, he sought to make peace. If your first reaction is to retaliate when a problem arises, your character needs help.

Later, when Lot was taken captive by a confederacy of kings, Abram proved to be *courageous—"he armed his trained servants...and pursued them"* (14:14). Imagine the bravery it took to chase an army with only 318 men at your disposal! How do you react when the odds are against you? The fact that Abram had *"trained servants"* shows that he was *conscientious.* He had foresight to prepare for trouble before it came. Do you often find yourself unprepared when trials come?

To develop strong character like Abram, perhaps it's time to cultivate a prayer life like he had. *"Abram called on the name of the LORD"* (13:4). Prayer changes things. Ask God to build your character.

JAN. 8	WAIT UPON THE LORD	GEN. 16-17

"Now Sarai Abram's wife bare him no children: and she had an handmaid, an Egyptian, whose name was Hagar" (Genesis 16:1).

How convenient! Abram wanted children, his wife was not able to bare any, and another woman just happened to be available to meet the need. The arrangement may have seemed appealing, but it was disastrous. Following human reasoning rather than God's will is a recipe for sin. The world's wisdom *"is earthly, sensual, devilish"* (James 3:15).

The Lord had previously promised to give Abram a son, and he believed God (15:4-6). However, after ten years of waiting, no child came, and he lost hope. His wife suggested Hagar as an option, and instead of reassuring her that God would keep His promise, he *"hearkened to the voice of Sarai"* (16:2). This reminds us that our weak faith prevents us from helping those who depend upon us.

Instead of trusting God to fulfill His promise, Abram took matters into his own hands and *"went in unto Hagar, and she conceived"* (16:4). This left lasting consequences. Strife arose between Sarai and Hagar, the wild man Ishmael was born, and Abram had to wait another fourteen years to receive his promised son. Sin always leaves scars. Therefore, wait upon the Lord instead of taking the convenient but sinful way.

GEN. 18-19   DON'T DOUBT GOD'S PROMISES   JAN. 9

"And he said, I will certainly return unto thee according to the time of life; and, lo, Sarah thy wife shall have a son" (Genesis 18:10).

The Lord is merciful. Despite Abram's debacle with Hagar, God changed his name to Abraham, meaning "father of many nations." The Lord had not withdrawn His *promise* of an heir. In fact, He clearly stated three times that Sarah would have a son (17:19; 18:10, 14). How many times does God have to say, *"I will"* before you believe?

What made the promise difficult to believe was their *problem*— *"Abraham and Sarah were old and well stricken in age; and it ceased to be with Sarah after the manner of women"* (18:11). Humanly speaking, it was not possible for them to have children. This led to Sarah's doubt and her consequent laughter at the notion of having a son. When God confronted her, she denied laughing. Unfortunately, we often act like Sarah, either doubting the Lord or covering up one sin with another.

Though their situation was impossible, God reminded them of His unfailing *power*. He asked, *"Is any thing too hard for the LORD?"* (18:14). Obviously, the answer was no. When God makes a promise to you, don't dwell on seemingly hopeless circumstances. Remember His great power! Abraham and Sarah ultimately had faith, and so can you.

GEN. 20-21   WHAT'S WRONG WITH YOU?   JAN. 10

"What aileth thee, Hagar? fear not; for God hath heard the voice of the lad where he is" (Genesis 21:17).

Hagar's situation was desperate. She and her son had been driven away from Abraham's home and were in danger of dying of thirst in the wilderness. Hagar cried out, *"Let me not see the death of the child"* and began weeping (21:16). She lost hope and was in despair.

It was at this point that God sent an angel to speak to her, saying, *"What aileth thee, Hagar?"* The modern-day equivalent would be, "What's wrong with you?" In light of her situation, that question almost seems insensitive. However, if Hagar just sat there and did nothing, they were both going to die. She needed to be confronted, not only comforted.

Though Hagar's trouble was serious, she had forgotten God's earlier promise that her son would grow to manhood (16:6-14). That would not have happened if he had died in the wilderness. As we have seen before, our faith in God's promises will often be tested by problems.

After getting Hagar's attention and reiterating His promise, *"God opened her eyes, and she saw a well of water"* (21:19). The well was there the entire time, but she had failed to see it. A lack of faith causes us to miss many blessings. When trouble comes, look for God's help.

JAN. 11   PASSING GOD'S TESTS   GEN. 22-23

"And it came to pass...that God did tempt Abraham" (Genesis 22:1).

In many cases, the word *tempt* refers to a solicitation to do evil. However, in this instance, it means "to test." God tested Abraham to see if he truly feared Him. Abraham was commanded to give up what was dear to him, which shows that the Lord wants our love for Him to exceed our affection for any other thing or person. We find two keys in this passage that will help us when we are tested by God.

The first key is *obedience*. How did Abraham respond to the sobering command to sacrifice his son? He *"rose up early in the morning...and went unto the place of which God had told him"* (22:3). If we ever hope to pass God's tests, we will have to do as Abraham and obey willingly and swiftly, regardless of the cost.

Another key is *faith*. When Isaac inquired about the lamb for the offering, Abraham responded, *"My son, God will provide himself a lamb"* (22:8). He fully expected to descend from the mountain with his son, believing that God could raise Isaac from the dead if necessary (Hebrews 11:17-19). It was not until Abraham reached for the knife that God provided a substitute for his son. Jehovah-jireh saw Abraham's faith and provided for his need. Oh, to have such unwavering faith!

JAN. 12   A FAITHFUL SERVANT   GEN. 24

"And he said unto me, The LORD, before whom I walk, will send his angel with thee, and prosper thy way" (Genesis 24:40).

Abraham's servant was given the important task of finding a bride for Isaac from the country and kindred of Abraham. The account provides some practical lessons about being a faithful servant.

First, remember God's provision—*"The LORD God of heaven...shall send his angel before thee"* (24:7). When God instructs us to do something, He also provides heavenly assistance to accomplish it.

Next, pray specifically—*"O LORD...I pray thee, send me good speed this day"* (24:12). The servant expected help that very day, and he got it. Amazingly, the answer came *"before he had done speaking"* (24:15). Notice also that God loves to answer requests made on behalf of others.

Third, praise God for His help. When the servant realized God had led him and answered his prayer, he *"bowed down his head, and worshipped"* (24:26). Never forget to thank God for all He does.

Finally, do what you know is right. You cannot expect God to reveal more of His will if you are not faithful to do what has already been revealed. The servant testified, *"I being in the way, the LORD led me"* (24:27). When we are going in the right way, God will lead us.

GEN. 25-26 — THE PLACE OF GOD'S BLESSING — JAN. 13

"And it came to pass after the death of Abraham, that God blessed his son Isaac; and Isaac dwelt by the well Lahairoi" (Genesis 25:11).

Isaac was blessed living by the well. *Lahoiroi* means "the well of him that lives and sees me." Oh, if we all lived in a state where we realize that God lives and sees us! Where God is present, blessings abound. Isaac had already been dwelling by the well when God gave him his wife (24:62-67). After his father had died, he realized the importance of continuing where God had already blessed him. Unlike Isaac, many people often look to move on to bigger and better opportunities with no regard for God's will. Until God directs us otherwise, it is best to stay in the place that His blessings are manifested.

Years later, a famine entered the land, and Isaac went to the king in Gerar. When the Lord appeared to him, He straightly charged, *"Sojourn in this land, and I will be with thee, and will bless thee"* (26:3). With the promise of God's presence and provision, Isaac remained there. He had already learned the importance of dwelling where God wanted him. What was the result? That year, Isaac planted in that land and reaped a bountiful harvest (26:12). Even in a famine, God can provide when we are obedient to Him. Stay close to the Lord, and your needs will be met.

GEN. 27 — LET GOD BE GOD — JAN. 14

"Now therefore, my son, obey my voice according to that which I command thee" (Genesis 27:8).

Before Jacob and Esau were born, God promised their mother that *"the elder shall serve the younger"* (25:23). As Isaac approached the end of his life, he determined to bless Esau, which Rebekah feared would have rendered God's promise void. So, Rebekah plotted with her younger son Jacob to deceive Isaac and steal the blessing from Esau.

What can we learn from this account? Let God be God. Since the Lord said that Esau would serve Jacob, it was bound to happen. Rebekah and Jacob should have exercised faith and trusted that God would bring to pass His plan in His timing. The blessing did not have to be stolen for God to accomplish His will.

It is never right to do wrong in order to produce a good outcome. If you have to break one of God's commandments to fulfill His will, either the thing was never God's will in the first place or you lack the faith to let Him do His job. Too often we think we have to help God.

Jacob reaped for his actions and fled for his life, living in fear for years. We will also suffer miserably for our self-willed actions. Be careful not to allow others, even family, to influence you to disobey God.

JAN. 15	GOD SEES YOUR AFFLICTION	GEN. 28-29

"And when the LORD saw that Leah was hated, he opened her womb: but Rachel was barren" (Genesis 29:31).

Mankind's selfishness is on full display in today's reading. First, *"Esau seeing that the daughters of Canaan pleased not Isaac his father"* went and married one of Ishmael's daughters (28:8-9). He acted out of spite towards his father. Next, we find Laban deceiving Jacob by giving him Leah to wife instead of Rachel. In each instance, people were hurt. Isaac was grieved because of Esau's actions, and Jacob was upset by Laban's underhandedness.

Our text speaks of another who was afflicted by selfish dealings— *"Leah was hated."* Selfishness always affects innocent people. Jacob had married Leah but did not love her. What a comfort it must have been when Leah realized that *"the LORD saw"* her plight and rewarded her with children! She acknowledged His blessing saying, *"Surely the LORD hath looked upon my affliction"* (29:32). When her fourth son was born, she said, *"Now will I praise the LORD"* (29:35).

Rest assured that if you are in a similar predicament, being wrongfully mistreated, God also sees your trouble. As He helped Leah, He will encourage you too. Take time to praise God for His aid.

JAN. 16	GO TO GOD FIRST	GEN. 30

"And she called his name Joseph; and said, The LORD shall add to me another son" (Genesis 30:24).

Rachel wanted children and demanded of Jacob, *"Give me children, or else I die"* (30:1). This she said because she *"envied her sister"* (30:1). Her motive was wrong; therefore, her method was wrong too. Always remember that selfish desires tend to lead to sinful actions.

Surely, her longing for a child was not bad, but Rachel's streak of envy led her to contention with her husband. Years later, Rachel did what she should have done in the first place. She went to God requesting a son. *"And God remembered Rachel, and God hearkened to her, and opened her womb"* (30:22).

Learn to bring all your burdens to the Lord first. Taking matters into your own hands leads to a barren and fruitless life. Rachel finally learned to exercise faith. She called her firstborn son Joseph, whose name means "adding." She was convinced that God would give her another son, which He did. Christians often plot, scheme, fuss, and feud to get what they want. If we would learn to simply cast our cares upon the Lord, we could avoid many prolonged heartaches. Don't forget that *"ye have not, because ye ask not"* (James 4:2). You can ask right now!

GEN. 31 — GO WHEN GOD SAYS TO GO — JAN. 17

"And the LORD said unto Jacob, Return unto the land of thy fathers, and to thy kindred; and I will be with thee" (Genesis 31:3).

It was time for Jacob to return to Canaan. Though he had heard the murmurings of Laban's sons and sensed the displeasure of Laban, he did not flee because of fear. It was because *"the LORD said...Return."* Jacob had served Laban for twenty years and been deceived by him repeatedly, but he did not leave until God directed him. When we find ourselves in a trying situation, it is best to stay put until God says, "Go."

The Lord's command to depart was tied to a promise—*"I will be with thee."* How comforting to know that when the Lord changes our surroundings He will also be there to sustain us. Never be afraid to follow His guidance.

God sent Jacob back to Canaan because He planned to multiply and bless his offspring there. The Lord reminded Jacob of the vow he had made years before while in Bethel. *"And Jacob vowed a vow, saying, If God will be with me...then shall the LORD be my God"* (Genesis 28:20-21). Realizing that God had been with him, Jacob wanted to continue to enjoy His presence. So, he returned to Canaan. Don't miss God's special presence and blessing by failing to follow Him.

GEN. 32-33 — TESTED FAITH — JAN. 18

"And he said, Thy name shall be called no more Jacob, but Israel: for as a prince hast thou power with God and with men, and hast prevailed" (Genesis 32:28).

It is easy to have faith when the sea of life is calm, but once troublesome waves threaten us, it is often a different story. Jacob had left Padanaram at the commandment of God and was assured of the Lord's protection. In fact, *"the angels of God met him"* (32:1). He even named the place Mahanaim, which means "two hosts," acknowledging that God's armies were traveling with his group. All was well so far.

When Jacob heard that Esau was travelling to meet him with four hundred men, he was *"greatly afraid and distressed"* (32:7). God had sent a trial to test and strengthen his faith, and it worked. Though Jacob faltered at first, he soon went to prayer and reminded God of His promise to multiply his seed. When troubled, we ought to find a promise and pray as Jacob did, *"thou saidst, I will surely..."* (32:12).

Jacob's faith was further strengthened and rewarded when he prayed, *"I will not let thee go, except thou bless me"* (32:26). Instead of a disastrous reunion with Esau, there was a delightful one. When God tests your faith, don't let go of Him. You will prevail through prayer.

JAN. 19	GET BACK TO BETHEL	GEN. 34-35

"And God said unto Jacob, Arise, go up to Bethel, and dwell there: and make there an altar unto God" (Genesis 35:1).

Jacob and his family were in disarray. His daughter, Dinah, was defiled shortly after desiring to *"see the daughters of the land"* (34:1). Her decision to be with the heathen appears to have led to her demise. Instead of dealing with the transgression against Dinah personally, Jacob remained silent while his sons handled it. Though rightfully upset, his sons reacted wrongly, deceiving and murdering the men of the city. Jacob's only concern seemed to be how their actions affected him. He said, *"Ye have troubled me to make me to stink among the inhabitants of the land"* (34:30). What a dysfunctional, carnal family they had become! They were in the land of blessing but were not prepared to be blessed.

What was God's solution for their lack of spirituality? He said to Jacob, *"Arise, go up to Bethel, and dwell there: and make there an altar unto God."* *Bethel* means "the house of God." It was time for Jacob and his family to dwell in God's presence and return to true worship. Then, they could experience His full blessing. Have you gotten out of sorts and begun to live selfishly? Do as Jacob did—*"Put away the strange gods that are among you"* and spend time with God once again (35:2).

JAN. 20	GENERATIONS TO COME	GEN. 36

"Now these are the generations of Esau, who is Edom" (Genesis 36:1).

Esau settled in the region south of the Dead Sea. He and his descendants inhabited the land of Edom. Because *"Esau took his wives of the daughters of Canaan"* his posterity was adversely affected (36:2). When carnal men choose worldly women, their children will not be raised in the fear of the Lord. His sin not only affected himself but his offspring. We must all realize that our fleshly decisions will impact the generations to come.

The entire populace of the land of Edom suffered because of Esau. In fact, the prophets record a future judgment on Edom because of his sin. God said, *"I will bring the calamity of Esau upon him"* (Jeremiah 49:8). The entire book of Obadiah discusses the coming judgment of Edom. Esau's negative influence has spanned thousands of years.

Let us be careful to live well, marry well, and raise our children well. Our foolish, fleshly decisions can impact many generations to come. Though Esau's brother Jacob was not perfect, he was mentioned in the "hall of faith" in the book of Hebrews. Through Jacob's seed came the Messiah, proving that faith makes a difference in our descendants. The decisions we make today will affect time and eternity. Choose wisely!

GEN. 37-38 — FAITHFUL IN ADVERSITY — JAN. 21

"And Joseph dreamed a dream, and he told it his brethren: and they hated him yet the more" (Genesis 37:5).

Many lessons can be learned from the life of Joseph by observing his sterling testimony in times of affliction. Perhaps the greatest character trait in his life was faithfulness. When his brothers had acted wickedly while feeding the flock, Joseph was bound by duty to tell his father (37:2). Certainly, that didn't go over well. Jacob's favoritism did not help matters either. However, despite the pressure of wanting to be accepted by his brothers, Joseph refused to act like them.

Joseph's brothers hated him, but when he shared the dreams God had given him, it only made the situation worse—*"they hated him yet the more."* Though it seemed like Joseph was punished for doing what was right, he never quit. When sent by his father to check on his brothers' welfare, it led to even greater adversity. This serves to remind us that following God is not always easy. In fact, it may lead to great hardship.

Another interesting point to consider is that God is the One who sent Joseph to Egypt as a slave (Psalm 105:17-19). Joseph maintained a good attitude and never wavered in spite of difficulty. How faithful are you? Do you willingly serve God at any cost, or are you quick to complain?

GEN. 39-40 — GOD'S PRESENCE — JAN. 22

"...the LORD was with him, and that which he did, the LORD made it to prosper" (Genesis 39:23).

Yesterday we noted that God sent Joseph into affliction. Today we see that *"the LORD was with him."* To make certain that we don't miss the point, God stated it four times in the chapter. What a consolation to know that God never leaves us or forsakes us!

Instead of fighting against God's plan for his life, Joseph welcomed it. In return, the Lord blessed him. Though your circumstances may be difficult, learn to accept them. If you make the best of your situation as Joseph did, you can be blessed like he was.

Notice three things God's presence does. First, it *prospers*—*"the LORD made all that he did to prosper in his hand"* (39:3). We can enjoy great success despite affliction. Second, God's presence *promotes*—Joseph began as a slave, but Potiphar *"made him overseer in his house"* (39:5). This teaches us that if we remain faithful to God, He can lift us up. Third, the presence of God *protects*. Though tempted by the provocative wife of Potiphar, Joseph escaped because he remembered God's presence. He exclaimed, *"how then can I do this great wickedness, and sin against God?"* (39:9). Remember God's presence!

JAN. 23   NOT FORGOTTEN   GEN. 41

"For God hath caused me to be fruitful in the land of my affliction"
(Genesis 41:52).

The closing words of chapter forty read, *"Yet did not the chief butler remember Joseph, but forgat him."* Though Joseph had served faithfully in prison for a crime he did not commit, he was forgotten by the one he had helped. Thankfully, God had not forgotten him. The Lord can make all things turn out right in the end. Notice how Joseph's humility led to honor and hope.

Joseph was *humble*. When asked to interpret Pharaoh's dreams, Joseph did not say, "I can do that." Instead, he responded, *"It is not in me: God shall give Pharaoh an answer of peace"* (41:16). Like Joseph, when we serve God, we should look up for help, not within. The Bible says *"before honour is humility"* (Proverbs 18:12). Since Joseph was humble, he was *honored.* Pharaoh promoted him and *"made him ruler over all the land of Egypt"* (41:43). Remain humble so that God can exalt you. Finally, Joseph's afflictions turned to *hope—"For God, said he, hath made me forget all my toil...God hath caused me to be fruitful in the land of my affliction"* (41:51-52). Stay faithful to God in your present trial and soon you will be able to forget your troubles too.

JAN. 24   HOW IS YOUR OUTLOOK?   GEN. 42-43

"Joseph's brethren came, and bowed down themselves before him with their faces to the earth" (Genesis 42:6).

Today's reading shows different ways people view problems. Let's consider Joseph and his family and see how their relationships with the Lord affected their outlook on life.

Joseph saw beyond problems. It took twenty years, but God's promise that his brothers would bow down to him came to pass. Like Joseph, we must keep our eyes on God's promises, not our problems.

Joseph's brethren saw problems as punishment. When things went wrong for them they said, *"We are verily guilty concerning our brother...therefore is this distress come upon us"* (42:21). For years they carried around the guilt of what they had done to Joseph, and they believed God was punishing them for their sin (42:28). Failure to deal with your sin can leave you guilt-ridden and defeated.

Jacob viewed problems as personal attacks. He cried out, *"Me have ye bereaved of my children...all these things are against me"* (42:36). In reality, God was for him. The Lord had sent Joseph to Egypt to save Jacob's family from hunger, but Jacob's selfishness had blinded him from seeing God's goodness. How do you see problems?

GEN. 44-45 — REPENTANCE MAKES A DIFFERENCE — JAN. 25

"Joseph could not refrain himself...And Joseph said unto his brethren, I am Joseph; doth my father yet live? And his brethren could not answer him; for they were troubled at his presence" (Genesis 45:1, 3).

Up to this point, Joseph had helped his brethren but had been harsh with them. It appears that he had hoped to bring Benjamin to be with him and may have sent his other brothers away with provision for their families. What caused him to finally reveal his true identity? He noticed a change in one of his brothers.

Judah demonstrated two traits of repentance—confession and concern. He confessed, *"God hath found out the iniquity of thy servants"* (44:16). Then he displayed a true burden for the welfare of his father. In order to spare his father grief, Judah was willing to become a slave in Benjamin's place. It was after Joseph observed a change in Judah's life that he *"could not refrain himself...And he wept"* (45:1-2).

Two great lessons are provided for us. First, those who have strayed from God for many years can still repent. Second, when people are seeking to turn from their sin, we should help and comfort them. Joseph forgave them and sought to relieve them saying, *"Now therefore be not grieved, nor angry with yourselves... for God did send me"* (45:5).

GEN. 46-47 — SEEK THE LORD — JAN. 26

"And Israel took his journey with all that he had, and came to Beersheba, and offered sacrifices unto the God of his father Isaac" (Genesis 46:1).

As Israel began his journey to Egypt, he took time to worship God. Instead of rushing toward his happy reunion with his son, he paused to acknowledge the One who had given him the blessing. When the Lord blesses you, be sure that you are more excited with the Giver than the gift. Our hearts should be filled with praise and adoration to our heavenly Father for His great goodness to us.

Our reading for today also shows us an example of the truth mentioned in James 4:8, *"Draw nigh to God, and he will draw nigh to you."* Notice that after Israel offered sacrifices, *"God spake unto Israel"* (46:2). What a comfort to know that when we seek the Lord, He will speak to us!

In Israel's case, God promised three blessings. First, *protection*—*"fear not to go down into Egypt"* (46:3). Second, *prosperity*—*"I will there make of thee a great nation"* (46:3). Third, *presence*—*"I will go down with thee"* (46:4). Israel was able to journey with confidence because he prayed. What promises await you? Seek God and find out!

JAN. 27 — FOLLOW GOD DESPITE PROTESTS — GEN. 48-49

"And Joseph said unto his father, Not so, my father: for this is the firstborn; put thy right hand upon his head" (Genesis 48:18).

It was a custom to give the family blessing to the firstborn. Since Jacob took Joseph's two sons as his own, he was responsible for the blessing. When he blessed them, he placed his right hand on Ephraim. Why did he give the prominent blessing to the younger son? Was it because Jacob had received the blessing as the younger son and identified better with Ephraim? Was he simply being carnal and causing strife in the family?

We find the answer in Hebrews 11:21, *"By faith Jacob, when he was a dying, blessed both the sons of Joseph; and worshipped, leaning upon the top of his staff."* Though Jacob received his blessing by deceit, he gave this blessing by faith, believing that God had great plans for Ephraim. What a blessing to see Jacob living by faith in his later years!

When Joseph protested his father's actions, he cried out, *"Not so."* However, Jacob refused to hearken to him. Here is a lesson for us. When God leads contrary to conventional wisdom, move forward by faith. Others may criticize and oppose you, but you must be more concerned with pleasing God than your fellows. Never allow anyone to hinder you from fulfilling God's will.

JAN. 28 — FRUITS OF FORGIVENESS — GEN. 50

"Now therefore fear ye not: I will nourish you, and your little ones. And he comforted them, and spake kindly unto them" (Genesis 50:21).

After Jacob died, Joseph's brothers feared, thinking Joseph would take revenge on them. They schemed and sent a messenger to Joseph saying what amounted to, "Dad said you need to forgive us." It is obvious that some of the brothers had never fully dealt with their sin. We must be sure to confess our sins daily so we don't live in guilt and fear for years as these men did. How did Joseph react?

"Joseph wept when they spake unto him" (50:17). Why? He had already forgiven them, but they had not realized it. How that must have hurt! Rather than getting bitter, Joseph lovingly reassured them.

Notice the fruits of forgiveness. First, Joseph refused to take revenge, saying, *"Fear not: for am I in the place of God?"* (50:19). Second, he focused on God's plan rather than his problems. He said, *"But as for you, ye thought evil against me; but God meant it unto good"* (50:20). Third, he repaid evil with good—*"I will nourish you, and your little ones"* (50:21). Fourth, he extended mercy—*"he comforted them"* (50:21). Fifth, he *"spake kindly unto them"* (50:21). Are you willing to take these five steps to show forgiveness to others?

EXODUS 1-2 — FEAR GOD — JAN. 29

"But the midwives feared God, and did not as the king of Egypt commanded them, but saved the men children alive" (Exodus 1:17).

God blessed Israel, and they *"were fruitful, and increased abundantly"* (1:7). When a new Pharaoh rose to power, he felt threatened by the Jews and persecuted them. However, *"the more they afflicted them, the more they multiplied and grew"* (1:12). After his plan to persecute God's people backfired, Pharaoh issued the heinous command to kill all the newborn Hebrew boys. The midwives were straightly charged, *"if it be a son, then ye shall kill him"* (1:16).

What a tough position to be in! If the midwives disobeyed Pharaoh, their lives would be in jeopardy. Thankfully, they made the right choice and *"feared God, and did not as the king of Egypt commanded them."* They were more afraid of disobeying God. Never let the fear of man prevent you from obeying God. Like the apostles, we can reply to all who threaten us, *"We ought to obey God rather than men"* (Acts 5:29).

Sometimes it takes courage to exercise faith, and those who trust the Lord will be greatly rewarded. Notice that *"God dealt well with the midwives"* (1:20) because of their faithfulness to Him. He even made houses for them! Unimagined blessings await those who put God first.

EXODUS 3 — GOD'S DELIVERANCE — JAN. 30

"And the LORD said, I have surely seen the affliction of my people...And I am come down to deliver them" (Exodus 3:7-8).

Things were difficult for God's people, but the Lord had not forgotten them. Perhaps you are facing hardships of your own. Take comfort in knowing that God has a *plan* for your trouble. He told Moses, *"I have surely seen the affliction of my people...And I am come down to deliver them."* He sees your need, too, and intends to run to your aid at just the right time.

In chapter two, we read about God's *providence*—He miraculously spared Moses from certain death and provided him with tremendous favor, training, and opportunities in Pharaoh's house. Though separated from his family, Moses was alive and well. Little did he realize that God was preparing him for a special task. Always remember that God's plans take time; as the Great Architect, He never misses one detail or deadline.

Notice last of all, God's *promise*—*"I will bring you up out of the affliction...unto a land flowing with milk and honey"* (3:17). Circumstances would become challenging for Moses in the coming days, but God provided a promise on which to cling. Learn to look past your affliction and by faith envision the *"milk and honey"* that will follow.

| JAN. 31 | EMPTY EXCUSES | EXODUS 4-5 |

"Now therefore go, and I will be with thy mouth, and teach thee what thou shalt say" (Exodus 4:12).

At times, God may require of us things that make us uncomfortable or seem impossible. Moses found himself in such a situation. God had charged him to confront the tyrant Pharaoh. A feeling of inadequacy immediately overwhelmed him, causing him to cry, *"Who am I, that I should go unto Pharaoh, and that I should bring forth the children of Israel out of Egypt?"* (3:11). The Lord responded, *"Certainly I will be with thee"* (3:12). However, Moses still objected to God's plan.

His first excuse was, *"they will not believe me"* (4:1). Of course, he was wrong because later we read, *"the people believed"* (4:31). The second excuse involved his personal ability—*"I am not eloquent"* (4:10). To that God replied, *"go, and I will be with thy mouth"* (4:12). Moses continued to resist, but *"the anger of the LORD was kindled"* (4:14).

God took away every excuse from Moses. Though we may think we have legitimate complaints or concerns about God's plans for our lives, He always knows better. God does not need your natural ability, only your availability. His power always makes up for your weakness. Stop making excuses and obey, or you may also kindle God's wrath.

| FEB. 1 | BE PATIENT | EXODUS 6-7 |

"Then the LORD said unto Moses, Now shalt thou see what I will do to Pharaoh: for with a strong hand shall he let them go, and with a strong hand shall he drive them out of his land" (Exodus 6:1).

In chapter five, we saw that Moses obeyed the Lord and spoke to Pharaoh, but instead of things getting better for the people, they got worse. Moses became discouraged and prayed, *"why is it that thou hast sent me?"* (5:22). He reminded the Lord that Pharaoh had not let the people go but afflicted them more. He added, *"neither hast thou delivered thy people at all"* (5:23). Oh, how tempting it is to find fault with God's plans when things don't go the way we think they should!

When following the Lord, we must realize that things may get worse for a season before they get better. However, we can rest assured that as God worked on Moses' behalf, He will work on ours too. Moses had to wait on God's timing, but the Lord gave him a comforting promise to sustain him—*"Now shalt thou see what I will do to Pharaoh."* In like manner, if we wait on the Lord, we shall see what He will do.

Our duty is to follow His prescribed plan, even when deliverance seems doubtful. As we shall see, the Lord worked wonders for Moses and Israel. Can we expect Him to do anything less for us?

EXODUS 8-9 — REGRET OR REPENTANCE? — FEB. 2

"And Pharaoh...said unto them, I have sinned this time: the LORD is righteous, and I and my people are wicked" (Exodus 9:27).

Pharaoh begged Moses to intercede with God to remove the frogs from his land. God was merciful, but *"when Pharaoh saw that there was respite, he hardened his heart"* (8:15). The wicked ruler was only grieved by the consequences of his sin, not with the sin itself. We know this because as soon as relief came, his arrogant demeanor returned.

After God sent hail to judge Egypt, Pharaoh made a meaningless confession—*"I and my people are wicked. Intreat the LORD (for it is enough)"* (9:27-28). He had the right words, but we know that it was not *"enough"* to convince him to let Israel go because *"when Pharaoh saw that the rain and the hail and the thunders were ceased, he sinned yet more"* (9:34). People will say just about anything to get relief from the consequences of their sin; but as we have seen, not all confessions are heartfelt. Beware not to just pay lip service to God.

Repentance is not expressed by the mere regret of unfavorable circumstances. True repentance is evidenced by a change in actions. If you act sorry only until God's judgment is lifted and return to your sinful ways, you are no better than Pharaoh. Regret is not repentance.

EXODUS 10-11 — HOW LONG WILL YOU REFUSE? — FEB. 3

"How long wilt thou refuse to humble thyself before me?"
(Exodus 10:3).

We mark the eighth demand for Pharaoh to release the children of Israel. He had already witnessed disastrous judgments upon his land, but he had not humbled himself nor submitted to Almighty God. It is easy for us to recognize the foolishness of his actions, but are we not guilty of the same thing at times?

How many times does God have to tell you to do something before you finally obey? It can almost be expected that a heathen king may attempt to defy God, but it should be unheard of for one of His children to act that way.

Are you struggling to submit in some area of your life today? Hear God's words, *"How long wilt thou refuse to humble thyself before me?"* Disobedience will lead to judgment. Notice what God said to Pharaoh, *"if thou refuse to let my people go, behold, to morrow will I bring the locusts into thy coast"* (10:4). Pharaoh was promised more trouble if he continued to disobey. Consider God's warning to you if you remain stubborn—*"if thou refuse...to morrow will I..."* What thing might God have to do to get your attention? It is better to obey than to find out!

| FEB. 4 | SAVED BY THE BLOOD | EXODUS 12 |

"...when I see the blood, I will pass over you" (Exodus 12:13).

The tenth judgment on Pharaoh and his people was the most severe of all. *"And it came to pass, that at midnight the LORD smote all the firstborn in the land of Egypt"* (12:29). As a result, Pharaoh finally let Israel go. What an awful price to pay for stubborn rebellion!

Before God's great deliverance occurred, He established a memorial for the event through the feast of the Passover. It provides not only a remembrance of what the Lord did for Israel but also a picture of the salvation which Jesus provides for us. Like the Israelites were slaves in Egypt, the lost are in bondage to sin. The lamb *"without blemish"* represents the sinless Son of God. Years later, when John the Baptist saw Jesus coming to him, he declared, *"Behold the Lamb of God, which taketh away the sin of the world"* (John 1:29). Christ is the Passover.

In order for the children of Israel to be spared the judgment of death in their homes, they had to apply the blood of the lamb to the doorposts and lintel. In like manner, the blood of Jesus the Lamb must be applied to our lives in order to avoid the judgment of eternal death in the lake of fire. If you will repent and receive Jesus' payment for your evil deeds, God's words apply to you—*"when I see the blood, I will pass over you."*

| FEB. 5 | GOD'S WAY | EXODUS 13-14 |

"God led them not through the way of the land of the Philistines, although that was near" (Exodus 13:17).

God delivered His people from Egypt by *"strength of hand...from the house of bondage"* (13:14). His intentions were to bring them *"into the land of the Canaanites"* (13:11), but they were not quite ready to inherit the land. He knew that they would return to Egypt at the first sign of war. So, instead of taking them directly to Canaan, God led them on a long journey in which He would teach them many vital lessons.

The quickest way to Canaan was to travel on the road known as *The Way of the Philistines*. It was a direct route from Egypt, making it faster and easier than the way God chose to lead His people. From this we learn that God does not always choose the easiest or most convenient course for our lives. He knows best what we need. The path of ease often leads to failure, while the difficult way builds needed character.

We are most useful to God when we are properly prepared, and such preparation often comes through trials that He leads us to face. If the path you are travelling is not easy, don't get discouraged. Simply realize that God is making you fit to fulfill His will and enjoy His rich blessings.

EXODUS 15-16	NO NEED TO COMPLAIN	FEB. 6

"And the people murmured against Moses, saying, What shall we drink?" (Exodus 15:24).

Chapter fourteen closes on a high note—*"Israel saw that great work...feared the LORD, and believed the LORD"* (14:31). Then they sang a glorious song of praise, acknowledging God's hand in their victory. Things were going well until three days later. After a great victory came a great trial—*"they went three days in the wilderness, and found no water"* (15:22). What followed was a great failure—*"the people murmured"* (15:24).

God had led His people to Marah, but they could not drink the bitter water. At times, the will of God may seem disturbing or disagreeable at first. However, as God made the bitter waters sweet for Israel, He can turn our difficult situations into delightful blessings.

A short distance from Marah was Elim, *"where were twelve wells of water"* (15:27). God had plenty of water waiting for them! In fact, there was one well for each of the tribes. Instead of complaining, they should have followed God, trusting His timing. Never doubt God's ability to provide for your need. By faith, follow Him until the need is met!

EXODUS 17-18	WATER FROM THE ROCK	FEB. 7

"Behold, I will stand before thee there upon the rock in Horeb; and thou shalt smite the rock, and there shall come water out of it, that the people may drink" (Exodus 17:6).

God's people faced another trial—*"there was no water for the people to drink"* (17:1). As God had a purpose for the previous time they lacked water, He had a plan for this difficulty too. Unfortunately, the Israelites did not remember God's former provision, nor did they look to Him for deliverance. What was God intending to show them this time? Satisfaction only comes from Him.

Notice the *great need*—*"the people thirsted there for water; and the people murmured"* (17:3). Their thirst was more than physical as revealed by their complaining spirit. God showed *great mercy* toward them despite their sinful condition. He lovingly offers undeserved blessings. The smitten rock represents Christ Who was wounded for our transgressions, and the water symbolizes the Holy Spirit Who flows from the Savior to quench the thirst of our barren souls.

Are you in a spiritual dry spell? Look to Jesus. He offers forgiveness of sin and a sweet, refreshing filling of His Spirit. Ask for it.

FEB. 8   A PICTURE OF REDEMPTION   EXODUS 19-20

"Ye have seen what I did unto the Egyptians, and how I bare you on eagles' wings, and brought you unto myself" (Exodus 19:4).

Set before us today is a beautiful picture of God's redemption. The blood sacrifice of the Passover lamb brought a tender deliverance—*"on eagles' wings."* God's *purchase* is evident—*"I bare you...and brought you unto myself."* All who are saved must acknowledge that God owns them and submit to His leadership.

Accordingly, God has a *purpose* for His purchased people—*"ye shall be a peculiar treasure unto me"* (19:5). The Lord has a special plan for each of His children. To be in His family is a tremendous honor, but to be His treasure is especially astounding, considering our utter unworthiness.

It is fitting that God would seek to *protect* His prized possessions. That is why He told Moses to *"set bounds unto the people"* (19:12) that He might prevent them from certain destruction. The Ten Commandments that follow in the next chapter were also given to protect them from sin. Never forget that since God owns you, He can make the rules for your life and that the boundaries He sets are for your own good.

FEB. 9   RIGHT OR WRONG?   EXODUS 21-22

"Now these are the judgments which thou shalt set before them" (Exodus 21:1).

Israel was a nation living under a theocracy, meaning that God governed their affairs. In addition to the Ten Commandments given to Moses on Mt. Sinai, God also issued many other *"judgments"* to be *"set before them."* A judgment in the Bible is God's ruling on a matter. What a blessing to know that God gives His people guidelines for living.

Some of the judgments issued to Israel were solely for them as a nation. Others have moral implications that apply to all mankind, despite the age in which they live. Additionally, God's laws have served as a model to follow. In fact, many of our country's laws are based on the decrees originally given to Israel. For instance, the concept of capital punishment for murder is based upon verses such as Exodus 21:12, *"He that smiteth a man, so that he die, shall be surely put to death."*

As believers, we are not left to wonder how we should act in this life. The Lord has revealed through His Word judgments that allow us to know what He thinks about certain matters. When we want to know if something is right or wrong, all we need to do is consult the Scriptures.

| EXODUS 23-24 | MUCH-NEEDED REST | FEB. 10 |

"Six days thou shalt do thy work, and on the seventh day thou shalt rest: that thine ox and thine ass may rest, and the son of thy handmaid, and the stranger, may be refreshed" (Exodus 23:12).

God has reasons for each of His commands. Today, we see two practical purposes for the Jews to observe the Sabbath day. First, God wanted His people to rest—*"thou shalt rest."* A lack of rest not only puts undue stress on the body but also on the mind, and when a person is completely run-down it can adversely affect his spiritual state.

A second consideration gleaned from this verse is that rest brings refreshment. The Lord showed compassion on His people, their animals, and their servants by commanding them to observe a day of rest. His goal was that they *"may be refreshed."* Though a workaholic thinks he has no time for a break, he would find that his work would be more productive if he took time to be refreshed. Certainly God does not want us to be lazy, but He does expect us to take a breather on a regular basis.

Though the Sabbath was given to Israel, rest and refreshment are still important to us. Further, always regard the wellbeing of those under your care by ensuring they also take time to be refreshed.

| EXODUS 25-26 | DWELLING WITH MEN | FEB. 11 |

"And let them make me a sanctuary; that I may dwell among them" (Exodus 25:8).

The tabernacle was an elaborate tent that God instructed Moses to make where He would *"dwell among them."* It was a picture of Jesus who later *"was made flesh, and dwelt among us"* (John 1:14).

The ark was a chest topped with the mercy seat, containing the Ten Commandments. God promised, *"I will meet with thee, and I will commune with thee from above the mercy seat"* (25:22). The ark pictures Christ in several ways. Our only means of communing with God is through His Son. The acacia wood speaks of His humanity and the gold testifies of His deity—He was the God-man. The golden crown around the top of the ark shows that Christ is the King of kings.

The table of showbread pictures Christ as the Bread of Life. God commanded, *"set upon the table shewbread before me alway"* (25:30). This reminds us that Jesus is always available to hungry souls. The golden candlestick pictures Him as the Light of the world.

Praise God that He desires to dwell among His imperfect people for their betterment! Let's enjoy His presence, fellowship, and light today.

FEB. 12 — A PICTURE OF OUR PRIEST — EXODUS 27-28

"And thou shalt make holy garments for Aaron thy brother for glory and for beauty" (Exodus 28:2).

Aaron was chosen by God to be a priest. His job was to offer sacrifices in the tabernacle to atone for the sins of the people. Since the Law only provided *"a shadow of good things to come"* (Hebrews 10:1), such sacrifices pointed to a better sacrifice offered by a better Priest. Hebrews 4:14 reminds us that *"we have a great high priest, that is passed into the heavens, Jesus the Son of God."* Let's consider two ways that Aaron's garments reveal some qualities of Jesus as our Priest.

First, on the shoulders of the ephod were two onyx stones engraved with the names of the children of Israel. Aaron was to *"bear the names before the LORD upon his two shoulders for a memorial"* (28:12). Truly, Jesus bears our names to His Father and intercedes on our behalf. Praise God we are never forgotten! Second, Aaron bore *"the names of the children of Israel in the breastplate of judgment upon his heart"* (28:29). How reassuring it is to think that we are upon the heart of Jesus!

Never forget that Jesus, as our Priest, appears *"in the presence of God for us"* (Hebrews 9:24). He is waiting to hear from you today.

FEB. 13 — PREPARING FOR SERVICE — EXODUS 29

"Then shalt thou take the anointing oil, and pour it upon his head, and anoint him" (Exodus 29:7).

Before Aaron and his sons could serve God as priests, they first needed to be prepared. Their consecration provides wonderful insight to all who wish to serve the Lord acceptably. Our service to God must start with being *cleansed.* The priests were washed in water outwardly, which symbolizes the inward cleansing that God expects of all His servants. We are purified by *"the washing of water by the word"* (Ephesians 5:26). By examining our lives in light of the Bible, our shortcomings will be exposed, allowing us to confess them and be clean.

Next, a servant must be *clothed.* As the priests were required to put on the holy garments, so must we *"put...on the Lord Jesus Christ"* (Romans 13:14) and be clothed with His righteousness. We have no goodness of our own and can only be of use to others when we abandon self and look to Jesus to fashion us. Another key to service is *consecration.* The priest had to be anointed with oil, picturing a filling of the Holy Spirit. All who seek to be used by God must be filled and energized by Him. Even Jesus was *"anointed...with the Holy Ghost and with power"* (Acts 10:38). If He relied upon the Spirit, so must we.

| Exodus 30-31 | **PRAYER AND FORGIVENESS** | Feb. 14 |

"And Aaron shall burn thereon sweet incense every morning: when he dresseth the lamps, he shall burn incense upon it" (Exodus 30:7).

Today's reading provides us with more information about the furnishings of the tabernacle. First, we see the altar of incense. It was located within the holy place *"before the vail that is by the ark"* (30:6). The sweet smelling incense speaks of prayer and praise. The priest had to pass by the altar of incense in order to enter the most holy place. This reminds us how we should enter God's presence. God wants us to *"come before his presence with singing"* (Psalm 100:2).

When we view the altar as a type of Christ, we see Him as our Mediator who intercedes on our behalf. Isn't it a blessing to know that Jesus prays for you? Since the incense speaks of prayer, we should pray in the same manner that the incense was offered—it was *"perpetual"* (30:8). In short, *"Pray without ceasing"* (1 Thessalonians 5:17).

The laver was located at the entrance of the tabernacle. The priests were required to wash each time before entering. God's requirement for the priests was, *"they shall wash with water, that they die not"* (30:20). The daily washing reminds us of our need to confess our sins each day. It also provides a warning—God punishes sin that is not cleansed.

| Exodus 32-33 | **REJECTING GOD** | Feb. 15 |

"They have turned aside quickly out of the way which I commanded them: they have made them a molten calf, and have worshipped it"
(Exodus 32:8).

It did not take long for Israel to turn away from God's commandments. Though they knew the Lord had told them not to make *"gods of gold"* (20:23), they did it anyway. In fact, *"they turned aside quickly."* How prone man is to reject God's clear, direct commands! What followed?

They soon plunged to the depths of sin. Their idolatry led to other vices. Along with their sacrifices to idols, they gave themselves over to pleasure—*"the people sat down to eat and drink, and rose up to play"* (32:6). They indulged in fleshly music, which was so unruly that Joshua confused it for the sound of war. The dancing and nakedness also indicate the sensuality of the music. Worldly music always promotes sin.

How did Israel's rebellion begin? It started *"when the people saw that Moses delayed to come down out of the mount"* (32:1). In other words, they took advantage of the absence of their authority. Do you try to get away with sin when nobody is looking? Once you enter the path of sin, you will travel on it further than you ever expected to go. If you are stubborn like Israel, you will kindle God's wrath as they did.

FEB. 16 — HELP FOR EACH TASK — EXODUS 34-35

"See, the LORD hath called...and he hath filled" (Exodus 35:30-31).

Our text provides great reassurance that what God calls us to do, He will also enable us to do. Bezaleel's commission to make the items for the tabernacle was accompanied by the necessary strength, wisdom, and skill he would require. If God calls you to a daunting task, He will supply what is needed to complete it. He promises, *"Faithful is he that calleth you, who also will do it"* (1 Thessalonians 5:24).

The name *Bezaleel* means "in the shadow of God." He lived up to his name as he worked in the power of the Holy Spirit, allowing God to get the glory. When God works through us, we should be satisfied with living in His shadow. Allow Him to get the preeminence.

Consider another encouraging thought. Though Moses was charged with the construction of the tabernacle, God did not expect him to do all of the work. The Lord will provide us with people to help us complete our appointed assignments. How often do you struggle with a load that you were not meant to carry alone? Learn to look for those that God has placed in your life to assist you, and then trust them to lend a hand. If you are overwhelmed with a particular duty today, ask God to either make you a "Bezaleel" or to give you one to help.

FEB. 17 — MORE THAN ENOUGH — EXODUS 36

"The people bring much more than enough for the service of the work, which the LORD commanded to make" (Exodus 36:5).

Great excitement filled the camp as God's people began working on the tabernacle. What a change of heart they had, considering not long before they were worshipping the golden calf! This reminds us of the mercy that God extends to His people—*"The LORD God, merciful and gracious, longsuffering, and abundant in goodness and truth"* (34:6). It is comforting to know that if we have strayed from God, He is willing and able to restore us. God gives second chances.

The repentance and revival of the people were evident in two ways. First, they worked—*"Then wrought Bezaleel...and every wise hearted man"* (36:1). Those whom God had called got busy. Lip service is not enough. We must demonstrate our commitment to God. Second, the people gave willingly. In fact, the offering they brought was *"much more than enough."* Giving is a lot easier when your heart is right.

Is your service or giving a bit lackluster? If so, you are a candidate for revival. When God reveals His will, be sure to get right at it! No cost of time or treasure should seem too high, especially since we have been forgiven so much. Once revived, service and sacrifice will be a joy.

| EXODUS 37-38 | STOP LOOKING AT YOURSELF | FEB. 18 |

"And he made the laver of brass, and the foot of it of brass, of the lookingglasses of the women assembling, which assembled at the door of the tabernacle of the congregation" (Exodus 38:8).

The laver was a large basin located in the court of the tabernacle used by the priests to wash their hands and feet. Both the laver and its stand were made of the brass from a special source. Many women donated their looking glasses, which were used as mirrors. Their sacrifice reminds us that those who would be used of God must cease to look at self.

No longer used for vain reflections, the mirrors had a new purpose. They were to hold and support the water that was used for cleansing. Rather than spending time looking at our imperfections, we should focus on the Word of God which is able to cleanse us. Jesus said, *"Now ye are clean through the word which I have spoken unto you"* (John 15:3).

The ladies' sacrifice also reminds us that if we hope to see God, we must give up all aspirations to gaze on self. James 1:25 says, *"But whoso looketh into the perfect law of liberty, and continueth therein, he being not a forgetful hearer, but a doer of the work, this man shall be blessed in his deed."* As we focus less on self, we will see more of God.

| EXODUS 39 | INSPECTION TIME | FEB. 19 |

"And Moses did look upon all the work, and, behold, they had done it as the LORD *had commanded, even so had they done it: and Moses blessed them"* (Exodus 39:43).

The craftsmen finished *"all the work of the tabernacle"* (39:32). Completing the job was no small task. The intricate artwork, embroidery, and engraving required skill and precision. As we noted earlier, God equipped His people with the ability to do the work. Once they finished every last detail, they presented the tabernacle to Moses.

This reminds us of our own work for the Lord. As Moses *"did look upon all the work,"* the Lord will one day inspect our labors. Will you be able to say that it was *"all"* done *"as the* LORD *had commanded"*? Too often, we only obey when it is convenient. This was not the attitude of Israel when it came to their appointed task. A job for the Lord is worth doing right!

Because of Israel's thorough obedience, *"Moses blessed them."* If we are faithful to do all that the Lord commands us, we can expect a blessing too. Let's work to hear, *"Well done, thou good and faithful servant: thou hast been faithful over a few things, I will make thee ruler over many things: enter thou into the joy of thy lord"* (Matthew 25:21).

FEB. 20 — KEYS TO OBEDIENCE — EXODUS 40

"Thus did Moses: according to all that the LORD commanded him, so did he" (Exodus 40:16).

As we conclude our reading of the book of Exodus, we observe that it ended on a high note. Why? Because Moses and the people obeyed the Lord. Let's consider two keys to obedience from this account.

First, obedience must be *timely*. God had commanded Israel to set up the tabernacle at the beginning of their new year, and they did not delay—*"on the first day of the month...the tabernacle was reared up"* (40:17). God's work must be done on His timetable, not ours.

Second, obedience must be *complete*—Moses did *"all."* In Scripture, the number seven is often used as a sign of completion. For example, God finished creation on the seventh day. In this chapter, God records the following words seven times, *"as the LORD commanded Moses."* Moses did not leave any detail of God's commands left undone, and neither should we. Notice that *"Moses finished the work"* (40:33).

What followed their obedience? God was glorified and the people were blessed with His presence—*"the glory of the LORD filled the tabernacle"* (40:34). Get excited about completing what God has commanded you to do and then await His reward.

FEB. 21 — IS YOUR ALL ON THE ALTAR? — LEV. 1-2

"...all on the altar...an offering made by fire, of a sweet savour unto the LORD" (Leviticus 1:9).

The imagery provided by the burnt offering is beautiful. First, we see Christ as a sacrifice offered *"without blemish"* in order *"to make atonement"* for our sins (1:3, 4). He presented Himself *"of his own voluntary will"* and put His *"all on the altar"* (1:3, 9). How we ought to praise our Savior for willingly laying down His life for us!

A second application speaks of the believer yielding himself to the Lord. In Romans 12:1, the parallels between our sacrifice and the burnt offering are too close to think they are coincidental. Paul exhorts, *"I beseech you therefore, brethren, by the mercies of God, that ye present your bodies a living sacrifice, holy, acceptable unto God, which is your reasonable service."* Let's consider a few comparisons.

As Christ put His *"all on the altar,"* so must we. Do not hold back any part of your life. Since Jesus gave up His life for us, we should be willing to make our lives a *"living sacrifice"* for Him. His offering was *"without blemish,"* and our life must be *"holy, acceptable unto God."* Are you willing to give up your sin to please Him? If you unreservedly give yourself to God, it will be *"a sweet savour unto the LORD."*

Peace and Forgiveness — Lev. 3-4 — Feb. 22

"...a sacrifice of peace offering" (Leviticus 3:1).

Yesterday, we spoke of the significance of the burnt offering. Today we will consider two other offerings. Some readers may be starting to see the sacrifices mentioned in the Old Testament in a new light. Each sacrifice is full of meaning and significance, providing insight to our relationship with the Lord Jesus Christ.

Notice that the peace offering refers to Christ's work of reconciliation. His sacrifice for our sin makes it possible for us to have peace with God. Paul mentioned that *"we have peace with God through our Lord Jesus Christ"* (Romans 5:1). If you have not received Jesus as your Savior, please do so without delay. You cannot make peace with God by any of your own sacrifices because *"the chastisement of our peace was upon him"* (Isaiah 53:5). Jesus *"is our peace"* (Ephesians 2:14). You can never enjoy the peace of God until you first make peace with Him. Trust Him today to forgive your sins.

The sin offering is also mentioned in today's reading. The word *"guilty"* is stated three times, serving as a reminder that Christ bore our guilt on the cross. If you admit your guilt, you can obtain His peace!

Make It Right — Lev. 5-6 — Feb. 23

"Then it shall be, because he hath sinned, and is guilty, that he shall restore that which he took violently away, or the thing which he hath deceitfully gotten" (Leviticus 6:4).

When a man stole from his neighbor, God considered it *"a trespass against the LORD"* (6:2). This proves that when we sin against our fellow man, we also sin against the Lord. Therefore, we must make the matter right with both man and God.

It is interesting that before God would accept the trespass offering from a thief, He first expected the man to *"restore that which he took."* Jesus taught a similar lesson regarding offering gifts to the Lord. He said, *"Therefore if thou bring thy gift to the altar, and there rememberest that thy brother hath ought against thee; Leave there thy gift before the altar, and go thy way; first be reconciled to thy brother, and then come and offer thy gift"* (Matthew 5:23-24).

These accounts in Scripture teach us that in order to be right with God, we must also make amends with people we have offended. It may be humbling to go to someone and seek restoration, but it is vital. Have you allowed a conflict with a fellow believer to hinder your fellowship with God? Delay no longer and go *"be reconciled to thy brother."*

FEB. 24 — TAINTED THANKFULNESS — LEV. 7

"But the soul that eateth of the flesh of the sacrifice of peace offerings, that pertain unto the LORD, having his uncleanness upon him, even that soul shall be cut off from his people" (Leviticus 7:20).

The peace offering pictures Jesus' sacrifice on the cross, which provides peace with God. If a person knowingly partook of the peace offering while being unclean, a severe punishment was imposed upon him. He was *"cut off from his people."* Why? It is hypocritical to celebrate forgiveness while showing no remorse for current sin.

A similar situation occurs when a Christian partakes of the Lord's Supper without first confessing his sin. Paul instructed, *"But let a man examine himself, and so let him eat of that bread, and drink of that cup"* (1 Corinthians 11:28). The same principle applies to New Testament believers as did to the Israelites: we should not continue with sin in our lives while supposedly expressing our thankfulness for God's forgiveness. This shows contempt for Christ's great sacrifice. If we are truly grateful for our salvation, we will change how we live.

God hates hypocrisy. He punished people in Moses' day, and He will do the same today. Thankfully, *"if we would judge ourselves, we should not be judged"* (1 Corinthians 11:31). Confess any known sin.

FEB. 25 — ANOINTED LABOR — LEV. 8

"And Moses took the anointing oil, and anointed the tabernacle and all that was therein, and sanctified them" (Leviticus 8:10).

It took a tremendous amount of work and sacrifice to complete the tabernacle. Though everything was in place, the tabernacle was not ready for service. It first had to be anointed with oil and sanctified. Even so, our labors are ineffective unless anointed by the Holy Spirit. Many Christians are quick to do their part but fail to seek God's blessing on their efforts.

Unfortunately, much work done by believers is carried out in their own strength. Jesus provides a wonderful example to follow. Before He *"went about doing good,"* He was first anointed with the Holy Ghost (Acts 10:38). You may make great sacrifices for God and pour countless hours into ministries at your church, but such effort will have limited success if not performed in God's strength.

In reality, the best work that we can do for God is not work that we do. It is work that Christ does through us. Paul expressed it this way, *"I am crucified with Christ: nevertheless I live; yet not I, but Christ liveth in me: and the life which I now live in the flesh I live by the faith of the Son of God"* (Galatians 2:20). Be sure that your labor is anointed by God!

LEV. 9-10 — MAKE PREPARATIONS — FEB. 26

"...to day the LORD will appear unto you" (Leviticus 9:4).

The Lord promised to appear to His people. However, He first expected Israel to fulfill a few conditions. They were to prepare to meet Him by making four distinct offerings. Each of the offerings was necessary in order to experience a special manifestation of God's presence. Consider how each offering represents steps we must take to enjoy a heavenly visitation.

The sin offering reminds us to deal with our sin. The promise of seeing God is made to *"the pure in heart,"* not to the defiled (Matt. 5:8). The peace offering suggests we give thanks for the peace we have with the Father through Jesus. The burnt offering speaks of our dedication as *"a living sacrifice, holy, acceptable unto God"* (Romans 12:1). The meat offering consisted of a sacrifice which came from the field, implying we must commit our labors to the Lord. He deserves our all.

If we hope to see God in a notable way, we must first confess our sin, be at peace with Him, and present our lives and labors to Him. In short, nothing can be withheld from our Creator. What happened when Israel met God's conditions? He visited them—*"the glory of the LORD appeared unto all the people"* (9:23). Make preparations for such a visit!

LEV. 11-12 — GOD'S PEOPLE SHOULD BE DIFFERENT — FEB. 27

"For I am the LORD that bringeth you up out of the land of Egypt, to be your God: ye shall therefore be holy, for I am holy" (Leviticus 11:45).

After giving a detailed list of animals that could and could not be eaten, God told His people the reason for His regulations. He wanted to be their God, but they first had to be holy since He is holy. The word *holy* refers to being set apart. God wanted Israel to be distinct from the nations around them. This required guidelines to help them *"make a difference between the unclean and the clean"* (11:47).

Peter quoted our text when explaining that Christians are to be different after salvation. Egypt was a place of bondage, but God delivered Israel. In like manner, Christ rescued us from sin. Therefore, as God no longer wanted Israel to resemble Egypt, He no longer wants us to live as we did before being saved. Peter exhorted the believers, *"As obedient children, not fashioning yourselves according to the former lusts"* (1 Peter 1:14).

Are you tempted at times to follow your former lusts? If so, remember that God expects you to make a clear distinction *"between the unclean and the clean."* When you think of the dietary laws given to the Jews, remember that God has activities you can and cannot partake of.

FEB. 28 — THE UNCLEANNESS OF SIN — LEV. 13

"And if the priest see that, behold, the scab spreadeth in the skin, then the priest shall pronounce him unclean: it is a leprosy" (Leviticus 13:8).

Leprosy was a plague of the skin that caused devastating effects to the body. In many ways, leprosy represents sin. Those in Israel infected by the disease were pronounced unclean by the priest and made to dwell alone outside of the camp (13:46). In the same way, sin is repulsive to God and causes separation. Never allow sin to become acceptable in your life; God hates it. Another similarity between leprosy and sin is that they both have a tendency to spread. If you let sin fester in one area of your life, it will soon show up in another. For example, a bad attitude will soon extend to your actions. Further, your sin will affect others too. For instance, if you display a critical spirit in your home, others in your family will also be infected.

When a plague turned white, the priest would pronounce a man clean (13:17). Praise God that Jesus is our great High Priest who has prevailed to wash us *"whiter than snow"* (Psalm 51:7) and declare us to be clean! If you have any unconfessed sin, turn to the Lord at once and ask for a cleansing. Don't allow sin to separate you from God's fellowship and rob you of His richest blessings.

FEB. 29 — SIN WITHIN — READ FAVORITE

"This is the law of the plague of leprosy in a garment of woollen or linen, either in the warp, or woof, or any thing of skins, to pronounce it clean, or to pronounce it unclean" (Leviticus 13:59).

As this day is unusual, occurring only every four years, so two words found in our text are also uncommon. When referring to leprosy in a garment, the words *warp* and *woof* are mentioned. They are weaving terms which describe the process of crossing threads. When the fibers of the garment were thoroughly ingrained with leprosy, the article of clothing was considered unclean. A contaminated garment was burned with fire, showing the danger that sin poses to us all. Without redemption, every sinner is doomed for eternal fire. However, there is hope. A garment thoroughly washed was spared and pronounced clean (13:58), and so are all who are cleansed by Jesus.

Our sinful flesh is much like the leprous warp and woof. Tightly woven into our old nature is the corrupting influence of sin. Paul expressed it this way, *"For I know that in me (that is, in my flesh,) dwelleth no good thing"* (Romans 7:18). Thankfully, Paul also gave us a solution. He exclaimed, *"the Spirit of life in Christ Jesus hath made me free from the law of sin and death"* (Romans 8:2). Ask Jesus to free you!

LEV. 14 — HOME INSPECTION — MAR. 1

"And he that owneth the house shall come and tell the priest, saying, It seemeth to me there is as it were a plague in the house" (Leviticus 14:35).

Today's reading continues the discussion about leprosy. The Lord instructed His people how to handle leprosy found in houses. Let's consider how leprosy in a house can be compared to sin in a home.

First, we see the *responsibility* of the head of the home. It was the duty of the owner of the house to report any suspicions he had that leprosy might be present. In like manner, every father who suspects sin creeping into his family must bring the matter directly to God. Ask the Lord to help you with the problems in your home.

Next, observe the *removal* of sin. If a plague was present, the infected stones were removed and the house was scraped (14:40-41). We cannot allow sin to be tolerated in our homes. We must take away every contaminating influence such as worldly music, videos, books, and attire.

Getting rid of sin is only the beginning. Something wholesome must be put in its place. Notice the principle of *replacement* at work in this situation. Clean stones replaced infected stones (14:42). As failure to deal with leprosy led to the *ruin* of houses, so sin destroys homes.

LEV. 15-16 — FORGIVENESS, FIRE, AND FRAGRANCE — MAR. 2

"And he shall take a censer full of burning coals of fire from off the altar before the LORD, and his hands full of sweet incense" (Leviticus 16:12).

After the death of Aaron's sons, Nadad and Abihu, God provided instructions for Aaron to observe while serving as priest *"that he die not"* (16:2). The chapter describes regulations to follow on the Day of Atonement, which provided *"an atonement for the children of Israel for all their sins once a year"* (16:34). Consider a few lessons.

Aaron had to be *forgiven*. Before making a sacrifice to atone for the sins of the people, he had to start with himself—his initial sacrifice was to *"make an atonement for himself, and for his house"* (16:6). Truly, none of us are fit to help others with their problems until we first deal with our own. Once you cast the beam out of your own eye, you can *"see clearly to cast out the mote out of thy brother's eye"* (Matthew 7:5).

Next, God expected him to use the right *fire*. Aaron's sons were judged because they *"offered strange fire...which he commanded them not"* (10:1). This serves as a reminder that we should not rely on fleshly energy but on God's power in our labors. God's work must be done His way. Last, Aaron's offering was to include *fragrance*, having his *"hands full of sweet incense."* Be sure your life and service are full of praise!

MAR. 3   DON'T LET THE WICKED AFFECT YOU   LEV. 17-18

"After the doings of the land of Egypt, wherein ye dwelt, shall ye not do: and after the doings of the land of Canaan, whither I bring you, shall ye not do: neither shall ye walk in their ordinances." (Leviticus 18:3).

Israel had been exposed to the wicked lifestyles and practices of the Egyptians for a few hundred years. Their final destination was the land of Canaan, which also was filled with evil customs. However, God made it clear that He did not want His people to live like the heathen.

Much like the children of Israel, we live among multitudes of ungodly people who carry on as if God does not exist. Our text reminds us that despite our corrupt surroundings, the Lord still expects us to live differently. Thankfully, when He commands us to do something, He also provides a way to get it done. So, what did God give to Israel that would help them? His Word! Notice that the wicked had *"their ordinances;"* yet God told His people, *"keep mine ordinances, to walk therein"* (18:4). Here's the point—we shouldn't allow the heathen to dictate how we live.

The world constantly pushes its corrupt values on us through the radio, television, and the Internet. It wants to tell us how to think, act, and talk. We must focus on God's Word, instead of the world. When we do, we will renew our minds and be shining lights in this dark world.

MAR. 4   THE MERCY OF THE LAW   LEV. 19-20

"And thou shalt not glean thy vineyard, neither shalt thou gather every grape of thy vineyard; thou shalt leave them for the poor and stranger: I am the LORD your God" (Leviticus 19:10).

Often times people speak of the harsh demands and severe regulations of the Law but fail to see the mercy of God in it. We display a limited understanding of the Bible when we think that the Old Testament is merely about judgment while the New Testament is all about liberty. God's character is the same through every dispensation of time. Even in the Mosaic Law, we see the mercy of God.

Chapter nineteen provides many rules that were meant to benefit mankind. *Provision* was made for the poor (19:9-10), *protection* was instituted for the handicapped (19:14), *peace* was encouraged in personal relationships (19:16-17), *politeness* was to be rendered to the elderly (19:32), *pity* was to be expressed to strangers (19:33-34), and *propriety* was to be exercised in business transactions (19:35-36). Clearly, many laws were instituted for the well-being of others.

Here are a couple of lessons for us. First, remember that the Lord has reasons for each of His laws. Second, consider God's commands as a means to express His mercy to others, not as oppressive restrictions.

REVERE THE HOLY THINGS — MAR. 5

"And they shall not profane the holy things of the children of Israel, which they offer unto the LORD" (Leviticus 22:15).

The priests were given specific instructions on how the offerings of the Lord were to be eaten. Those who were unclean were forbidden to partake of the sacrifices (22:3). What God separates and sanctifies must be held in high esteem by His people. The word *profane* refers to misusing something or making it common. The *"holy things"* of God must remain holy. We must never be flippant about the things of God.

What are some *holy things* that we must always revere? First, God's Word must be respected. He warned, *"They shall therefore keep mine ordinance, lest they bear sin for it, and die therefore, if they profane it"* (22:9). Ignoring His Word leads to judgment. Therefore, we must love it, read it, heed it, crave it, share it, defend it, and treasure it!

Second, God's name must not be used carelessly—*"Neither shall ye profane my holy name"* (22:32). A good rule to follow is to only speak the name of the Lord when you are either talking to Him or about Him in a respectful manner. Don't use His name as an exclamation such as, "Oh my...." Using His name in a frivolous way offends Him, and *"the LORD will not hold him guiltless that taketh his name in vain"* (Exodus 20:7).

A PATTERN FOR FORGIVENESS — MAR. 6

"...there shall be a day of atonement...ye shall afflict your souls, and offer an offering made by fire unto the LORD" (Leviticus 23:27).

The Day of Atonement was a solemn event held yearly by Israel to atone for their sins. The word *atone* means "to cover or appease." The sacrifices of the priest were limited because *"it is not possible that the blood of bulls and of goats should take away sins"* (Hebrews 10:4). While the sacrifices of the Jewish high priest appeased God, they also pointed to a better sacrifice. When Jesus came, He *"appeared to put away sin by the sacrifice of himself"* (Hebrews 9:26). Today, no animal sacrifices are needed because Christ's sacrifice was perfect. Truly, forgiveness is only obtained through Jesus.

Looking at the Day of Atonement, let's consider a picture of how we obtain forgiveness. First, *repentance* is required—*"ye shall afflict your souls."* All who seek to be cleansed of sin must first express genuine sorrow for offending God. Second, *rest* is important—*"ye shall do no work in that same day"* (23:28). The command to abstain from work on the Day of Atonement reminds us that our good works cannot secure forgiveness (see Ephesians 2:8-9 and Titus 3:5). Finally, forgiveness brings *rejoicing*—*"from even unto even, shall ye celebrate"* (23:32).

MAR. 7 — FAIR BUSINESS — LEVITICUS 25

"Ye shall not therefore oppress one another; but thou shalt fear thy God: for I am the LORD your God" (Leviticus 25:17).

Our text condemns buying and selling dishonestly. God's people were strictly forbidden to oppress each other in any business transactions. Observe three practical lessons we can apply to our lives.

First, God expects us to be *fair*—*"Ye shall not therefore oppress one another."* It is never right to knowingly cheat someone out of money. In order to gain a bit more money, you may be tempted to be dishonest or withhold an important detail about something you are selling. However, using shady tactics stems from covetousness, and God commands, *"let it not be once named among you, as becometh saints"* (Ephesians 5:3).

Second, the right kind of *fear* in our lives will prevent us from being unfair to others—*"thou shalt fear thy God."* When we remember that God sees all of our dealings, it will change how we act. Always look up!

Finally, we can avoid being unfair to people by showing *favor* to them. Israel was commanded, *"And if thy brother be waxen poor, and fallen in decay with thee; then thou shalt relieve him"* (25:35). Giving is the opposite of taking; and by considering how to be a blessing to someone, we can avoid any temptation to profit unjustly from them.

MAR. 8 — BROKEN BANDS — LEVITICUS 26

"I am the LORD your God, which brought you forth out of the land of Egypt, that ye should not be their bondmen; and I have broken the bands of your yoke, and made you go upright" (Leviticus 26:13).

The above statement appears in a pivotal point in the chapter. It comes between God's promise of blessing for obedience to His commands and His warning of punishment for disobedience. It is as if He said, "I delivered you so that I could bless you; but if you refuse to follow me, I will have to persuade you with judgment." The freedom which Israel enjoyed should have been enough to convince them to obey.

If every Christian would stop to consider what God has already done for him, he would think twice before turning back to sin. The bands in our text refer to the hefty poles used in a yoke. They were oppressive and placed a heavy burden on the neck. When God delivers us from the bondage of sin, He totally breaks the bands that fasten us to our burdens. We are truly set free from our sin. Further, He makes us to *"go upright"* instead of bowed down with the guilt of our sin. We no longer have to go through life stooped over!

Since salvation provides such wonderful relief, don't return to the broken yoke and put it back on. Enjoy your freedom and run from sin.

LEVITICUS 27	**DOES IT APPLY TO US?**	MAR. 9

"These are the commandments, which the LORD commanded Moses for the children of Israel in mount Sinai" (Leviticus 27:34).

The book of Leviticus contains many rules and regulations regarding worship and daily living. Some might ask, "Are Christians obligated to observe all of the ceremonies and rituals found in the Law?" The key to answering that question is found in the last verse of Leviticus. Notice to whom these commands were given—*"the children of Israel."* Christians are not held to the ceremonial aspects of the Law such as animal sacrifices, dietary laws, and observing Jewish feasts. The main purpose of the Law today is to show people their sin (Romans 3:20) and to point them to Christ for salvation (Galatians 3:24).

As we have seen over the past weeks, many moral lessons can be gleaned from the Law and applied to our lives. Never regard any portion of the Bible as unworthy of your attention. Paul exhorted, *"All scripture is given by inspiration of God, and is profitable"* (2 Timothy 3:16). Truly, much can be learned from the Old Testament. Timeless principles of right and wrong, types of Christ, and examples of faith and failure are mingled throughout its pages. Your understanding of the New Testament will increase as you learn more of the Old Testament.

NUMBERS 1	**GET READY TO FIGHT**	MAR. 10

"From twenty years old and upward, all that are able to go forth to war in Israel: thou and Aaron shall number them by their armies" (Numbers 1:3).

One of the purposes of numbering Israel was to establish who would compose their fighting forces. Women and children were excluded from the front lines in God's armies, and every young man was to be available for battle when the time came. The numbering was a warning that war was ahead, and the Lord wanted His troops ready.

The life of a Christian, in some ways, follows the path that the children of Israel journeyed. First, we are rescued from the bondage of sin as they were delivered from Egypt. Next, we are taught *"to observe all things"* (Matthew 28:20) in discipleship as they were instructed to learn the Law. Finally, once redeemed and prepared, we are expected to engage in spiritual warfare as they were expected to fight for their nation.

Unlike Israel, every Christian is expected *"to go forth to war."* Women and children are not exempt from spiritual combat. Paul spoke to the entire church of Ephesus when he said, *"Put on the whole armour of God, that ye may be able to stand against the wiles of the devil"* (Ephesians 6:11). Are you numbered as a faithful soldier in God's army?

MAR. 11	GOD CHOOSES	NUMBERS 2

"And on the east side toward the rising of the sun shall they of the standard of the camp of Judah pitch throughout their armies: and Nahshon...shall be captain of the children of Judah" (Numbers 2:3).

Before reaching the Promised Land, the children of Israel faced many journeys. Each time they travelled, they had to set up the tabernacle and pitch their tents. The Lord divided the whole congregation into four camps which were stationed on the east, south, west, and north of the tabernacle. Let's see how the camp of Israel can compare to a church.

First, God chooses our position. As each tribe was placed in a specific part of the camp, God has a particular place for each member of a church to serve. Paul explained this to the Corinthians, *"But now hath God set the members every one of them in the body, as it hath pleased him"* (1 Corinthians 12:18). Be content with your position.

Next, God chooses our leaders. In Israel, the Lord appointed one captain for each camp. Like Israel followed their captain, we must submit to our pastor. It is the job of sheep to follow, not lead.

Finally, God chooses our function. Each tribe in Israel knew their position when it came to march. Likewise, every member of a church must fulfill his specific duty for which God equips him (Romans 12:4-8).

MAR. 12	LEARN FROM LOSS	NUMBERS 3

"And Nadab and Abihu died before the LORD, when they offered strange fire before the LORD...and Eleazar and Ithamar ministered in the priest's office in the sight of Aaron their father" (Numbers 3:4).

When you lose what is precious in your life, things that remain suddenly tend to take a higher priority. Thus was the case with Aaron. Two of his sons died because they had disobeyed the Lord. Since Aaron did not die with them, we deduce that he had not participated with the offering of strange fire. We must conclude that Nadab and Abihu were not under his direct supervision at the time.

Aaron did not want such a terrible thing to happen again. So, he became more involved with his remaining two sons. Observe that they *"ministered in the priest's office in the sight of Aaron their father."* He kept a better eye on them than he had on the sons he had lost.

Let us learn from Aaron's example. When failure or loss comes, do all that you can to prevent it from happening again. Failure with one child does not have to lead to missteps with another. Neither do financial disasters have to be repeated. Many other examples could be given, but one thing is certain—we must *"strengthen the things which remain"* before we lose them too (Revelation 3:2).

| NUMBERS 4 | **FULFILL YOUR ROLE** | MAR. 13 |

"This shall be the service of the sons of Kohath in the tabernacle of the congregation, about the most holy things" (Numbers 4:4).

When it was time for Israel to travel, the tabernacle had to be disassembled and transported. The descendants of the three sons of Levi were commissioned to carry the items of the tabernacle. The Kohathites were given charge of the most holy things, but strict regulations were established to prevent them from touching or seeing the hallowed objects.

A clear distinction was made between the priests and the laity. The sons of Kohath were not priests. Therefore, they could not intrude into matters reserved for the sacred office of the priest. It was the duty of the priests to pack the most holy things of the tabernacle, and the Kohathites were expected to fulfill their role of carrying the items on poles.

A great principle is provided for us in today's reading. In every sphere of life, you must learn to know your place and fulfill your role. Too often people like to meddle with matters that do not pertain to their calling in life. Deacons try to run churches, women attempt to lead their homes, and employees undermine their managers at work. When God's order is not followed, trouble is just around the corner. Stick to your job.

| NUMBERS 5-6 | **LET GOD JUDGE** | MAR. 14 |

"And this water that causeth the curse shall go into thy bowels, to make thy belly to swell, and thy thigh to rot: And the woman shall say, Amen, amen" (Numbers 5:22).

The case of a woman suspected of being unfaithful to her husband was to be settled by going to the priest. After presenting her to the Lord, the priest would give her bitter water to drink and offer a jealousy offering. If she was guilty, her stomach would swell and her thigh would rot. If she was innocent, she was set free from the curse and made clean. This is certainly not a prescription for today; it was meant only for Israel. Nevertheless, the account provides principles worthy of consideration.

First, we should resolve our conflicts. As the jealous husband sought God's help through the priest, we should take our problems directly to God. If we have suspicions about others, it is not good to take matters in our own hands. Leave judgment in the hands of the Lord. *"For God shall bring every work into judgment, with every secret thing, whether it be good, or whether it be evil"* (Ecclesiastes 12:14).

This account also serves as a reminder that God reveals sin. His methods may not be the same as in Moses' day, but we can be sure that *"whatsoever a man soweth, that shall he also reap"* (Galatians 6:7).

Mar. 15   Forget the Wagons   Numbers 7

"And Moses took the wagons and the oxen, and gave them unto the Levites...But unto the sons of Kohath he gave none" (Numbers 7:6, 9).

Have you ever thought that someone else had it easier than you? It is a common weakness in many of us. Once we begin thinking that way, we will be tempted to utter those familiar words, "That's not fair."

To make things easier for the families assigned to transport the tabernacle, God told Moses to give six donated wagons to them. Instead of dividing them equally, two were given to the Gershonites, four were given to the Merarites, and none were reserved for the Kohathites. It was as if Moses had said to the Kohathites, "No wagons for you." Right now, you might be thinking, "That doesn't seem fair." Unfortunately, we are selfish creatures living in a society that teaches we are entitled to what everybody else has. Remember that the Lord is *"a God of truth and without iniquity, just and right is he"* (Deuteronomy 32:4). He is fair.

As always, God has reasons for what He does. No disservice was done to the sons of Kohath. Their calling to carry the most holy things meant that they would bear them upon their shoulders. Have you been called to carry a heavier load than others? Instead of whining, rejoice! Bigger sacrifices tend to yield greater rewards. So, forget the wagons.

Mar. 16   God's Guidance   Numbers 8-9

"And when the cloud was taken up from the tabernacle, then after that the children of Israel journeyed: and in the place where the cloud abode, there the children of Israel pitched their tents" (Numbers 9:17).

God gave Israel a visible token of His presence. A cloud covered the tabernacle by day and appeared as fire at night. It also led them on their journeys. Consider a few lessons about God's guidance.

Have a right relationship with God's house. God's presence was manifested in the tabernacle. The cloud rested above the tabernacle to keep Israel's focus on Him. For the Christian, God provides much guidance through the local church as He speaks through His Word.

Move when God moves. When the cloud moved, God's people were expected to follow—*"whether it was by day or by night that the cloud was taken up, they journeyed"* (9:21). Israel had to be ready to journey at a moment's notice. Following God may not always be convenient, but it is the only way to continue to enjoy His presence. Be quick to follow.

Don't put your comfort above God's command. Israel never knew when they would travel again—it may have been *"two days, or a month, or a year"* (9:22). We should enjoy where God leads us but must never get so comfortable that we are unwilling to leave. Always go with God.

| NUMBERS 10 | WATCH YOUR MOTIVES | MAR. 17 |

"Also in the day of your gladness...ye shall blow with the trumpets over your burnt offerings, and over the sacrifices of your peace offerings; that they may be to you for a memorial before your God" (Numbers 10:10).

On special occasions when offerings were made, the children of Israel were told to blow trumpets. Music is often used to express gladness. So, when the trumpets accompanied sacrifices from a thankful heart, God took special notice. The Lord likes sacrifice, praise, and thanksgiving. Be certain, therefore, when you give your time, talent, and treasure to God that it comes from a heart full of praise.

In the New Testament, Jesus condemned some people for blowing trumpets when they helped the poor. He said, *"Therefore when thou doest thine alms, do not sound a trumpet before thee, as the hypocrites do in the synagogues and in the streets, that they may have glory of men"* (Matthew 6:2). How could blowing the trumpet be right in one case and wrong in another? Much of it has to do with motives. In the first case, people were sounding the trumpet in praise to God. In the second instance, folks were seeking the attention of men. Have you ever done something good, hoping that others would see it? It is possible to do a good thing for the wrong reason. Always guard your motives.

| NUMBERS 11 | A COMPLAINING SPIRIT | MAR. 18 |

"And when the people complained, it displeased the LORD: and the LORD heard it; and his anger was kindled" (Numbers 11:1).

Shortly after leaving Sinai, the people started to complain. The fact that we are not told what was so unsettling to them indicates that the matter was of little importance. In reality, all of our complaints about God's plan for our lives are unfounded.

One thing we do know is that their attitude *"displeased the LORD."* God destroyed many of them. Sadly, many Christians do not realize how offensive the sin of murmuring is to the Lord. It is an attack on His love, wisdom, and character. To complain is to put our will and wellbeing before God. It is selfishness. Further, it becomes a habit—*"the children of Israel also wept again"* (11:4). Be very careful about developing a pattern of negative thinking and fault finding. It can kindle God's anger.

Complaining leads to other sins. The people said, *"our soul is dried away: there is nothing at all, beside this manna"* (11:6). Notice that they exaggerated their problem. They were not starving; they had manna. Also, they despised God's provision, calling it *"nothing at all."* They even became delusional saying, *"it was well with us in Egypt"* (11:18). If you have allowed a complaining spirit to develop in your life, repent.

| MAR. 19 | ARE YOU ABLE? | NUMBERS 12-13 |

"And Caleb stilled the people before Moses, and said, Let us go up at once, and possess it; for we are well able to overcome it. But the men that went up with him said, We be not able" (Numbers 13:30-31).

Faith affects your outlook on life. The twelves spies surveyed the land and brought back their report to Moses. The facts showed that it was a fruitful land with fortified cities and strong people. Full of faith, Caleb declared, *"Let us go up at once, and possess it; for we are well able to overcome it."* Knowing that God had promised Canaan to them, he focused on the possibilities.

Ten of the spies looked at the problems. They told Moses, *"We be not able."* All they could envision were the giants in the land. The more they thought about the giants, the larger they seemed to become in their minds. They let their imaginations run wild, saying, *"we were in our own sight as grasshoppers"* (13:33). When you begin to focus on your difficulties and doubt God, you will tend to blow your problems out of proportion. The larger they become, the more you will fear them.

God has many blessings waiting for you. Though huge obstacles may intimidate you, don't allow fear to hinder you. With God, you are *"well able to overcome."* Possess the land that God has promised you.

| MAR. 20 | BE DIFFERENT | NUMBERS 14 |

"But my servant Caleb, because he had another spirit with him, and hath followed me fully, him will I bring into the land" (Numbers 14:24).

The Lord recognized Caleb as being different from the others. The ten faithless spies had discouraged the people and persuaded them not to enter the Promised Land. The entire congregation wept, murmured, and planned to overthrow Moses and return to Egypt (14:1-4). Not only did Caleb refuse to yield to peer pressure, he also led the effort to convince the people to obey the Lord. Notice how a different attitude led to different actions, which resulted in a different reward.

Caleb's attitude was different—*"he had another spirit with him."* When others are full of discouragement, fear, and rebellion, we must rise to the occasion and display a sensible, spiritual nature. Is your attitude easily influenced by others? If so, it is time to get *"another spirit."*

Caleb also had different actions. God testified of him, *"he...hath followed me fully."* Caleb rebuked the people and encouraged them—*"Only rebel not ye against the LORD, neither fear ye the people...their defence is departed from them, and the LORD is with us"* (14:9). Instead of following the crowd, try to challenge it. Finally, Caleb earned a different reward. Only he and Joshua were allowed to enter the land.

| NUMBERS 15 | IGNORANCE OR PRESUMPTION | MAR. 21 |

"But the soul that doeth ought presumptuously...the same reproacheth the LORD; and that soul shall be cut off from among his people" (Numbers 15:30).

God made a difference between sins of ignorance and sins of presumption in Moses' day. Those who sinned ignorantly were instructed to present a sin offering to make atonement. This teaches us that being ignorant of right and wrong does not make a person less accountable. Reconciliation with God must be made.

A presumptuous sin refers to one's attitude. The word implies acting in a proud manner with no regard for God's commands. It is further defined in the following verse, *"he hath despised the word of the LORD, and hath broken his commandment"* (15:31). Under the Law, swift judgment was passed on those guilty of blatantly defying God.

As Christians, we must realize that both types of sins are an offence to God. When you sin ignorantly, confess it once you are aware of it and amend your ways. If you sin on purpose, you can be forgiven (1 John 1:9), but you will reap what you have sown (Galatians 6:7). Don't think you will get away with it. Learn to pray as David did, *"Keep back thy servant also from presumptuous sins"* (Psalm 19:13).

| NUMBERS 16 | "SPIRITUAL" JEALOUSLY | MAR. 22 |

"...they gathered themselves together against Moses and against Aaron, and said unto them, Ye take too much upon you...wherefore then lift ye up yourselves above the congregation of the LORD?" (Numbers 16:3).

Korah was a Levite who led a revolt against God's leadership. He and some others had become disgruntled with their positions and were jealous of the men of God. This account provides warnings to the flock and an exhortation to leaders.

Be content with the opportunities of service that God gives to you. Moses asked Korah's group, *"Seemeth it but a small thing unto you...to do the service of the tabernacle...?"* (16:9). Remember that no task is small when it is appointed by God. Do your job and let others do theirs.

As the rebels in Korah's day recruited famous men in the congregation, so backslidden members seek notable people in the church to join their opposition to leadership. Don't be caught up in their rebellion. If you join in their sin, you will partake of their punishment.

After God killed the rebels, the rest of Israel blamed it on Moses and Aaron. Therefore, God sent a plague and many died. Instead of being bitter, God's men remained true to their calling and helped the people who had turned against them. Let every leader follow their example.

MAR. 23 — GOD'S STAMP OF APPROVAL — NUMBERS 17-18

"And it shall come to pass, that the man's rod, whom I shall choose, shall blossom: and I will make to cease from me the murmurings of the children of Israel, whereby they murmur against you" (Numbers 17:5).

Yesterday we read about the uprising against Moses and Aaron. Today, we see how God put His stamp of approval on their leadership. This serves as a reminder of the tender mercies that the Lord extends to His servants.

God did not want any more murmurings about the priesthood. The tribe of Levi had just learned their lesson that only those of Aaron's house were to be priests. To ensure that nobody from the other tribes had similar thoughts, God commanded that a rod from each tribe be placed in the tabernacle. The rod which budded would reveal God's choice. Aaron's rod not only budded but also blossomed and bore fruit. God made it clear who He had chosen.

We may experience opposition at times for serving God, but we can be assured that the Lord will work to silence our adversaries as He did in Moses' day. How comforting to know that when we suffer wrongfully, God will take up our cause! Be faithful and remember that when God makes your works to blossom, others will know that He is on your side.

MAR. 24 — A SAD LAPSE OF FAITH — NUMBERS 19-20

"And Moses and Aaron went from the presence of the assembly unto the door of the tabernacle of the congregation, and they fell upon their faces: and the glory of the LORD appeared unto them" (Numbers 20:6).

Sadly, Israel failed another test and reacted as they had previously on many occasions. Instead of trusting God to meet their needs, they complained and *"gathered themselves together against Moses and against Aaron"* (20:2). Always remember that God will continue to test you in a similar manner until you learn the lesson and respond in faith.

Moses and Aaron acted appropriately when they were confronted by the angry congregation. They went straight to the tabernacle and *"fell upon their faces."* What was the result? God met with them—*"the glory of the LORD appeared unto them,"* and He gave them a plan to follow. When trouble comes, go directly to God, and He will manifest His presence to you and provide a solution for your problem.

Although Moses and Aaron started out well, they allowed self to interfere with their service. Instead of speaking to the rock as instructed, Moses hit the rock twice out of rage. He and Aaron let the sin of others affect their attitude and lost their opportunity to enter the Promised Land. One lapse of faith can cause you to lose precious blessings. Be careful.

NUMBERS 21 — LOOK PAST YOUR TROUBLE — MAR. 25

"...the soul of the people was much discouraged because of the way" (Numbers 21:4).

Things were going well for Israel. They had just defeated the king of Canaan and were on their way to possess the Promised Land. After forty years of wandering in the wilderness, their journey was nearly over. They had much to look forward to. However, we read that *"the soul of the people was much discouraged."* Notice why—*"because of the way."*

Instead of looking at the problems on the path, Israel should have been looking to God. It was *"the way"* that He had planned for them. So, it must have been good, regardless of a few hardships. Rather than anticipating the blessing of inheriting the land, the people focused on the hardships of the journey. Are we not often like Israel, living in discouragement while on the path to God's blessing? We must learn to look past our problems and focus on the prize set before us.

As usual, one sin leads to another. Israel's discouragement resulted in anger at God, opposition to leadership, and complaints about God's provision. Instead of coddling them in their sorrow, God judged them. Discouragement can take you far from God and bring His judgment. Guard against it. Stop looking at *"the way"* and move forward by faith.

NUMBERS 22 — ACCEPT GOD'S ANSWER — MAR. 26

"Now therefore, I pray you, tarry ye also here this night, that I may know what the LORD will say unto me more" (Numbers 22:19).

Balak, the king of Moab, feared Israel because of what they had done to the Amorites. Therefore, he sent messengers to hire the prophet Balaam to curse God's people in order to secure Moab's victory. That night, the Lord clearly commanded Balaam, *"Thou shalt not go with them; thou shalt not curse the people: for they are blessed"* (22:12). Balaam obeyed, but Balak was persistent and offered him great rewards.

Balaam knew God's will on the matter, but the promise of promotion seemed too great to give up on so easily. He told the king's messengers, *"tarry ye also here this night, that I may know what the LORD will say unto me more."* The Lord had already spoken. What more would He say? Balaam was hoping that God would change His mind.

The Lord did permit him to go, but it was apparently so He could judge him for his stubbornness. *"God's anger was kindled because he went"* (22:22), and the angel would have killed Balaam if the donkey did not have more sense than his master. The lesson for us is simple. Accept God's first answer, or you will be humbled and have to live with the consequences of getting your own way. Never try to manipulate God.

| MAR. 27 | SATAN'S TACTICS | NUMBERS 23-25 |

"I thought to promote thee unto great honour; but, lo, the LORD hath kept thee back from honour" (Numbers 24:11).

Balak's quest to curse God's people consumed him, but the Lord confounded him by turning the would-be curse into a blessing. The persistence of Balak reminds us how Satan relentlessly attacks us. Thankfully, this account assures us that neither man nor devil can stop us when God has determined to bless us! You can march confidently to your assigned task today without fear of the enemy.

Our text reveals how Balak mirrored another of Satan's attacks. He sought to entice Balaam through false accusations against God—*"the LORD hath kept thee back from honour."* One of the devil's oldest tricks is to try to get us to believe that we are missing a good life by following God. He tricked Eve in a similar manner. We must remember that God is the One who promotes us. Satan has never been the source of any true blessing for anyone. His ways end in humiliation, not honor.

Lastly, Satan seeks to contaminate those he cannot curse. Balak enticed God's people. Israel committed *"whoredom with the daughters of Moab"* and *"joined himself unto Baalpeor"* (25:1, 3). Though Satan cannot curse you, he seeks to ruin you through self-indulgence. Beware.

| MAR. 28 | REASONS FOR NUMBERING | NUMBERS 26 |

"Take the sum of all the congregation of the children of Israel, from twenty years old and upward, throughout their fathers' house, all that are able to go to war in Israel" (Numbers 26:2).

This chapter contains the second account of the numbering of Israel. Though some people might find this passage of Scripture laborious or inapplicable to their lives, God saw fit to include it in His Word. With God, every detail matters. Consider three reasons for this record.

First, God reminded them of coming battles. Those numbered were all that were *"able to go to war."* The numbering of the tribes provided organization for combat. We, too, should be prepared to engage in spiritual warfare each day. What steps have you taken to be ready?

Second, the Lord promised them victory, giving instructions on how to divide the territory before it was even conquered. God spoke as if the battle had already been won, which provided confidence to His people. Let us anticipate and envision certain triumph in our spiritual battles.

Finally, this chapter is a reminder that promises of God's judgment are always fulfilled. With the exception of Caleb and Joshua, none of the people numbered in the wilderness of Sinai were part of the second numbering because they had died. Let this be a solemn warning to obey.

| NUMBERS 27-28 | **INTERCESSORY PRAYER** | MAR. 29 |

"And Moses brought their cause before the LORD" (Numbers 27:5).

The daughters of Zelophehad were to be left with no possession in the land because their father had died in the wilderness, and he had no sons. The women were helpless, having no father or brothers to provide for them. Therefore, they approached the leaders of Israel and requested that they would receive what should have been their father's inheritance. What follows is a beautiful picture of intercession and intervention.

Though many heard their request, only Moses brought the matter to the Lord in prayer. How do you respond when those in need ask for help? Are you quick to bring *"their cause before the LORD"*? Surely we can lift those who are downhearted, sick, or mistreated. Let us pray for all who are vulnerable, including widows, orphans, and new believers.

After Moses prayed to God, *"the LORD spake unto Moses saying, The daughters of Zelophehad speak right"* (27:6-7). When a request is *"right"* we can expect an answer! Since God has instructed us to pray for others, He has obligated Himself to intervene. Moses' prayer secured a possession for the daughters, proving that there is power in intercessory prayer. Who needs your prayers today? If you intercede, God will intervene. Don't delay; bring *"their cause before the LORD."*

| NUMBERS 29-30 | **ACCOUNTABLE TO GOD** | MAR. 30 |

"Every vow, and every binding oath to afflict the soul, her husband may establish it, or her husband may make it void" (Numbers 30:13).

Vows are promises made to God. Since the Lord faithfully kept His Word to Israel, He expected them to keep their promises to Him. Moses commanded, *"If a man vow a vow unto the LORD...he shall not break his word, he shall do according to all that proceedeth out of his mouth"* (30:2). Exceptions, however, were given to women under their father's or husband's authority. Our topic of consideration today is the importance of authority and accountability.

First, notice that God established man as the authority in the home. When a man heard his wife or daughter make a promise to God, he could authorize it or annul it. If the vow was disallowed, God forgave the wife because it was in her heart to obey though hindered by her husband.

Second, with authority comes accountability. Although the husband had power to cancel his wife's vows after authorizing them, God held him accountable—the man would *"bear her iniquity"* (30:15). If you have been given authority over another, be very careful with that power. Be considerate of those under your watch-care, knowing that God will hold you accountable for hindering someone's service to Him.

MAR. 31 — BLURRED VISION — NUMBERS 31

"And Moses said unto them, Have ye saved all the women alive?" (Numbers 31:15).

Moses was angry because the men of war had saved the Midianite women for themselves. The men either forgot or did not care that such women had previously turned many Israelites to idolatry through their whoredoms. Moses protested, *"Behold, these caused the children of Israel...to commit trespass against the LORD in the matter of Peor, and there was a plague among the congregation of the LORD"* (31:16). That plagued killed 24,000 people in Israel, and Moses did not want God's wrath kindled once again. Praise God for faithful leaders!

Fleshly desires tend to blur spiritual eyesight. Those who do not learn from the folly of others are bound to reap the same results. Sadly, many Christians are much like the men of war, who sought to fulfill their lusts with no regard for the consequences. For example, multitudes are falling into immorality through unfiltered content on the Internet, but many believers are slow to establish safeguards to prevent their own fall.

What wrong desires are you seeking to fulfill? Consider God's admonition, *"For if ye live after the flesh, ye shall die: but if ye through the Spirit do mortify the deeds of the body, ye shall live"* (Romans 8:13).

APR. 1 — DON'T SETTLE FOR LESS — NUMBERS 32

"...let this land be given unto thy servants for a possession, and bring us not over Jordan" (Numbers 32:5).

God wants the best for our lives, but oftentimes we settle for less. The children of Israel were preparing to cross the Jordan River and inherit the land they had been waiting to possess for 40 years. Much to Moses' surprise, two and a half tribes requested not to enter the Promised Land. Understanding what led to their decision will show us why we often miss out on God's best.

First, they walked by sight, not by faith. They noticed that the country that the Lord smote east of Jordan was *"a land for cattle,"* and they reasoned with Moses, *"thy servants have cattle"* (32:4). In other words, they were satisfied with what they had seen and had no desire to follow God, thinking it could not get any better. The world may appeal to us, but God's provision is much better! Don't settle for less.

Second, they wanted an easy path. They were content to let others fight for Canaan while they enjoyed their inheritance. In the end, they still had to cross the Jordan and fight, but they did not partake of the Promised Land. When your way seems easier than God's, think again. His way is always best. Go where God leads. The fight will be worth it.

NUMBERS 33-34	**DRIVE OUT SIN**	APR. 2

"Then ye shall drive out all the inhabitants of the land from before you, and destroy all their pictures, and destroy all their molten images, and quite pluck down all their high places" (Numbers 33:52).

The Lord did not want His people to be adversely affected by the inhabitants of the land. Therefore, His instructions to Israel were clear. He told them to leave no remnant of the Canaanites or their abominations in the land. God warned, *"those which ye let remain of them shall be pricks in your eyes, and thorns in your sides, and shall vex you in the land wherein ye dwell"* (33:55). In other words, failure to obey the Lord would lead to distorted vision, pain, and trouble.

Sin will have the same devastating effect on a Christian as the Canaanites did on Israel. If we allow any vice or carnal pleasure to remain in our lives, it will hurt and trouble us. Through God's help, we must strive to *"drive out all the inhabitants"* of sin from our lives.

The text mentions pictures, idolatrous images, and places of worship. What forms of worldly entertainment linger in your home? Are there ungodly pictures on a wall, in a magazine, or on a computer that must be destroyed? Renounce worldly entertainment and anything that comes before God. Deal thoroughly with sin, or it will lead to your downfall.

NUMBERS 35-36	**GOD'S REFUGE**	APR. 3

"...he should have remained in the city of his refuge until the death of the high priest" (Numbers 35:28).

The Lord showed mercy on those who unintentionally took another man's life by establishing six cities of refuge where they could find safety. Once in the city, the slayer had to remain until the death of the high priest. Then he was free to return home and move about Israel. However, if he left prematurely, the man who was designated to take revenge for the dead man's life was allowed to kill the slayer.

Obviously, it would have been foolish for a slayer to leave the city of refuge. It would be far better to endure a temporary loss of freedom than to lose one's life. This leads to an important lesson for us. We must never complain about the restrictions that God places on our lives, knowing that they are for our own good. If the slayer ignored God's warnings, it was at his own peril. Likewise, when we cast aside the Lord's commands, we do so at great risk.

As the psalmist, we should regard the Lord as our refuge and enjoy the protection that He offers. *"I will say of the LORD, He is my refuge and my fortress: my God; in him will I trust"* (Psalm 91:2). Instead of straying from our Refuge, let us run to Him!

APR. 4 — POSSESS THE LAND — DEUT. 1

"Behold, the LORD thy God hath set the land before thee: go up and possess it, as the LORD God of thy fathers hath said unto thee; fear not, neither be discouraged" (Deuteronomy 1:21).

God wanted Israel to possess the land of Canaan. It was a *promised* land; they should have been anxious to inherit it. It was a *pleasant* land; the fields were fruitful and the cities were already built for them. There was one hindrance—it was a *possessed* land. The enemy stood between them and their possession.

The Lord has special blessings prepared for each of His children. He has spiritual territory that must be conquered. What land does God want you to possess? It could be victory over a besetting sin, a better home life, financial stability, or fruitful ministries. Whatever it is, God commands, *"go up and possess it."* Sometimes the task is not easy, but we must fight the battles that God chooses for us.

Great victories require great faith. Israel had allowed fear to hinder their obedience. As they had no need to fear, neither do we. Fear is a choice. When we look at the size of the enemy, we tremble; but when we consider the greatness of God, our faith is renewed. We are able to do all that God commands us. So, *"fear not, neither be discouraged."*

APR. 5 — WILDERNESS BLESSINGS — DEUT. 2-3

"For the LORD thy God hath blessed thee…he knoweth thy walking through this great wilderness: these forty years the LORD thy God hath been with thee; thou hast lacked nothing" (Deuteronomy 2:7).

Even when God's people are chastened, they are still blessed. This is true because chastisement is meant to correct, not destroy believers. Israel wandered through the wilderness because of their rebellion, but Moses pointed out that the Lord had been faithful to them. Notice three comforting truths that each believer can rest upon.

First, *God's providence leads us.* Despite Israel's refusal to enter the land, God had not completely given up on them. The next generation would inherit Canaan. When you stray from the Lord, He will direct your wilderness wanderings to correct you and work His will.

Second, *God's presence remains with us.* Though Israel walked through the wilderness, they were not alone. Even when chastened, can you not admit that *"the LORD thy God hath been with thee"*?

Third, *God's provision sustains us.* Though God disciplined His people, He still provided for them and they *"lacked nothing."* Although the blessings of the milk and honey were delayed, the people still had the manna in the wilderness. God is merciful in His discipline.

DEUT. 4	LISTEN AND OBEY	APR. 6

"Now therefore hearken, O Israel, unto the statutes and unto the judgments, which I teach you, for to do them, that ye may live, and go in and possess the land" (Deuteronomy 4:1).

Though the previous generation refused to possess the land, God renewed the charge to the group who survived the time in the wilderness. His instructions were simple—*"hearken"* and *"do."*

In order to succeed in the Christian life, we must listen and obey. The word *hearken* means "to listen attentively." As the Lord had given Israel detailed instructions to follow, He provides principles in the Bible for us to observe. Success is only promised to those who pay close attention to all that God commands. We have no right to *"add unto the word"* or *"diminish ought from it"* (4:2). We must follow it all.

Many in Jesus' day listened to His message when it was acceptable; but when it was difficult they said, *"This is an hard saying; who can hear it?"* (John 6:60). Because they did not like what He said, *"many of his disciples went back, and walked no more with him"* (John 6:66). Once you start picking and choosing which portions of Scripture you will follow, you set yourself in opposition to God. Before long, you will walk *"no more with him."* Don't be a casualty—*"hearken"* and *"do."*

DEUT. 5-6	DON'T FORGET	APR. 7

"Then beware lest thou forget the LORD, which brought thee forth out of the land of Egypt, from the house of bondage" (Deuteronomy 6:12).

Because the Lord loves us, He *"daily loadeth us with benefits"* (Psalm 68:19). However, when our hearts and homes become *"full of all good things"* (6:11), we can be distracted by our blessings and forget the very One who gave them to us. Knowing the selfishness of human nature, the Lord included the warning in our text, not only for Israel, but for us, too. Let's consider how to stay focused on the Lord.

Put Him first. *"And thou shalt love the LORD thy God with all thine heart, and with all thy soul, and with all thy might"* (6:5). How simple!

Second, remember the captivity from which you were delivered. As the Lord brought forth Israel *"from the house of bondage,"* He also rescued us from sin. By reflecting on our lives prior to salvation, we realize that all that we have is completely undeserved. Take a moment and thank the Lord for His pardon, peace, and provision.

Third, never allow possessions to possess you. Each time you enjoy one of the *"good things"* God has allowed you to have, lift your heart with praise and thank Him for His abundant blessings. As you acknowledge Him, you honor Him and get your eyes off self.

APR. 8   CONFIDENCE IN BATTLE   DEUT. 7-8

"Thou shalt not be afraid of them: but shalt well remember what the LORD thy God did unto Pharaoh, and unto all Egypt" (Deuteronomy 7:18).

Fear in battle is not a winning strategy. However, it can creep in when God's people lack faith. Therefore, the best way to combat fear is to promote faith in the living God. Our text shows how the Lord sought to build Israel's confidence in Him for the battle. This is the key to victory.

First, we need confidence in the *power of God*. The Lord told His people to remember what He had done to the mighty army of Pharaoh. The same God would fight for them in Canaan too. You may be facing a strong enemy, but you do not have to be overwhelmed. By rehearsing past victories, your faith will be bolstered for the present conflict. After all, what God has done before, He is able to do again.

Second, we need confidence in the *plan of God*. The Lord told the people that He would drive out the nations *"by little and little"* (7:22). Victory is not usually gained by one battle. As little victories add up, they ultimately lead to triumph. Be patient with God's plan and be happy with small victories in your life. Even little ones prove you are gaining ground, not losing it. Any victory is better than defeat.

APR. 9   UNDESERVED BLESSINGS   DEUT. 9-10

"Speak not thou in thine heart, after that the LORD thy God hath cast them out from before thee, saying, For my righteousness the LORD hath brought me in to possess this land" (Deuteronomy 9:4).

Man's pride causes him to think that he deserves every blessing he receives. This was the problem that the Lord sought to prevent with Israel. He made it clear that they were not inheriting the land because of their goodness. In fact, He said, *"Understand therefore, that the LORD thy God giveth thee not this good land to possess it for thy righteousness; for thou art a stiffnecked people"* (9:6).

Too often people try to gauge their spirituality by the size or number of their blessings. They think, "I must not be too bad since God has been so good to me." Such reasoning can lead to trouble. The truth is that even wicked people enjoy the favor of God as they breathe His air, bask in His sunshine, and drink His water. Therefore, when we consider God's blessing as an approval of our lifestyle, we may wrongly think that all of our ways please Him. Be careful not to think too highly of self.

We must remember that every blessing is undeserved. What we have is because of God's grace, not because of our merit. Have you begun to think that God owes you something? Think again.

DEUT. 11-12 — TEACH YOUR CHILDREN — APR. 10

"And ye shall teach them your children, speaking of them when thou sittest in thine house, and when thou walkest by the way, when thou liest down, and when thou risest up" (Deuteronomy 11:19).

The greatest thing parents can do for their children is to teach them the Word of God. If Israel made it a priority, God promised to multiply their days in the land. In fact, they would be *"as the days of heaven upon the earth"* (11:21). Do you want such a blessing for your family?

By teaching your children the principles, precepts, and promises of the Lord, you can ensure that they will be equipped to please God. Our text not only stresses the importance of teaching God's words but also suggests how to do it. We must be *"speaking of them"* throughout the day. Look for opportunities to apply Biblical principles to daily life while at home or out and about. Discussing God's Word with your children in the morning starts their day off right, and reading the Bible with them at night will help clear their minds of worldly influences.

Of course, we cannot teach our children properly if we have not made the Bible a priority in our own lives. Before instructing Israel to teach their children, God first said, *"Therefore shall ye lay up these my words in your heart and in your soul"* (11:18). Let's do likewise.

DEUT. 13-14 — FOLLOW GOD — APR. 11

"Thou shalt not hearken unto the words of that prophet…for the LORD your God proveth you, to know whether ye love the LORD your God with all your heart and with all your soul" (Deuteronomy 13:3).

God warned His people that a prophet must not be followed merely because of his ability to perform signs and wonders. The key to knowing if a prophet was from God rested in his message. If he in any way tried to persuade people to serve other gods, he was to be rejected, regardless of his apparent power.

In our day, false prophets abound. Their message may not be as bold as, *"Let us go after other gods, which thou hast not known, and let us serve them"* (13:2), but the effect will be the same. Preachers of the modern-day prosperity gospel are false teachers because they lead people to the gods of materialism and covetousness. Paul rebuked the believers in Galatia for accepting another gospel and exhorted, *"But though we, or an angel from heaven, preach any other gospel unto you than that which we have preached unto you, let him be accursed"* (Galatians 1:8).

Resist any temptation to follow those who claim miraculous power. Satan presents himself as an angel of light and weaves a little bit of truth with toxic error. Test all doctrine by the Bible, not by miracles.

APR. 12	A HEART FOR THE NEEDY	DEUT. 15-16

"If there be among you a poor man of one of thy brethren within any of thy gates in thy land...thou shalt not harden thine heart, nor shut thine hand from thy poor brother" (Deuteronomy 15:7).

What is your attitude toward poor people? Many times the poor are despised by those who are blessed in this world. Pride causes people to look down on the less fortunate. In severe cases, the poor are belittled by those who have much. Too often, we salve our consciences by expressing superficial pity instead of providing tangible assistance.

Giving is a matter of the heart. The Lord warned His people, *"If there be among you a poor man...thou shalt not harden thine heart."* Refusing to help someone with a true need is a willful decision. Let us be sure not to harden our hearts when prompted by God to help another.

Our heart's attitude is further revealed by the manner in which we give to the needy. The Lord said, *"thine heart shall not be grieved when thou givest unto him"* (15:10). Give from a heart of compassion, not merely out of duty. Those who honor the Lord by caring for the poor will be blessed for their sacrifice—*"for this thing the LORD thy God shall bless thee in all thy works"* (15:10). Don't miss God's blessing by failing to give with a right motive. Have a heart for God and the needy.

APR. 13	LIKE A KING	DEUT. 17-18

"And it shall be with him, and he shall read therein all the days of his life: that he may learn to fear the LORD his God, to keep all the words of this law and these statutes, to do them:" (Deuteronomy 17:19).

The Lord provided important instructions for Israel's kings to follow regarding His Word. They were to read it daily and follow it. Such advice is good not only for sovereigns but also for subjects. We would do well to do as Israel's kings were instructed.

First, we must read God's Word daily. Observe two things that we will gain by careful study of the Bible. We will *"learn to fear the LORD."* As we understand more about our Creator, we will become more dependent upon Him. Next, we will learn *"to keep"* His words. The word *keep* means "to guard." As we discover the wisdom, comfort, and guidance in God's Word, we will treasure it and guard our time in it. The king was to have his own copy of the Law, which was a luxury not all in his day could enjoy. Today, God's Word is available to multitudes, giving us a privilege previously reserved for kings and priests.

Second, not only must we read God's commands, we must *"do them."* The man who is *"blessed in his deed"* is a doer of the Word, not merely a hearer (James 1:25). Put into practice all that God teaches you.

DEUT. 19-21	JUDGMENT DETERS SIN	APR. 14

"...behold, if the witness be a false witness, and hath testified falsely against his brother; then shall ye do unto him, as he had thought to have done unto his brother" (Deuteronomy 19:18-19).

Tolerance of sin tends to breed more tolerance. When a society is soft on wrongdoing, corruption spreads like cancer. The Lord had a very strict policy in Israel to help combat the sin of bearing false witness. He who testified falsely against another, hoping to bring judgment upon him, would receive the very punishment he wished on the other.

The result of this *"eye for eye"* retribution was that others would be deterred from bearing false witness. The Lord said, *"And those which remain shall hear, and fear, and shall henceforth commit no more any such evil among you"* (19:20). When enforced, it made people think twice before repeating the same offence.

Though the harsh demands of the Law given to Israel are not meant for us to follow, we can see the importance of executing appropriate judgment. As believers, we must not be influenced by the world's philosophy of accepting and excusing sin. For example, if we allow our children to be disobedient, disrespectful, or dishonest without correcting them, not only will they continue to sin but their siblings will too.

DEUT. 22-23	DISTINCTION	APR. 15

"The woman shall not wear that which pertaineth unto a man, neither shall a man put on a woman's garment: for all that do so are abomination unto the LORD thy God" (Deuteronomy 22:5).

The lines of distinction between the sexes are seemingly becoming blurrier with each passing day. While an increasing number of people claim to struggle with gender identity, God's Word has remained constant about the subject. Consider two principles of distinction from the Scriptures.

First, we are distinct by creation. *"But from the beginning of the creation God made them male and female"* (Mark 10:6). A person's gender at birth is his or her gender. God made you either male or female.

Second, we are to reflect God's distinction by our appearance. Our text verse clearly draws a contrast between men's and women's clothing. Over the past several decades, it has become common for women to wear clothing that *"pertaineth unto a man."* Now it is acceptable for men to dress effeminately. Such behavior destroys God-intended distinction and contributes to gender identity problems. Instead of excusing this command in the Bible, every believer should strive to be as distinct in his/her appearance as God desires. Failure to do so is an abomination.

| APR. 16 | LEAVE A LITTLE | DEUT. 24-25 |

"When thou cuttest down thine harvest in thy field, and hast forgot a sheaf in the field, thou shalt not go again to fetch it: it shall be for the stranger, for the fatherless, and for the widow: that the LORD thy God may bless thee in all the work of thine hands" (Deuteronomy 24:19).

Once again we see the mercy of God on display as He made provision for the vulnerable. Those who had no means to provide for themselves were allowed to gather the remnants of another's harvest. One more sheaf to a man with much would have been insignificant, but it may have made a huge difference to a person struggling to survive. Let us not neglect to spare a bit of our abundance for the less fortunate. They will benefit from it far more than we will.

A heart that wants everything for self is greedy. As Christians, our focus in life should not be strictly upon ourselves. Paul reminded us to consider the needs of others—*"Look not every man on his own things, but every man also on the things of others"* (Philippians 2:4). Don't live to snatch up all that you can; purposefully leave a little for others.

A special promise is given to those who are thoughtful of others. A small deed of kindness can bring abundant rewards. Help the needy *"that the LORD thy God may bless thee in all the work of thine hands."*

| APR. 17 | HONOR THE LORD | DEUT. 26-27 |

"And now, behold, I have brought the firstfruits of the land, which thou, O LORD, hast given me. And thou shalt set it before the LORD thy God, and worship before the LORD thy God" (Deuteronomy 26:10).

The above words were to be spoken by God's people after inheriting the Promised Land. They were to bring the first fruits that the Lord had provided for them and worship Him for His abundant provision. Certainly, every believer should honor the Lord with their words and their wealth. After all, it is because of Him that we possess any good thing—*"for it is he that giveth thee power to get wealth"* (8:18).

As we acknowledge the Lord for His supply, we remember the source of our blessings. When was the last time you took inventory of your many material and spiritual blessings and proclaimed, *"'thou, O LORD, hast given me'* these things"? Giving to God is good, but doing so with a grateful heart is better. Too often Christians give but fail to honor the Lord because their motive was duty, not gratitude.

It was only after the people honored God that they were free to enjoy His blessings. After our text we read, *"thou shalt rejoice in every good thing which the LORD thy God hath given unto thee"* (26:11). Keep your focus on the Lord, not merely the blessings He bestows.

Deut. 28	IT'S YOUR CHOICE	Apr. 18

"And all these blessings shall come on thee, and overtake thee, if thou shalt hearken unto the voice of the LORD thy God" (Deuteronomy 28:2).

The word *Deuteronomy* means "second law." Forty years had passed since the Law had been given the first time, and this new generation needed to hear it for themselves. Therefore, this book repeats much of what we have read earlier in the Pentateuch. After letting His people know what was required of them, the Lord explained that they would be blessed for their obedience and cursed for their rebellion.

The blessings included provision, protection, prestige, and power. The Lord promised to open *"his good treasure"* for them to enjoy (28:12). The curses for disobedience were more numerous than the blessings for obedience, obviously to encourage compliance to the Law.

The word *curse* involves the calling of trouble upon a person. God does not needlessly trouble His people, but He has no choice when they disregard His loving instructions. The chastisement listed is horrifying. In addition to losing the blessings mentioned above, the destruction of all that was dear unto them, including their families, was promised.

God's blessings or curses will *"come on"* and *"overtake"* each of us. You cannot escape the goodness or chastisement He intends for you.

Deut. 29-30	THE SECRET THINGS	Apr. 19

"The secret things belong unto the LORD our God: but those things which are revealed belong unto us and to our children for ever, that we may do all the words of this law" (Deuteronomy 29:29).

Diligent Bible study is commendable, but some mysteries are simply not meant to be understood. Our text says it quite aptly—some things *"belong unto the LORD"* and other things *"belong unto us."* It is dangerous to speculate about subjects the Bible is silent about.

Despite the revelations given to Paul, he realized that his knowledge of the Most High was limited. He said, *"For now we see through a glass, darkly; but then face to face: now I know in part; but then shall I know even as also I am known"* (1 Corinthians 13:12). Some things we will not know until we get to heaven and see the Lord face to face.

Perhaps the area with which people get the most distracted is prophecy. Rather than speculate about things we are unsure about, we are to continue in the things we have *"been assured of"* (2 Timothy 3:14). How will it help a person to know about the end times if he fails to gain victory over sin? The Bible is a practical Book. It is not merely for information but for application. Instead of getting preoccupied with the *"secret things,"* obey what God has clearly revealed (30:11-14).

APR. 20 — PROMISES FOR THE BATTLE — DEUT. 31

"And the LORD, he it is that doth go before thee; he will be with thee, he will not fail thee, neither forsake thee: fear not, neither be dismayed" (Deuteronomy 31:8).

Moses would soon die, and Joshua would have some big shoes to fill! He could have easily been overwhelmed with the responsibility of leading the entire nation of Israel to conquer Canaan, but God encouraged him. When you face a task that seems beyond your ability, reflect upon the three promises which were given to Joshua.

First, *"he will be with thee."* The reason we know the Lord will be with us in battle is because He goes before us to prepare the way. Whatever God calls you to do, you have the assurance of His presence. He will be with you whether He leads you across the street or across the sea to witness for Him. Our duty is to *"fear not, neither be dismayed."*

Second, *"he will not fail thee."* Since we have God's presence, we are also assured of His power. He has never lost a battle. The only way we can fail is to refuse to go to war with God or follow His instructions.

Third, He will not *"forsake thee."* Not only will God enter the battle with you, He will remain with you until the victory is secured. Though we often disappoint the Lord, He is too noble to abandon us.

APR. 21 — CONSIDER YOUR LATTER END — DEUT. 32

"O that they were wise, that they understood this, that they would consider their latter end!" (Deuteronomy 32:29).

The song of Moses was given to Israel as a reminder of God's fairness in judgment—*"He is the Rock, his work is perfect: for all his ways are judgment: a God of truth and without iniquity, just and right is he"* (32:4). The Lord knew that Israel would rebel, and He wanted them to realize that His judgment upon them would be justified.

Contained in the song is God's desire for His people—*"O that they were wise."* He lamented their lack of wisdom and shortsightedness. He longed for His people to enjoy all of the blessings that He had planned for them, but their disobedience brought judgment instead of favor. How often we miss God's best for our lives!

One of the main problems of the people was that they would not *"consider their latter end."* It is not just that they *did not* consider it but that they *would not*. This implies that they willfully refused to think about their future. In other words, they knew that their actions were wrong but did not want to think about the consequences. How often do you act the same way? Never forget that today's decisions will produce tomorrow's results. Be careful! Live for the future, not the present.

Deut. 33-34 — Uniquely Blessed — Apr. 22

"And this is the blessing, wherewith Moses the man of God blessed the children of Israel before his death" (Deuteronomy 33:1).

The majority of chapter 33 records the blessings that Moses pronounced on the twelve tribes before his death. It is interesting to note that each tribe received their own unique blessing, teaching us that we are not all blessed in the same manner. When we look on the favor God has shown to others, we must refuse to be jealous; and when we see God's special blessing in our own lives, we must guard against pride.

The Lord, in His wisdom, knows exactly what each of us needs and will supply us with what is necessary to accomplish His will. Too often Christians focus on the blessings that others receive and feel sorry for themselves, thinking they have been shortchanged by God. Though you may not have what someone else has, you certainly enjoy privileges that others do not. Focus on what you have, not on what you lack!

God never makes mistakes—*"his work is perfect...just and right is he"* (32:4). You have been uniquely blessed. Rejoice in the talents, gifts, and means that God has granted you. Don't compare yourself to anyone else. The Lord made you for a purpose and has equipped you to fulfill it. So, seek to accomplish His will each day.

Joshua 1-2 — Divine Assistance — Apr. 23

"Now after the death of Moses the servant of the LORD it came to pass, that the LORD spake unto Joshua the son of Nun" (Joshua 1:1).

When Moses died, God was not taken by surprise. He had a man prepared to fill the vacancy in leadership. Along with calling Joshua, the Lord also reassured him with several promises. Notice what we can expect when God calls us to a task:

God's provision—*"that have I given unto you"* (1:3). As the Lord promised to provide land to Israel, we can expect to gain spiritual territory in our lives. What has He called you to possess for Him?

God's power—*"There shall not any man be able to stand before thee all the days of thy life"* (1:5). None of the mighty kings of Canaan could defeat Joshua, and the same God stands with and fights for us.

God's presence—*"as I was with Moses, so I will be with thee"* (1:5). Moses never had to face a foe without the assurance of God's divine presence. When the battle rages and fear begins to creep into your heart, remember the strengthening words, *"I will be with thee."*

God's prosperity—*"thou shalt make thy way prosperous, and then thou shalt have good success"* (1:8). If we meditate in God's Word day and night as Joshua did, we can be confident of similar success.

| APR. 24 | STEPS OF FAITH | JOSHUA 3-5 |

"And it shall come to pass, as soon as the soles of the feet of the priests...shall rest in the waters of Jordan, that the waters of Jordan shall be cut off" (Joshua 3:13).

What stands between you and God's blessing? For Israel, it was the Jordan River. Perhaps you face an overwhelming obstacle today. As the Lord had a plan for Israel to forge ahead, He also has one for you.

God promised that once the priests stepped into Jordan, the waters would be cut off. Fear may have hindered the priests and caused them to wonder if the plan was safe or even feasible. In order to succeed, the priests needed faith to take the first step. It is important to note that the waters did not stand on a heap until they obeyed. Once their feet touched the water, God began to work. Since obedience precedes blessing, never hesitate to follow God's instructions.

The Lord wants you to take steps of faith. At times, He will lead you to do things exceedingly difficult or against conventional wisdom. However, when you follow His commands, you can expect results. Troubled waters that stand between you and God's blessing will only be *"cut off"* as you take steps of faith. Be sure to follow the priests' example and base your actions on God's Word, not on your whims.

| APR. 25 | SIN IN THE CAMP | JOSHUA 6-7 |

"And the LORD said unto Joshua, Get thee up; wherefore liest thou thus upon thy face?" (Joshua 7:10).

At the end of chapter six we read, *"the LORD was with Joshua"* (6:27). However, a few verses later we see Israel defeated in battle. What happened? *"Israel committed a trespass in the accursed thing"* (7:1). Sin always ruins things. Let's consider what occurs when sin enters the camp.

Notice the *reaction* of Joshua. He questioned God, saying, *"Alas, O Lord GOD, wherefore hast thou at all brought this people over Jordan, to deliver us into the hand of the Amorites, to destroy us?"* (7:7). If that wasn't enough, Joshua then complained about the loss, *"would to God we had been content, and dwelt on the other side Jordan!"* (7:7). Do you ever find yourself blaming God when things go wrong? That won't help.

Next we see God's *rebuke*—*"Get thee up."* There was a reason for their defeat in battle. Joshua should have been searching for the cause, not blaming the Lord. The *reason* for their failure was plain. God said, *"Israel hath sinned"* (7:11). When we cannot stand before the enemy, we should examine our lives to see if a particular sin is the cause.

The *remedy* is simple—*"take away the accursed thing"* (7:13).

JOSHUA 8-9	FIGHTING GOD'S WAY	APR. 26

"And the LORD said unto Joshua, Fear not, neither be thou dismayed: take all the people of war with thee, and arise, go up to Ai" (Joshua 8:1).

Yesterday we read about Israel's loss in the battle of Ai. They had not consulted the Lord before the assault and presumed they could win with a small detachment of soldiers. After their loss, they learned a valuable lesson—God's battles must be fought God's way.

Attacks must be *complete*. For this second assault on Ai God commanded, *"take all the people of war with thee."* Israel was overconfident the first time, only sending three thousand men to battle. Victory is not secured by half-hearted efforts. We must be fully committed, throwing all we have into the fight. Use every spiritual weapon you have against the enemy if you hope to be victorious.

Attacks have to be *concentrated*. The Lord commanded Joshua, *"Stretch out the spear that is in thy hand toward Ai"* (8:18). This is a beautiful picture of focusing our attack on the enemy. Single out a particular sin to defeat and direct all your resources toward conquering it.

Attacks need to be *continued*. Joshua did not draw back his spear until *"he had utterly destroyed all the inhabitants of Ai"* (8:26). If you hope to win your battles, you must persevere in the fight. Don't quit!

JOSHUA 10	PEACE FOLLOWS THE BATTLE	APR. 27

"And all the people returned to the camp to Joshua at Makkedah in peace" (Joshua 10:21).

Five powerful kings conspired to attack Gibeon because they had made peace with Israel. When Joshua went to defend the city, he entered the battle with a promise from God. The Lord said, *"Fear them not: for I have delivered them into thine hand; there shall not a man of them stand before thee"* (10:8). With assurance of victory, Joshua gathered the men of valor and engaged the enemy.

After the battle we read that *"all the people returned to the camp…in peace."* Not one of Israel's soldiers was injured or slain in the battle! This provides wonderful reassurance to all of us who are soldiers of Jesus Christ. The Lord may have skirmishes for us to encounter, but we will not be worse for wear. God sends us not to be slain or disfigured but to gain victory. Our end will be as Israel's. At the conclusion of the battle, we will possess more spiritual territory and enjoy God's peace.

Do not dread the conflict that God has led you to face. Rest upon His promises and trust His goodness for a decisive victory. If you are weary in battle, remember that peace awaits those who stay in the fight and win. Further, like Israel, you will gain confidence for future battles.

APR. 28   SLAY THE GIANTS   JOSHUA 11-12

"There was none of the Anakims left in the land of the children of Israel: only in Gaza, in Gath, and in Ashdod, there remained" (Joshua 11:22).

The Anakims were the giants that caused Israel to fear entering the Promised Land after the ten spies gave their evil report. As a result, God's people had to wander in the wilderness for forty years until the faithless generation died off. Allowing the giants to remain in the land could have given Israel more problems in the future. Therefore, Joshua did well when he *"destroyed them utterly with their cities"* (11:21).

Unfortunately, Israel stopped short of expelling all of the giants. Some remained in Gaza, Gath, and Ashdod. This was not a failure on Joshua's part because *"he left nothing undone of all that the LORD commanded Moses"* (11:15). The individual tribes who divided the inheritance failed to drive out the remaining inhabitants from these three cities. Thus, the giants continued to pose a threat for decades. Sadly, Israel did not defeat these Philistine cities until the days of David.

It is important that we deal thoroughly with whatever may hinder our service to God. Perhaps you face a giant that strikes fear in your heart. Determine to root out any attitude, association, or action in your life that prevents you from inheriting the full portion of God's promised blessing.

APR. 29   I WANT THAT MOUNTAIN   JOSHUA 13-14

"Now therefore give me this mountain" (Joshua 14:12).

God rewards His faithful servants. Joshua and Caleb were the only adults to enter the Promised Land from the previous generation. Finally, Caleb was to receive the inheritance that the Lord had promised. This account provides an example for all of us to follow.

Notice the *great dedication*. God had promised a blessing to Caleb because he *"wholly followed the LORD"* (14:9). The reason many miss God's best is because they only half-heartedly serve the Lord. If you want His full blessing, hold nothing back and follow Him completely.

Next, consider the *great deliverance*. Caleb testified, *"the LORD hath kept me alive, as he said, these forty and five years"* (14:10). Those words *"as he said"* are a precious reminder that God will do what He has pledged. You may have to wait many years as did Caleb, but rest assured that the Lord will deliver on His promise.

We also observe a *great discovery*. As an old man, Caleb had strength to fight the giants who had reinvaded the high country. He proclaimed, *"I am as strong this day as I was in the day that Moses sent me"* (14:11). God can strengthen you to do the impossible. Only show *great determination* and say as Caleb did, *"give me this mountain."*

| Joshua 15-16 | Give Me a Blessing | Apr. 30 |

"Give me a blessing; for thou hast given me a south land; give me also springs of water" (Joshua 15:19).

Achsah, Caleb's daughter, sought springs of water for the land her father had already given. She made a simple petition—*"Give me a blessing."* This was not a disrespectful demand. On the contrary, it showed the confidence she had in her father. She reasoned that since he had provided the south land, he would also give her the necessary springs to water it. This account provides a beautiful picture of prayer.

When Achsah approached her father, he said, *"What wouldest thou?"* (15:18). In today's language we would say, "What would you like me to do?" Does this not remind us of our heavenly Father's invitation to pray? He said, *"Call unto me, and I will answer thee, and shew thee great and mighty things, which thou knowest not"* (Jeremiah 33:3). God awaits your requests. Go to Him at once with all your needs!

Consider what Achsah requested—*"springs of water."* Is this not a reminder of our need for the Holy Spirit? Jesus said of each believer, *"out of his belly shall flow rivers of living water"* (John 7:38). As Caleb's daughter boldly requested *"springs of water"* from her father, let us ask for a daily filling of the Spirit from our heavenly Father.

| Joshua 17-18 | Stop Whining | May 1 |

"Why hast thou given me but one lot and one portion to inherit, seeing I am a great people...?" (Joshua 17:14).

The children of Joseph were appointed a portion of the land from God. Instead of being thankful and setting out to take possession of it, they wanted more. Joshua directed them to the hill country, but they cried, *"The hill is not enough for us"* (17:16). Oh, how many of God's people utter those ungrateful words—*"not enough"*!

Selfishness is often accompanied by other sins. The people were lazy and fearful. Twice Joshua had to tell them to go up to the wood country and cut down an area large enough to settle in. They seemed reluctant to work for it. Some are prone to complain about that which requires work; they are always looking for an easier path.

Setting their eyes on the open valleys, the people saw problems there too. They were afraid of the Canaanites who were defended by formidable chariots of iron. So, everywhere they looked, they seemed to be unsatisfied with their prospects. Does that sound like you?

It is easy to complain about our portions in life or the areas of service God chooses for us. However, we must not allow laziness or fear to hinder us from taking possession. Let's stop whining and get busy!

| MAY 2 | LOOSEN YOUR GRIP | JOSHUA 19 |

"Out of the portion of the children of Judah was the inheritance of the children of Simeon: for the part of the children of Judah was too much for them" (Joshua 19:9).

Yesterday we read about the children of Joseph who thought their portion was too small. Today, we see a tribe that had too much land to possess. Consequently, the Lord gave part of Judah's inheritance to Simeon. How would you have reacted if you were Judah?

It is human nature to cling to one's possessions. For example, many of us have a lot of junk sitting around our homes that we *might* use in the future, even though it serves no immediate purpose. We would never think of getting rid of it simply because it belongs to us. Consider the words that Jesus used to encourage us not to hold too tightly to material blessings, *"freely ye have received, freely give"* (Matthew 10:8).

We should learn to loosen our grip on our treasure. Don't be upset when the Lord directs you to share some of what you have been given with others. In Judah's case, it was not even a case of giving. God took it and gave it to another. Should the Lord choose to take some of your earthly goods away, would you be bitter? Like Judah, what we have is only an inheritance. Our heavenly Father decides what we get of His.

| MAY 3 | ALL CAME TO PASS | JOSHUA 20-21 |

"There failed not ought of any good thing which the LORD had spoken unto the house of Israel; all came to pass" (Joshua 21:45).

Our text comes at the conclusion of the division of the land. In today's reading the cities of refuge were chosen and the Levites received their cities. Everything that God promised before the children of Israel conquered Canaan came to pass. God keeps His promises.

As promised, He gave *possessions*—*"the LORD gave unto Israel all the land which he sware to give unto their fathers"* (21:43). When God says He will provide for your needs, rest assured that He will.

As promised, He gave *peace*—*"the LORD gave them rest round about"* (21:44). Though they had to wander in the wilderness for forty years and then fight many battles once they entered the Promised Land, they finally had rest. Life may seem tiresome and troublesome at times, but God gives refreshing seasons when we need them.

As promised, He gave *power*—*"there stood not a man of all their enemies before them"* (21:44). God gave them the ability to defeat their foes. He will strengthen you too. Notice that not one *"good thing"* God promised to His people failed; it *"all came to pass."* What *"good thing"* has He promised you? Wait patiently for Him to bring it to pass.

JOSHUA 22-23   JUMPING TO CONCLUSIONS   MAY 4

"And when the children of Israel heard of it, the whole congregation of the children of Israel gathered themselves together at Shiloh, to go up to war against them" (Joshua 22:12).

After the land was divided, the men of war from the two and a half tribes were allowed to return to their possessions east of Jordan. When they came to the border, they built *"a great altar to see to"* (22:10). Thinking they did so out of rebellion to the Lord, Israel prepared to go to war in order to prevent God's judgment on the nation.

Thankfully, before descending into battle, Israel sent a small delegation of leaders to confront the tribes on the other side. Though they were accusative at first, they soon realized that they had misunderstood the intentions of their brethren. In the end, Israel rejoiced to learn that the altar was built as a witness to the true God, not in rebellion against Him.

When you have a conflict with another, go to him personally and listen to his side of the story. Do not react foolishly by forming a plan of attack against him. Never allow pride to lead you to think the worst of others. Speaking face to face in a civilized manner can clear up misunderstandings and prevent needless battles between brethren.

JOSHUA 24   DIVIDED HEARTS   MAY 5

"Now therefore put away, said he, the strange gods which are among you, and incline your heart unto the LORD God of Israel" (Joshua 24:23).

Joshua gathered Israel and rehearsed the Lord's dealings with His people. He reminded them of the great deliverance from Egypt and the blessings of the Promised Land. With all that God had done for them, they should have served Him gladly. Joshua challenged the people, *"Now therefore fear the LORD, and serve him in sincerity and in truth...choose you this day whom ye will serve"* (24:14-15). He told them to decide between their false gods and the Lord. Joshua concluded by saying, *"as for me and my house, we will serve the LORD"* (24:15).

The people responded with the right words, saying, *"we also serve the LORD; for he is our God"* (24:18). However, they were still clinging to strange gods. Their hearts were divided, wanting the benefits of serving God along with the pleasure of following worldly pursuits.

Do you ever struggle with a divided heart? Perhaps you want God's blessings but are drawn to the worldliness around you. If so, it is time to *"put away...the strange gods"* and *"incline your heart unto the LORD God."* In other words, get rid of your sin and seek God wholeheartedly. Jesus made it clear, *"No man can serve two masters"* (Matthew 6:24).

MAY 6	THE NEXT GENERATION	JUDGES 1-2

"...there arose another generation after them, which knew not the LORD, nor yet the works which he had done for Israel" (Judges 2:10).

Israel failed to drive out the inhabitants of the land as commanded and suffered terribly as a result. God said, *"they shall be as thorns in your sides, and their gods shall be a snare unto you"* (2:3). Though Israel later *"served the LORD all the days of Joshua, and all the days of the elders that outlived Joshua"* (2:7), they failed their children in two ways.

First, they neglected to teach their children about God and His Word. Consequently, *"there arose another generation after them, which knew not the LORD."* How sad! As a result, the next generation *"forsook the LORD, and served Baal and Ashtaroth"* (2:13). Then God's anger was kindled and *"the hand of the LORD was against them for evil...and they were greatly distressed"* (2:15). Is that what you want for your children? When we fail to help them develop a personal relationship with God, they will serve the gods promoted by our culture and reap the results.

Second, their disobedience made it easier for their descendants to sin. If Israel had driven out the Canaanites, their children would never have learned about Baal worship. When we allow sin to remain in our lives, it will eventually influence our children. Consider your family.

MAY 7	TURN TO THE LORD	JUDGES 3-4

"And when the children of Israel cried unto the LORD, the LORD raised up a deliverer" (Judges 3:9).

After the death of Joshua, the children of Israel forsook the Lord. What followed was a pattern of judgment, deliverance, rebellion, and further judgment. During this period, God raised up judges to deliver His people from their oppressors when they turned back to Him.

As noted yesterday, the Lord left some of the heathen in the land. This was a *test* for Israel—*"they were to prove Israel...to know whether they would hearken unto the commandments of the LORD"* (3:4). God may use the ungodly to test us too. Will you follow Him or the world?

We also notice Israel's *trespass*. They failed God's test and *"did evil in the sight of the LORD"* (3:7). Never excuse your disobedience as a mistake; it is *"evil in the sight of the LORD."*

The result of their sin was *trouble*—*"the anger of the LORD was hot against Israel"* (3:8). They were oppressed by Mesopotamia for eight years. How long do you endure hardship before you repent?

Finally, we see *turning*—*"Israel cried unto the LORD."* He was merciful and gave them a deliverer. We may ask why they waited so long to seek God's help. A better question is why do we wait so long?

| JUDGES 5-6 | CONSEQUENCES OF SIN | MAY 8 |

"And the children of Israel did evil in the sight of the LORD: and the LORD delivered them into the hand of Midian seven years" (Judges 6:1).

Israel enjoyed forty years of peace after the victory led by Deborah and Barak. Instead of remaining faithful to God, they *"did evil in the sight of the LORD."* This time God allowed the Midianites to oppress them. Let's observe the consequences of their sin to avoid similar troubles.

Sin leads to *fear.* Israel made dens, caves, and strong holds to hide from the Midianites. Did not Adam and Eve hide from God in the Garden of Eden after they sinned? Sin puts us in retreat mode, running from our enemies and hiding from God.

Sin leads to *fruitlessness.* When *"Israel had sown...the Midianites came up...and destroyed the increase of the earth"* (6:3-4). They did not get to enjoy the fruits of their labor. If we get away from the Lord, He can make all of our best efforts futile. Does it ever seem like you are spinning your wheels, getting nowhere in life? Check your heart for sin.

Sin leads to *failure.* Instead of experiencing great blessings, *"Israel was greatly impoverished"* (6:6). Christians who backslide can become bankrupt financially, emotionally, and spiritually. Have you strayed from God? If so, do what Israel did—they *"cried unto the LORD"* (6:7).

| JUDGES 7-8 | FICKLE HEARTS | MAY 9 |

"And it came to pass, as soon as Gideon was dead, that the children of Israel turned again, and went a whoring after Baalim" (Judges 8:33).

The Lord called Gideon to deliver Israel from the Midianites. When he gathered his army, the Lord said, *"The people that are with thee are too many"* (7:2). God knew that they were proud and would take credit for the victory by saying, *"Mine own hand hath saved me"* (7:2). Therefore, He chose a small band of men to lead an unconventional attack on the enemy. After God provided a great victory, Israel said to Gideon, *"Rule thou over us"* (8:22), but he declined and said, *"the LORD shall rule over you"* (8:23). He wanted them to serve God, not him.

Despite God's mercy, Israel proved that they did not want God to rule over them. Notice how quickly they turned back to Baalim—it was *"as soon as Gideon was dead."* How sad! They only did right because of Gideon. As soon as they could, they went back to their sin.

Unfortunately, many people in our day are no different. They superficially serve God as long as an authority in their lives compels them to do so. However, at their first opportunity, they run full steam ahead into sin. Be careful that your service is motivated by love for God, not merely by fear of man. Watch for the same attitude in your children.

May 10   Sin's Payday   Judges 9

"Thus God rendered the wickedness of Abimelech, which he did unto his father, in slaying his seventy brethren" (Judges 9:56).

The life of Abimelech illustrates how sin catches up to people. His father was Gideon, but he did not have a place of prominence among his brethren because his mother was a concubine. Abimelech's name means "of a king," and he wanted to live up to his name and be a ruler. With the help of the men of Shechem, he conspired to kill his seventy brothers. Managing to escape, Jotham confronted his brothers' murderers and pronounced God's judgment upon them.

Abimelech reigned for three years, and then the Lord troubled him. *"God sent an evil spirit between Abimelech and the men of Shechem; and the men of Shechem dealt treacherously with Abimelech"* (9:23). In the end, Abimelech and others involved in the evil plot were dead.

We can learn a couple of lessons from this account. First, selfish aspirations can lead to disregard for others. If we are not careful, we will harm others to achieve our goals. Second, God notices every sin. Nothing escapes His attention, and He will trouble those who break His commandments. Third, though judgment may be delayed for a season, it will come. You will always reap what you sow. Sin has a payday.

May 11   Carnal Service   Judges 10-11

"Jephthah vowed a vow unto the LORD" (Judges 11:30).

The Lord chose Jephthah to deliver Israel from the Ammonites. Though God's Spirit enabled Jephthah to defend Israel, he was not a godly man. Consider how his terrible vow illustrates fleshly service.

It was *selfish*. He asked God, *"deliver the children of Ammon into mine hands"* (11:30). It wasn't for Israel; it was all about him. Be careful that your service is not for promotion of self.

It was *foolish*. He promised to offer as a burnt offering the first thing that met him out of his house when he returned from battle. What normally comes out to meet someone? A person! No doubt it would have been his wife or daughter. Never make careless promises to God.

It was *harsh*. When his daughter rejoiced to see him, he scolded her for greeting him, saying, *"thou art one of them that trouble me"* (11:35). It was his fault, not hers! Don't blame others for your bad decisions.

It was *baseless*. God's directions for burnt offerings did not include human sacrifices. Jephthah was askew to insist on breaking one of God's commands to keep an unscriptural promise. It is never right to do wrong.

It was *callous*. The Bible says that he performed *"his vow which he had vowed"* (11:39). Though wrong, he thought he was right. How sad!

| JUDGES 12-14 | SELF-WILLED SERVANTS | MAY 12 |

"And Samson said unto his father, Get her for me;
for she pleaseth me well" (Judges 14:3).

Though Samson was strong physically, he was weak morally. He is another example of people who serve God the way they see fit. Notice Samson's disregard for God's Word.

First, he sought to marry a heathen woman, which was forbidden in the Law (Deuteronomy 7:1-3). Further, he chose her simply because, as he put it, *"she pleaseth me well."* Was that not a fleshly desire? Though God used Samson's decision for His glory, it does not mean He condoned it. Second, he disregarded his Nazarite vow by eating honey out of a dead lion. Third, after marrying the Philistine, he abandoned her when in a fit of rage. Samson repeatedly put his interests first.

It is difficult to understand why God used such self-willed people like Samson until we remember how merciful He is to use us. Lest we think that selfishness is blessed in the end, read tomorrow's Scripture passage and see that Samson's life ended in self-destruction. Be careful not to assume that God is obligated to bless or use you when you are not fully submitted to His will. The account of Samson should serve as a reminder that God can withdraw His power from us at any moment.

| JUDGES 15-16 | THE HUMBLED HERO | MAY 13 |

"But the Philistines took him, and put out his eyes, and brought him down to Gaza, and bound him with fetters of brass" (Judges 16:21).

Samson provides a dilemma for many believers. On one hand, he seems like a hero, but on the other hand he is a terrible role model. As a hero, he defeated God's enemies, the Philistines. He was strong and zealous. He captured three hundred foxes to use to burn the fields of his adversaries, killed one thousand people with a jawbone of a donkey, and carried away the city gates of Gaza on his shoulders. While he seems heroic, we also see a dark side of the man. He had unbridled lust for ungodly women; he committed fornication with a harlot and loved the deceptive Delilah (16:1-4). What can we conclude from Samson's life?

First, we should not glorify men. As Samson deserves no credit for his power, neither do others in our day. Learn to admire the mighty power of God's Spirit upon a man more than a man's exploits. Second, remember that sin is destructive. God allowed Samson's lust to defeat him. As Delilah conquered Samson, so your lust will put you to shame. In the end, Samson lost his eyes which he used for lust and his freedom which he used to pursue his passions. Worst of all, he lost his ministry as judge. What will you lose because of your sin? Fear your passions!

MAY 14   WAYWARD WORSHIP   JUDGES 17-18

"In those days there was no king in Israel, but every man did that which was right in his own eyes" (Judges 17:6).

The above verse speaks of the religious climate of Israel. People worshipped God how they pleased, regardless of what the Lord had prescribed in His Word. For instance, Micah had idols in his home and disregarded the Ten Commandments which forbid idolatry. Further, he hired a personal priest to give him favor with God but ignored God's guidelines for the priesthood. Man's attempts to please God are always in vain when they veer from the principles set forth in Scripture.

Today, people try to worship God in their own way too. Let's consider a few examples. Many mainline denominations practice infant baptism even though there is no basis for it in Scripture. Other churches emphasize gifts such as tongues, prophecy, and "on demand" healings, ignoring that the Bible clearly states that such gifts ceased upon the completion of the New Testament (1 Corinthians 13:8-10). Sadly, many fundamental churches have joined the bandwagon by incorporating worldly "worship" music in their services, despite God's command to *"abstain from fleshly lusts, which war against the soul"* (1 Peter 2:11). Beware that you do not try to worship God your own way.

MAY 15   CONSIDER, LEARN, AND SPEAK UP   JUDGES 19

"...consider of it, take advice, and speak your minds" (Judges 19:30).

The moral decline in Israel had reached new lows. The depravity of man is on full display in this chapter. We see whoredom, the bold demands of sodomites, an old man offering his daughter to the sodomites, a man giving his concubine to be abused by the perverts, the murder of the concubine, and the heartless reaction of her husband.

When we look around our nation today, we see similar wicked practices. Immorality, sexual perversion, and murder abound. In Israel's case, it was seemingly uncommon. Notice the testimony of the people who witnessed the terrible deeds mentioned above. They said, *"There was no such deed done nor seen from the day that the children of Israel came up out of the land of Egypt unto this day"* (19:30). In other words, it was not as prevalent as sin has become in our day.

If we are shocked and appalled by the deeds recorded in today's reading, we should be doubly offended by what has become acceptable in our own society. The chapter concludes with a challenge that we would do well to follow—*"consider of it, take advice, and speak your minds."* Never become tolerant of the sin around you. Consider it lest you indulge in it, and don't fear to voice your objections to others.

JUDGES 20	**STAND WITH THE RIGHTEOUS**	MAY 16

"But the children of Benjamin would not hearken to the voice of their brethren the children of Israel" (Judges 20:13).

When the children of Israel heard of the evil act committed by the sons of Belial in Gibeah, they rose to action and sought to *"put them to death, and put away evil from Israel"* (20:13). Their purpose was not revenge but to purge the wickedness from their nation.

The tribe of Benjamin, however, rallied to the defense of Gibeah and waged war against Israel. Why? Because *"the men of the place were Benjamites"* (19:16). In other words, they defended wickedness on the basis of kinship.

Too often we hear people say, "I know they are wrong, but they are my relatives. Don't criticize them." If you have to choose sides, base your decision on your faith, not family ties or friendship. It is the duty of every believer to side with righteousness. This is not to say that we turn our backs on family and friends. We are not an army like Israel out to destroy evil doers. Our tactics are different. We should *"restore such an one in the spirit of meekness"* (Galatians 6:1), not condone his sin. Because Benjamin sided with wickedness, they suffered great loss. When you choose the wrong side, you might partake of their judgment.

JUDGES 21	**MISGUIDED PRAYER**	MAY 17

"And the people came to the house of God...and lifted up their voices, and wept sore; And said, O LORD God of Israel, why is this come to pass...?" (Judges 21:2-3).

We learned yesterday of Benjamin's punishment for defending the evildoers who had abused and killed a man's concubine. As a result, the men which remained of the tribe of Benjamin lacked wives, and Israel worried that the tribe would dwindle to nothing. Having previously sworn not to give their daughters to the Benjamites, they faced a dilemma. So, they went to the house of God and mourned.

Unfortunately, they offered the wrong prayer. They asked, "Why did this happen?" They already knew why. They should have inquired, "What shall we do to fix the problem?" Their prayer was misguided.

Be careful not to repeat Israel's error when you pray. When the cause of your problem is already known, do not ask why as if to imply that it is God's fault. Instead, seek a solution from Him. Israel never asked what to do about their problem, leaving them to figure it out on their own. Perhaps they would have received a better plan than allowing their daughters to be randomly snatched away. When we make decisions without consulting God, we miss His divine direction.

MAY 18 — BLESSINGS FOR THE BEREAVED — RUTH 1-2

"The LORD recompense thy work, and a full reward be given thee of the LORD God of Israel, under whose wings thou art come to trust" (Ruth 2:12).

The above words were spoken to Ruth, the daughter-in-law to Naomi. When her husband died, she could have easily returned to her mother's home to find comfort and consolation. Instead, she left her homeland and journeyed with Naomi, saying, *"thy people shall be my people, and thy God my God"* (1:16). Why? She wanted a relationship with the Lord more than personal comfort, and God took notice of her faith. So did Boaz.

In Ruth's time of sorrow, she chose to seek refuge under Jehovah's wings. All who put their trust in Him will be handsomely rewarded. Are you grieving today? Turn to the Almighty, and *"a full reward be given thee."* Your loss may be the door that leads to a great blessing. Do not miss God's provision for your need by seeking comfort more than God's direction for your life. In the end, Ruth was given a new husband.

Little did Ruth know that she would be the great grandmother of King David from whom would spring an even greater Ruler—the Messiah! God has a plan for your troubles. Trust and follow Him.

MAY 19 — CHANGE YOUR FOCUS — RUTH 3-4

"Then Naomi her mother in law said unto her, My daughter, shall I not seek rest for thee, that it may be well with thee?" (Ruth 3:1).

Our text marks the turning point in Naomi's life. After losing her husband and two sons, she had returned to her native land with a bitter heart. When her friends greeted her, she said, *"Call me not Naomi [which means "pleasant"], call me Mara [which means "bitter"]: for the Almighty hath dealt very bitterly with me"* (1:20). Her focus was on herself and her problems, which made her miserable. It was not until she considered the needs of Ruth that she found comfort.

We will all experience grief and loss. It can be devastating at times. However, we must realize that relief comes when we change our focus. Dwelling on our troubles makes us bitter, not better. Naomi forgot that Ruth also suffered a great loss. Instead of seeking the Lord and helping Ruth, she felt sorry for herself. It is impossible to be happy when bitter.

Was not Job's captivity turned when he stopped having a pity party and prayed for his friends? God always has a plan for our tragedies. Though Naomi initially thought she returned empty, she finally realized she still had Ruth. In the end, we find Naomi rejoicing with a grandson. Change your focus, and life will be much brighter.

| 1 SAMUEL 1-2 | **HELP FROM HANNAH** | MAY 20 |

"And she was in bitterness of soul, and prayed unto the LORD, and wept sore" (1 Samuel 1:10).

Hannah was barren, and to make matters worse, her husband's other wife mocked her for being unable to bear children. We read, *"her adversary...provoked her sore, for to make her fret"* (1:6). Do you have problems? If so, consider some lessons from the life of Hannah.

First, realize the source of your problems. Notice where her biggest problem came from—*"the LORD...shut up her womb"* (1:5). God intended on using this trial to draw Hannah closer to Himself and to bless her with a special child, Samuel. Never get angry at the Lord for troubles that come into your life. He always has a purpose.

Second, don't carry your burdens longer than you have to. Observe that this trial occurred *"year by year"* (1:7). She allowed it to control her emotions and affect her health as she *"wept, and did not eat"* (1:7).

Third, pour out your heart to God. Hannah finally brought her trouble to the Lord in prayer and asked specifically for a son. After she *"poured out"* her *"soul before the LORD"* (1:15), she received an answer of peace and *"was no more sad"* (1:18). Even though she still had an adversary, she was no longer depressed. Heartfelt prayer changes things!

| 1 SAMUEL 3-4 | **RESPOND TO GOD'S CALL** | MAY 21 |

"...the LORD called Samuel: and he answered, Here am I" (1 Samuel 3:4).

The spiritual state of Israel was low. The priesthood had been corrupted by Eli's sons who *"made themselves vile"* (3:13). Thus, the Lord chose Samuel to be His prophet. Consider how it came about.

First, we see God's *revelation*—*"the LORD called Samuel."* It was uncommon for God to speak directly to people at that time (3:10). So, it is not surprising that the Lord had to address Samuel a few times before he understood Who was talking to him. Rest assured that when God is recruiting you for a task, He will make it clear.

Second, we note Samuel's *response*. He replied, *"Here am I,"* revealing his availability. He further said, *"Speak; for thy servant heareth"* (3:10). This demonstrated his attentiveness to God's voice and his anticipation for God's direction. When the Lord speaks to you, be ready to listen and be excited about following His plan for your life.

Finally, consider the *results*—*"And Samuel grew, and the LORD was with him"* (3:19). Maturity and God's presence follow submission to the Lord. Further, since Samuel was willing to serve, God paved the way for him. Soon, *"all Israel...knew that Samuel was established to be a prophet of the LORD"* (3:20). Answer God's call—the rewards are great!

MAY 22 — RETURNING TO GOD — 1 SAMUEL 5-7

"Hitherto hath the LORD helped us" (1 Samuel 7:12).

Israel suffered a great loss to the Philistines. As a result, the ark of God was taken. Though God allowed Israel to be judged, He defended His name by plaguing the Philistines. Eventually, the ark was returned, *"and all the house of Israel lamented after the LORD"* (7:2). However, sorrow was not enough. The people needed to face their sin.

Therefore, Samuel called the people to repentance—*"If ye do return unto the LORD with all your hearts, then put away the strange gods"* (7:3). Returning to God requires turning from sin. Your fellowship with the Lord is dependent on your attitude toward your sin.

The people responded and confessed their wrongdoing. They fasted and cried out, *"We have sinned against the LORD"* (7:6). Though fasting was not necessary for their forgiveness, it reveals that they were serious about getting right with the Lord. Too often our confession of sin is shallow and flippant. Shouldn't repentance be noticeable?

In the midst of revival, Israel was attacked. However, God gave a great victory. The people set up a memorial and called it *"Ebenezer, saying, Hitherto hath the LORD helped us."* Satan puts up a fight when you turn from your sinful ways, but God will help you as He did Israel.

MAY 23 — LIKE THE WORLD — 1 SAMUEL 8-9

"...now make us a king to judge us like all the nations" (1 Samuel 8:5).

Samuel was getting old, and the elders of Israel requested a king to rule over them instead of judges. Notice their main argument—they wanted to be *"like all the nations."* They had forgotten that God called them to be *"an holy people...a peculiar people unto himself, above all the nations that are upon the earth"* (Deuteronomy 14:2). God wanted them different, not the same as the other nations.

When God's people desire to be like the world around them, something is wrong. It is because they do not want to be *"holy people."* The Lord says of such individuals, *"they have rejected me, that I should not reign over them"* (8:7). Do you have a longing to look, talk, dress, act, or be like the world? Such desires stem from a rejection of God.

Even after Israel was warned that their king would oppress them, they replied, *"Nay; but we will have a king over us"* (8:19). *Nay* means "no." Their continued stubbornness led to a blatant refusal of God's authority and warnings. How often do you say no to God? If you insist on having your way long enough, God may give it to you; however, you will regret it. Eventually, *"ye shall cry out"* in your affliction, but *"the LORD will not hear you in that day"* (8:18). Choose God, not the world!

1 SAMUEL 10-11	TRANSFORMING POWER	MAY 24

"And the Spirit of the LORD will come upon thee, and thou shalt prophesy with them, and shalt be turned into another man"
(1 Samuel 10:6).

The above words were spoken to Saul after he was anointed king over Israel. The promise was that God's Spirit would come upon him and change him. Our text serves as a reminder that we need the Holy Spirit to empower us for service. As the Lord prepared Saul to fulfill his role as king, He will enable you to accomplish your duties for Him. Claim the same promise given to Saul—*"the Spirit of the LORD will come upon thee."* Jesus promised something similar to His disciples, *"ye shall receive power, after that the Holy Ghost is come upon you"* (Acts 1:8).

Not only does the Spirit empower us for service, He also transforms our character. Saul was *"turned into another man."* God is in the life-changing business. With Him, the weak become powerful, the fearful become brave, the discouraged become hopeful, and the caustic become compassionate. The Spirit produces *"love, joy, peace, longsuffering, gentleness, goodness, faith, meekness, temperance"* (Galatians 5:22-23). Through Him, love replaces hatred, joy conquers discouragement, and peace overcomes anger. Allow God's Spirit to change you today.

1 SAMUEL 12-13	GRAB YOUR SWORD	MAY 25

"So it came to pass in the day of battle, that there was neither sword nor spear found in the hand of any of the people" (1 Samuel 13:22).

The Philistines wanted to ensure they had the upper hand against God's people. Their strategy was simple; they made sure that there were no blacksmiths *"throughout all the land of Israel"* (13:19). Since the Israelites could not make swords or spears, they were easier to defeat.

As Christians, we face spiritual battles every day, and God has given us an unbeatable weapon to use—the Bible. In fact, the Word of God is called *"the sword of the Spirit"* (Ephesians 6:17) and has power to defend us from Satan's attacks. As the Philistines sought to keep swords out of the hands of Israel, the devil works hard to prevent every believer from arming himself with the Word of God. He knows that we will be vulnerable if we enter the battlefield weaponless.

Each morning, you must pick up your Sword and prepare your heart for *"the day of battle."* As the Israelites had tools in their hands instead of swords, many Christians have laid down their Bibles and picked up tools of a different nature. People spend more time in the morning with their phone than their Bible. Satan has convinced multitudes that time with technology is more valuable than time with God. Don't be fooled!

| MAY 26 | FAITH BRINGS VICTORY | 1 SAMUEL 14 |

"...it may be that the LORD will work for us: for there is no restraint to the LORD to save by many or by few" (1 Samuel 14:6).

The day came when Jonathan was tired of doing nothing about the threat that the Philistines posed to Israel. So, he said to his armor bearer, *"Come, and let us go over unto the garrison of these uncircumcised"* (14:6). It takes a brave man to engage an entire garrison with only one helper. Jonathan was not only a man of courage but also a man of faith. He was convinced that the Lord was able to give him a victory, regardless of the size of his band of men.

Faith brings confidence. Knowing that there was *"no restraint to the LORD,"* Jonathan figured that God could work on their behalf. Once we are convinced that God is able to assist us, we will be emboldened to put our faith into action.

We may look at the spiritual darkness that abounds in this world and see ourselves outnumbered. Instead of being filled with fear, let us say, *"it may be that the LORD will work for us."* Jonathan's belief that God would help him led to a great victory. Though the battle started with only Jonathan and his armor bearer, soon many others *"came to the battle"* (14:20). Your faith may inspire others to join the fight.

| MAY 27 | REJECTING GOD | 1 SAMUEL 15-16 |

"For rebellion is as the sin of witchcraft, and stubbornness is as iniquity and idolatry. Because thou hast rejected the word of the LORD, he hath also rejected thee from being king" (1 Samuel 15:23).

Witchcraft and idolatry are unacceptable sins to most believers. However, rebellion and stubbornness, which God hates, are commonly practiced by Christians. In God's sight, attitudes can be just as repulsive as actions. Subtle sins of omission due to our stubbornness are as bad as overt ones such as witchcraft and idol worship.

King Saul was surprised to be condemned by God. In his mind, he had obeyed. However, his obedience was incomplete. As a result of rejecting God's command, God rejected him. Is this not a warning to us?

Has the Lord instructed you to do something which you have been reluctant to do? Perhaps you have only partially obeyed His will. One of the reasons Christians do not fully follow God is that they fear man. This was Saul's problem—he *"feared the people, and obeyed their voice"* (15:24). Has this been a factor in your disobedience? If so, remember the words of Solomon, *"The fear of man bringeth a snare: but whoso putteth his trust in the LORD shall be safe"* (Proverbs 29:25). It is much better to stay in favor with God. Don't risk being rejected of Him.

1 SAMUEL 17 — BE YOURSELF — MAY 28

"And he took his staff in his hand, and chose him five smooth stones out of the brook, and put them in a shepherd's bag which he had, even in a scrip; and his sling was in his hand" (1 Samuel 17:40).

When David went to fight Goliath, he was first sent in Saul's armor. However, David refused to use the unproved weaponry of another man. It stood to reason that if Saul would not trust his own armor to fight the giant, David should not trust it either. So, David equipped himself with what he was familiar with—his sling, shepherd's bag, and a few stones. What he had in battle was not as important as Who he had.

If God wanted to use a soldier to fight Goliath, He would have chosen one; but instead He chose a shepherd boy. Therefore, David had no reason to try to act like a soldier. All he had to do was be himself and trust God for the results. What he lacked in formal training he made up with faith. Willingness often makes a man more useful than skillfulness. A new convert can be a better witness than a fearful theologian. Saul's men knew how to fight but they lacked the heart to do so.

When God calls you to a task, never try to act like someone else. God chose you because He wants you. Acting like someone else would spoil His plan. As David used the things *"which he had,"* so must you.

1 SAMUEL 18-19 — WHEN GOD IS WITH US — MAY 29

"And Saul was afraid of David, because the LORD was with him, and was departed from Saul" (1 Samuel 18:12).

Those who are chosen by God are assured of His presence. Three times in this Scripture passage it mentions that God was with David. Let's consider what God's presence did for him and can do for us.

The presence of God instills fear in the hearts of our adversaries. Why was Saul afraid of David? He saw the Lord active in David's life. Allowing God to shine through you will do more to put fear in your enemies than any scheme you can devise to intimidate them. Trust God.

The presence of God causes the ungodly to separate from us. Notice that Saul *"removed him* [David] *from him"* (18:13). The ungodly do not feel comfortable around us when we are close to God. Never take personal offence when this lost world excludes you from their company.

The presence of God makes us wise. Because God was with him, *"David behaved himself wisely in all his ways"* (18:14). Fellowship with God always affects our actions. Let wisdom direct your ways.

The presence of God creates animosity in the hearts of our enemies. As it led to Saul's desire to kill David, it may lead to trouble for you. However, don't fear. You will be blessed in the end as was David.

| MAY 30 | WALK CAREFULLY | 1 SAMUEL 20-21 |

"...truly as the LORD liveth, and as thy soul liveth, there is but a step between me and death" (1 Samuel 20:3).

Life is fragile, and serving the Lord often increases the number of threats made by our spiritual enemies. David had been anointed by the prophet to serve as the next king. However, Saul was still on the throne. Seeing David as a threat to his kingdom, Saul was determined to kill him.

David understood that one wrong step could lead to an untimely death. Perhaps that is why he later wrote, *"The steps of a good man are ordered by the LORD: and he delighteth in his way"* (Psalm 37:23). It is only as we follow God's ordained steps that we can be assured of safety. Do you delight in His way? If not, you are walking dangerously and could be closer to destruction than you may have imagined.

Though David was a step away from death, God's presence preserved him. Stay close to the Lord, and He will protect you too. As the vast numbers of troops in Saul's army could not destroy David, neither can the hosts of Satan stop you when you stay close to the Lord.

Being chosen by God for a special task does not exempt you from trouble. However, if you walk carefully, you will have great success.

| MAY 31 | THE DANGER OF SELF | 1 SAMUEL 22-23 |

"...all of you have conspired against me, and there is none that sheweth me that my son hath made a league with the son of Jesse, and there is none of you that is sorry for me" (1 Samuel 22:8).

Saul's hatred of David led him down the dark path of self-centeredness. Our text reveals how sin can distort one's thinking and emotional stability. Saul became irrational and delusional, thinking that everyone was against him. Self-pity and paranoia often accompany one another. Saul had a case of both, and if we don't guard against bitterness, we can be affected the same way.

Once self becomes our focus, everyone else becomes our enemy, even good people. Not only was Saul determined to kill David, he murdered 85 priests whom he falsely accused of conspiring against him. Be careful not to allow love for self to lead to hatred of others. Failing to deal with selfishness can lead to outrageous acts of wickedness and will ultimately end in self-destruction.

Saul's problem was not David. It was himself. Do you currently have a problem with someone? Be sure not to make matters worse by building a case against him in your heart. Get your eyes off self and you will be able to think clearly to manage each of your relationships.

1 SAMUEL 24-25   LET GOD BE THE JUDGE   JUN. 1

"The LORD judge between me and thee, and the LORD avenge me of thee: but mine hand shall not be upon thee" (1 Samuel 24:12).

In the wilderness, Saul sought to rest in a cave while hunting for David. Little did he know that the one he was pursuing was in the same cave! David's men encouraged him to take the life of Saul, but he refused to stretch forth his hand against *"the LORD'S anointed"* (24:6).

Let the Lord be judge in your skirmishes. Decline to take matters into your own hands, even when you have an opportunity to do so. An occasion that affords us a convenient chance at revenge must be seen as a test of our faith, not as a means to fulfill our unbridled desires.

Remember the proverb of the ancients, *"Wickedness proceedeth from the wicked"* (24:13). Do not allow yourself to stoop to adopt the evil methods of your adversaries. Allow God to take vengeance while you trust Him to work all things for good. Though Joseph's brothers meant evil against him, he realized that *"God meant it unto good"* (Genesis 50:20). Arm yourself with the same attitude, and it will prevent you from the bitter consequences of seeking revenge.

Though David succeeded with Saul, he almost took revenge against Nabal (25:13-33). Since we will be tested repeatedly, we must be alert.

1 SAMUEL 26-27   VIGILANCE AFTER VICTORIES   JUN. 2

"And David said in his heart, I shall now perish one day by the hand of Saul: there is nothing better for me than that I should speedily escape into the land of the Philistines" (1 Samuel 27:1).

Sadly, men of great faith have been known to stumble after major victories. For instance, Elijah was discouraged shortly after praying down fire on Mt. Carmel, Noah got drunk after escaping destruction by the flood, and Peter began to sink after walking on water.

David also suffered a lapse of faith after a spiritual victory. He had refused to kill Saul and chosen to wait on God's timing, saying, *"the LORD shall smite him; or his day shall come to die; or he shall descend into battle, and perish"* (26:10). However, shortly thereafter David feared for his life and went to seek refuge with the enemy, the Philistines.

God had promised that he would become king and preserved him from death on numerous occasions. However, despite all that, David said, *"I shall now perish one day by the hand of Saul."* Notice his faulty reasoning—*"there is nothing better for me than that I should speedily escape."* It would have been better for him to pray for wisdom. Instead, his decision led to deception and compromise. Let us beware lest we fall into the same snare. Great victories must be followed by great vigilance.

JUN. 3	FAR FROM GOD	1 SAMUEL 28-29

"And Saul answered, I am sore distressed...and God is departed from me, and answereth me no more" (1 Samuel 28:15).

King Saul feared when the armies of the Philistines gathered to fight against Israel. In desperation, he enlisted the help of a witch in an attempt to get counsel from the deceased prophet Samuel. While theologians debate whether or not the witch actually brought up Samuel or an evil spirit that impersonated him, let us not miss the point of the passage. Saul's disobedience brought great distress.

When trouble came, Saul realized how terrible life had become without God's abiding presence. He declared, *"God is departed from me."* Do you ever feel far from God? Sin always leads us away from His comfort, counsel, and care.

Saul also felt helpless. He cried, *"God...answereth me no more."* Have you ever thought that God stopped answering your prayers? Living in disobedience has consequences. When we refuse to listen to the Lord, He is under no obligation to listen to us. Had Saul repented, God would have forgiven him; but his hard heart is revealed by his willingness to seek help from a witch. Are you far from God? If so, sincerely return to Him. *"Draw nigh to God, and he will draw nigh to you"* (James 4:8).

JUN. 4	RESPONDING TO GRIEF	1 SAMUEL 30-31

"And David was greatly distressed; for the people spake of stoning him, because the soul of all the people was grieved...but David encouraged himself in the LORD his God" (1 Samuel 30:6).

David and his men faced a time of great loss and disappointment. Their families and possessions had been taken by looters, and what remained had been burned with fire. Grief filled their hearts, and they wept *"until they had no more power to weep"* (30:4). Though the same trouble befell them all, they did not all respond in the same manner.

David's men allowed their sorrow to overwhelm them. This led them to lash out at their leader. They became irrational, forgetting that it was the Amalekites, not David who had caused their trouble. We must never seek to take our frustrations out on other people.

When fiery trials take us by surprise, we must act as David did. In great distress, he sought the Lord. As a result, he found solace for his heartache and a solution for his hardship. The Lord strengthened his heart and assured him of victory. God said that they would *"without fail recover all"* (30:8). Perhaps more of our losses could be regained in life if we would learn to seek God in the midst of our troubles. Don't wait for others to console you; encourage yourself by consulting God.

| 2 SAMUEL 1-2 | **BATTLING BRETHREN** | JUN. 5 |

"Then Abner called to Joab, and said, Shall the sword devour for ever? knowest thou not that it will be bitterness in the latter end? how long shall it be then, ere thou bid the people return from following their brethren?" (2 Samuel 2:26).

After Saul's death, David became king over Judah, but Saul's son, Ishbosheth, was anointed king over Israel. For sport, the captains of Judah and Israel, Joab and Abner, each sent a few soldiers into a skirmish. The fight escalated into a full-blown battle between the two armies. Needless carnage resulted. Among the many who died was one of David's mighty men, Asahel, whom Abner had slain.

Realizing how foolish it was for brethren to be fighting, Abner uttered the words in our text. Can we not learn a lesson from this account? Too often, God's people engage in petty arguments that will certainly lead to *"bitterness in the latter end."* We need more folks like Abner who will come to their senses and realize the futility of attacking each other. Paul warned, *"But if ye bite and devour one another, take heed that ye be not consumed one of another"* (Galatians 5:15). If you have a disagreement with another believer, lay down your arms and settle your dispute today. *"How long shall it be"* until you make peace?

| 2 SAMUEL 3-4 | **WAIT ON GOD** | JUN. 6 |

"...the LORD liveth, who hath redeemed my soul out of all adversity"
(2 Samuel 4:9).

Two brothers slew Ishbosheth, king of Israel, hoping to gain favor with David. However, instead of rejoicing his heart, they kindled his anger. Though David was destined to be king over all Israel, he was determined to let God put him on the throne in His timing. The Lord had already promised him that he would be king, and he believed that God was alive and able to keep His promises.

The world's philosophy is to promote self and conspire against all who are in the way of success. However, God's people must remember that *"promotion cometh neither from the east, nor from the west, nor from the south. But God is the judge: he putteth down one, and setteth up another"* (Psalm 75:6-7). The only direction we need to look for advancement is up. Let God do His work and never try to "help" Him by taking matters into your own hands.

Waiting on God is a lost art. It requires faith that the Lord will intervene on our behalf. When faith is lacking, our actions will eventually be sinful. Let us remember as did David that *"the LORD liveth"* and is quite able to deliver us *"out of all adversity."*

JUN. 7 — SPIRITUAL INSIGHT — 2 SAMUEL 5-6

"David perceived that the LORD had established him king over Israel, and that he had exalted his kingdom for his people Israel's sake"
(2 Samuel 5:12).

David was chosen by God to be king over all Israel, and he did well to guard against conceit. Saul's downfall began when he focused on himself, and following his example would have led to similar destruction. Consider two things that David realized about his reign.

First, he recognized the Source of his blessing—God had promoted him. David had not worked his way up through the ranks to his elevated position. The Lord had shown mercy upon him and *"established him king over Israel."* When we realize that our blessings come from God, we have little to boast about.

Second, David perceived the purpose of his promotion—God had *"exalted his kingdom for his people Israel's sake."* The Lord wanted him to use his office to serve others, not himself. We handle our positions best when we understand that God blesses us so we can be a blessing to others. Use what the Lord has given you to serve others as David did, not to serve self like Saul. Every parent, pastor, and politician would do well to use their authority to help those in their care.

JUN. 8 — HUMILITY BRINGS BLESSINGS — 2 SAMUEL 7-9

"Who am I, O Lord GOD? and what is my house, that thou hast brought me hitherto?" (2 Samuel 7:18).

It was in David's heart to build an elaborate house for the ark of God, but the Lord had other plans. The subject quickly changed from what David hoped to do for God to what Jehovah intended to do for David. The Lord promised to establish David's house forever. What a blessing! The response of the king provides instruction to all who hope for similar assistance from God.

Be humble. Like David, we should cry out, *"Who am I, O Lord GOD?"* Too often our attitude is "Don't you know who I am?" instead of "Who am I?" Rather than thinking we deserve much from God, we should realize that humility is the key that unlocks the door to heaven's treasures. After all, *"God resisteth the proud, and giveth grace to the humble"* (1 Peter 5:5).

Be confident. When we meet God's condition of humility, we are assured of His blessing. As David talked with the Lord, he said, *"the word that thou hast spoken...establish it for ever, and do as thou hast said"* (7:25). Be bold to believe all that God promises. Though humility opens the hand to receive God's blessing, faith is necessary to grasp it.

| 2 SAMUEL 10-11 | DISPLEASING GOD | JUN. 9 |

"...the thing that David had done displeased the LORD" (2 Samuel 11:27).

How sad to read the words of our text! David had served God faithfully and provided a godly example for many years. However, today's reading reminds us that good people are vulnerable to sin when they fail to follow God's appointed steps. Let's learn some important lessons from this account lest we also displease our Lord.

First, neglecting our duties can lead to defeat. Instead of going to battle, David tarried in Jerusalem. Had he fought that day's battle, he would have avoided seeing Bathsheba. Too often we get comfortable and let our guard down, exposing ourselves to temptation. What counts is not what we did yesterday for God but what we are doing today.

Second, lusts must be denied, not indulged. Though David saw Bathsheba, he did not have to pursue a relationship with her. He should have gotten away from the temptation as swiftly as Joseph fled from Potiphar's wife. Instead, he lingered and inquired about her.

Third, reproof must be accepted. When David was told that Bathsheba was married, he should have realized that others were trying to prevent him from going into sin. When people care enough to warn you of the error of your way, do not shrug off their objections to your sin.

| 2 SAMUEL 12-13 | HERE COMES TROUBLE | JUN. 10 |

"Behold, I will raise up evil against thee out of thine own house"
(2 Samuel 12:11).

Yesterday we read of David's despicable sin of adultery and murder. Today we see God's response. You may appear to get away with sin for a while as it seemed that David did for several months, but your actions will catch up to you. Consider the *confrontation of sin—"the LORD sent Nathan unto David"* (12:1). After giving a parable about a heartless man who stole another's sheep, the prophet implicated David as the culprit who had stolen another man's wife. David's heart surely sank when he heard those sobering words, *"Thou art the man"* (12:7). Be thankful that God loves you enough to send someone to reveal your sin.

Notice also the *confession of sin*. After being rebuked by Nathan, David said, *"I have sinned against the LORD"* (12:13). This was not a flippant admission of guilt but heartfelt repentance as revealed in Psalm 51. As the sweet psalmist of Israel had soured, so will you until you turn from your sin and seek forgiveness. Have you anything to confess?

Lastly, we observe the *consequences of sin*. Though David was forgiven, he still reaped the results of his actions. What man does secretly will be exposed by God openly (12:12). Beware. You will reap.

JUN. 11 — THE FOLLY OF FLATTERY — 2 SAMUEL 14-15

"Absalom stole the hearts of the men of Israel" (2 Samuel 15:6).

Abasolom's mother was the daughter of a heathen king, and she obviously had more influence on his upbringing than David did. Instead of following his father's godly example, he showed no signs of spirituality. After murdering his brother, Absalom fled to Geshur and sought refuge with his grandfather, king of Geshur, for three years.

Though Absalom was not repentant, David brought him back to Jerusalem. Once there, *"Absalom stole the hearts of the men of Israel"* and conspired to overthrow his father. How? He used the wicked device of flattery. When people came to David for judgment, Absalom spoke well to them, saying *"thy matters are good and right"* (15:3). Beware of smooth talkers! Those who flatter you usually want something from you. Flattery is often in partnership with deceit. Truly, *"a flattering mouth worketh ruin"* (Proverbs 26:28). Solomon watched his brother Absalom dethrone their father and issued this warning: *"meddle not with him that flattereth with his lips"* (Proverbs 20:19).

Flattery may be effective, but it is also devilish. As a Christian, you must steer clear of using it. You may be able to manipulate people by showering undue praise on them, but that is not a tactic of the righteous.

JUN. 12 — LOOK FOR GOOD — 2 SAMUEL 16-17

"It may be that the LORD will look on mine affliction, and that the LORD will requite me good for his cursing this day" (2 Samuel 16:12).

David had his fair share of trouble. Absalom's rise to power had encouraged evil elements in Israel to rebel against righteousness. As David went into exile, Shimei was emboldened to cast stones at him and curse him. How true were the words which David penned, *"The wicked walk on every side, when the vilest men are exalted"* (Psalm 12:8). We would do well to follow David's example when the evil generation about us mistreats us.

Look to God. Like David, we should say, *"It may be that the LORD will look on mine affliction."* Trust that the Almighty will consider your plight and intervene on your behalf. Don't take matters into your own hands as Abishai sought to do. Instead, wait on God for deliverance.

Look for good. When trouble comes into your life, learn to say, *"the LORD will requite [repay] me good."* Jesus promised that He would reward us handsomely in heaven for our troubles here. He said, *"Blessed are ye, when men shall revile you…for great is your reward in heaven"* (Matthew 5:11-12). Learn to anticipate good to come out of every trial. Remember that *"all things work together for good"* (Romans 8:28).

2 SAMUEL 18 — RESULTS OF SIN — JUN. 13

"And the king was much moved...and wept: and as he went, thus he said, O my son Absalom, my son, my son Absalom! would God I had died for thee, O Absalom, my son, my son!" (2 Samuel 18:33).

Though David's army had been victorious in battle, things did not end as he had hoped. His son Absalom was killed, and it broke his heart. David's lamentation indicates that he felt responsible for his son's death. Today's reading records the results of sin: reaping, remorse, and regret.

Sin brings reaping. David's failure to raise Absalom in the ways of the Lord came to full fruition, reminding us that *"sin, when it is finished, bringeth forth death"* (James 1:15). Certainly, David was not the only one to blame. As an adult, Absalom was responsible for his own actions.

Sin brings remorse—*"the king was much moved...and wept."* No amount of weeping can undo the consequences of sin. We tend to dismiss God's promptings to amend our ways until it is too late. If you deal with your sin today, you can prevent a harvest of misery later.

Sin brings regret. David's heart smote him because he knew he had not done his best as a father. Unless you follow the Lord in your daily duties, you will also say one day, *"would God I had...."* Repentance can curb reaping, remorse, and regret. What are you waiting for?

2 SAMUEL 19 — CHECK MOTIVES — JUN. 14

"...why should the king recompense it me with such a reward?" (2 Samuel 19:36).

Barzillai assisted David when he hid from Absalom in Mahanaim. He provided beds, dishes, and an abundance of food for David and his men (17:27-29). When it came time for the king to return to Jerusalem, Barzillai went down to meet him. Was he hoping to collect a reward for his earlier service? He was far too noble for that. David thought to richly repay his kindness, but Barzillai declined saying, *"why should the king recompense it me with such a reward?"* He was surprised that the king would make such an offer to him, proving that his intentions of helping David were selfless, not selfish. This should inspire each of us to check our motives.

When Solomon became king, he learned that people sought to be on his good side, hoping to gain privileges from him. He said, *"Many seek the ruler's favour"* (Proverbs 29:26). What drives your relationship with your leaders? Do you help them only when you think there is a chance of future repayment? As Barzillai sought to be a blessing to David with no strings attached, let us seek what we can do for others rather than what we can gain from them.

JUN. 15   INSPIRING FAITH   2 SAMUEL 20-21

"These four were born to the giant in Gath, and fell by the hand of David, and by the hand of his servants" (2 Samuel 21:22).

Long before David became king, Goliath terrorized the armies of Israel. His presence struck fear in the hearts of every soldier. As a shepherd boy full of faith, David did what no man of valor was willing to do. With God's help, he faced and defeated the giant. As an old man, he was still willing to fight the Philistines. Though his body *"waxed faint"* (21:15), his spirit was strong. Whether as a youth or an elderly man, David provided an example of courage and faith for others to follow.

Prior to David's confrontation with Goliath, no man dared oppose a giant, but his faith influenced others. Years later, four of his men slew giants of their own. One man's courage emboldened others to attempt great things for God.

This should challenge us in two ways. First, we too can defeat every giant that we face. Your giant may be a towering trial or a tantalizing temptation. Regardless of its size or strength, it is no match for the Lord Who stands with you. Second, our faith can challenge others to do great things for God. Our families, churches, and communities need examples of faith and courage to inspire them. How are you impacting others?

JUN. 16   DISTRESSED?   2 SAMUEL 22

"In my distress I called upon the LORD, and cried to my God: and he did hear my voice out of his temple, and my cry did enter into his ears"
(2 Samuel 22:7).

In today's reading, David recounts how God delivered him from all his enemies. While this song of praise records many lessons, we will limit our discussion to the importance of seeking the Lord in seasons of distress. The word *distress* means "narrow" and implies the trouble and sorrow associated with being in a tight place. As a person with claustrophobia is overwhelmed when space is limited, we often have a similar reaction when troubles seem to pile on top of us.

Are you presently distressed, dwelling on problems or having a pity party? It is not God's plan for us to be filled with anxiety; neither does He want us to ignore our troubles or try to entertain them away. Failing to deal with our problems Biblically only makes matters worse. It is far better to call upon God and cast your care upon Him! If you do, you will soon exclaim as David, *"He did hear my voice."* Consider God's response to David's prayer—*"the earth shook and trembled"* and the Lord *"came down"* (22:8, 10). Get excited about God moving on your behalf and intervening in your life. He wants to come down and help.

| 2 SAMUEL 23-24 | **MIGHTY MEN NEEDED** | JUN. 17 |

"But he stood in the midst of the ground, and defended it...and the LORD wrought a great victory" (2 Samuel 23:12).

In every army, there are certain men who rise to the top. They are the elite forces. Though David had hundreds of thousands of soldiers, a relatively small number were listed as his mighty men. Those who attained to such a title had one thing in common—they defied the enemy despite great odds against them. Among them was Shammah. Notice what made him mighty—*"he stood in the midst of the ground, and defended it"* when others had fled.

If you ever hope to be mighty in God's service, you must stand for righteousness and defend the truth. The world needs Christians who will be mighty for God, willing to stand alone against those who seek to destroy their families, churches, and nation. Are you quick to retreat and give up the ground that God wants you to possess for Him? If so, it is time to stand. Paul urges us, *"Put on the whole armour of God, that ye may be able to stand against the wiles of the devil"* (Ephesians 6:11).

When you stand your ground, the Lord will do for you what He did for Shammah—*"the LORD wrought a great victory."* God fights on behalf of those who stand for Him. Are you ready for a victory? Stand!

| 1 KINGS 1 | **DISCOURAGE SELF-PROMOTION** | JUN. 18 |

"And his father had not displeased him at any time in saying, Why hast thou done so?" (1 Kings 1:6).

Adonijah's aspirations to be king were known to David, but he was not discouraged by his father. The Scripture reveals two problems with Adonijah's desire: pride and rebellion. Notice that he *"exalted himself"* (1:5). Any time a person promotes himself, he is going in a direction opposite to his best interest. After all, *"God resisteth the proud"* (James 4:6). If God wanted Adonijah to be king, the man had no need to plot and scheme for the position. We would do well to learn to wait upon the Lord for any promotion we hope to gain.

Since David had previously declared that Solomon would reign in his stead, he erred by not discouraging Adonijah's ambition. When people are not confronted with their wrongdoing, they are more likely to continue in it. Silence from authority is often perceived as a message of consent. We need more spiritual and civil leaders who will oppose those who are self-willed.

Adonijah's rebellion came when he said, *"I will be king"* (1:5). The throne was never promised to him. We must all be careful not to utter, *"I will"* when it is not God's will. All who do will be humiliated in the end.

| JUN. 19 | TRUE MANLINESS | 1 KINGS 2 |

"...be thou strong therefore, and shew thyself a man" (1 Kings 2:2).

David charged Solomon to be strong and manly. The picture that immediately comes to mind when describing strength is a tough man with bulging muscles. While some men strive to be big, brash, and brawn, that is not exactly what David had in mind for Solomon.

God defines strength and manliness in terms of the inner man, not the physique. Notice what David said after challenging Solomon to be a strong man—*"And keep the charge of the LORD thy God, to walk in his ways, to keep his statutes, and his commandments, and his judgments, and his testimonies, as it is written in the law of Moses"* (2:3). This put the emphasis on spirituality, not carnality. In other words, obedience to God and His commands is what makes a strong man.

Unfortunately, many Christians have allowed the world to define manliness in terms of physical qualities instead of spiritual character. This does not mean that a man should neglect his body. He should exercise and stay fit, but that must not be his focus. Though Samson was physically strong, it did little to help him fight temptation. Be sure to use God's measuring stick of godliness rather than the world's emphasis on the flesh when determining the strength of a man.

| JUN. 20 | AN OUTSTANDING OFFER | 1 KINGS 3-4 |

"In Gibeon the LORD appeared to Solomon in a dream by night: and God said, Ask what I shall give thee" (1 Kings 3:5).

The Lord gave Solomon an opportunity to have whatever he wanted. Perhaps you wish a similar offer would be made to you. Well, it has! Jesus said, *"If ye abide in me, and my words abide in you, ye shall ask what ye will, and it shall be done unto you"* (John 15:7). However, there are conditions. Let's learn from the Lord's dealing with Solomon.

Consider the *reason for the offer*. Before God made this offer, Solomon loved God, obeyed Him, and offered a generous sacrifice (3:3-4). This teaches us that those who wish to receive big blessings from God must first show themselves worthy. Holiness precedes blessedness.

Observe also the *response to the offer*. Solomon showed great humility and dependence, saying, *"I am but a little child: I know not how to go out or come in"* (3:7). Further, his request was not primarily for himself; he asked for wisdom in order to better serve God's people. If we humbly ask God to make us a better servant, we shall not be denied.

Finally, notice the *results of the offer*. God answered his request, *"Behold, I have done according to thy words"* (3:12). In fact, Solomon received more than he asked for! What will you ask God to do for you?

1 KINGS 5-6 — THE REASON FOR REST — JUN. 21

"But now the LORD my God hath given me rest on every side, so that there is neither adversary nor evil occurrent" (1 Kings 5:4).

David fought many wars during his reign, but Solomon enjoyed extended peace. Knowing the Lord had a purpose for providing him rest, Solomon used it wisely. He said, *"I purpose to build an house unto the name of the LORD my God"* (5:5). Here we find that the reason for rest is to labor for the Lord.

Much of our time may seem to be spent engaged in spiritual battles, which detract us from fulfilling our life's calling. We would rather be building than battling. The adversary attacks us on every side to prevent us from making progress in God's appointed tasks. Was it not so in Nehemiah's day when the men had to build the walls with one hand and carry a sword in the other? Their efforts to build were hindered by the constant threat of the enemy.

What a blessed season when we have *"rest on every side."* Let us use such times to strengthen our hearts, homes, and houses of worship. Rest is given for greater service. Do not miss opportunities to build for God when battles subside. Redouble your efforts in prayer, soulwinning, discipleship, and giving. Build before the adversary strikes again.

1 KINGS 7 — RIGHT CHOICES — JUN. 22

"And king Solomon sent and fetched Hiram out of Tyre" (1 Kings 7:13).

When it came time to finish the temple, Solomon chose Hiram to fashion all the works of brass. Since we all make choices in life, let us reflect on Solomon's selection of Hiram.

First, it was a *settled choice*. The king had authority to choose whom he would. He did not waver but *"sent and fetched Hiram."* When you are responsible to make a decision, do not be indecisive. We know that a *"double minded man is unstable in all his ways"* (James 1:8). Learn to make decisions without fretting and fearing the results. Act decidedly and confidently once you have weighed your options.

Second, it was a *sensible choice*. Though Solomon was decisive, he was not hasty. His decision was well thought out. He chose a man who was *"filled with wisdom, and understanding, and cunning"* (7:14). Because the work in the temple was for God's glory, it had to be done well. Think through your decisions to find the best possible solutions. Wise decisions are rarely made accidentally.

Third, it was a *sympathetic choice*. Hiram was *"a widow's son of the tribe of Naphtali"* (7:14). By hiring him, Solomon managed to assist the fatherless and a widow. Let us also look for ways to help the needy.

JUN. 23	WHAT PLAGUES YOU?	1 KINGS 8

"What prayer and supplication soever be made by any man, or by all thy people Israel, which shall know every man the plague of his own heart... hear thou in heaven thy dwelling place, and forgive" (1 Kings 8:38-39).

Plagues are troublesome diseases that can bring misery and death. Over the centuries, terrible plagues have ravaged communities and nations. What disease can do to a body, sin can do to a heart. Therefore, we should fear plagues of a spiritual sort as much as we dread those of a physical nature.

When Solomon dedicated the temple, his prayer included a plea for mercy for those who would acknowledge their sin and repent. The key was that *"every man"* had to first know *"the plague of his own heart."* Do you know what has come between you and the Savior? If so, you are a prime candidate for revival.

Is sin currently plaguing your heart? You may not be aware of every sin you have committed, but you probably know the one that is bringing your present trouble. How long will you remain in pain and misery? Whatever the cause, confess it and return to the Lord. He is ready to restore you and bring healing to your soul. If you are not sure of the plague that haunts you, ask God. He knows and is willing to reveal it.

JUN. 24	WHO GETS THE GLORY?	1 KINGS 9-10

"And all the earth sought to Solomon, to hear his wisdom, which God had put in his heart" (1 Kings 10:24).

At times, God bestows an abundance of grace on individuals and blesses them far beyond their peers. Solomon was one such man. People came from far distances to hear his wisdom and lavish him with costly gifts, yet the Lord did not choose to bless him because He loved him more than others. When God elevates a man, He has a purpose—to glorify Himself.

Don't overlook the reason Solomon was admired by *"all the earth."* His admirers wanted to hear the wisdom *"which God had put in his heart."* They recognized the Source of his greatness. What caused the queen of Sheba to travel to Jerusalem from Africa? She *"heard of the fame of Solomon concerning the name of the LORD"* (10:1). She primarily wanted to know more about God.

When the Lord blesses you with wisdom, talent, or substance, remember it is for His glory, not your own. If men seek our opinion or assistance because they see God in us, that is an honor which exceeds any earthly title or treasure. When seeking a blessing from God, see to it that your motive is His glorification, not your advancement.

1 KINGS 11 — FROM BLESSING TO ADVERSITY — JUN. 25

"And the LORD was angry with Solomon, because his heart was turned from the LORD God of Israel" (1 Kings 11:9).

Yesterday, we read of Solomon's exaltation. Today, we read of his downfall. After numerating all the blessings bestowed upon him in chapter ten, today's chapter begins with a pivotal word—*"But."* What did he allow to ruin things? He permitted something else to steal his affection. Earlier, we saw that *"Solomon loved the LORD"* (3:3). Now we read, *"Solomon loved many strange women"* (11:1).

The Lord had previously commanded His people not to meddle with women of other nations. Solomon replaced his love for God with love for the world. He loved what God hated. Unfortunately, our flesh also craves things that the Lord forbids; and when we disregard His warnings, we will lose the blessings that we now enjoy.

As God had predicted, Solomon's wives *"turned away his heart"* (11:3). Once we turn from God, we will do *"evil in the sight of the LORD"* as he did (11:6). What followed? The *"LORD was angry with Solomon"* and *"stirred up an adversary"* to oppose him (11:14). Can we expect anything less when we turn from following God? It is far better to love the Lord than to enjoy the pleasures of sin.

1 KINGS 12-13 — LISTEN TO GOOD ADVICE — JUN. 26

"And they spake unto him, saying, If thou wilt be a servant unto this people this day, and wilt serve them, and answer them, and speak good words to them, then they will be thy servants for ever" (1 Kings 12:7).

When it came time to make Rehoboam king, Jeroboam led a group that presented its grievances. Rehoboam wisely consulted *"the old men, that stood before Solomon"* (12:6). Unfortunately for him, he forsook their counsel and *"consulted with the young men that were grown up with him"* (12:8). The old men had spent years in Solomon's presence and gleaned from his wisdom. Why did Rehoboam refuse their counsel? He did not like it. The young men told him what he wanted to hear; so, he followed their advice. We should be careful not to reject wise counsel simply because we do not like it. It can lead to destruction.

Another important lesson for us to consider is the advice the old men gave to Rehoboam. They wisely said, *"If thou wilt be a servant unto this people...then they will be thy servants for ever."* The older generation understood that leaders were meant to serve, not to oppress. If God has given you authority in your home, church, workplace, or community, use it to help those you lead. Jesus taught the same thing, *"And whosoever will be chief among you, let him be your servant"* (Matthew 20:27).

JUN. 27   DROP THE DISGUISE   1 KINGS 14-15

"...why feignest thou thyself to be another?" (1 Kings 14:6).

Jeroboam had committed more wickedness than all the rulers before him. God's indictment upon him was, *"thou hast gone and made thee other gods, and molten images, to provoke me to anger, and hast cast me behind thy back"* (14:9). Jeroboam's sin was especially heinous because he led the nation of Israel to depart from God. Despite how wicked he was, he knew who to turn to when he needed help.

When Jeroboam's son fell sick, he sent his wife in a disguise to the prophet Ahija to find out if the boy would live. Why the disguise? He wanted help from God without humbling himself and repenting of his sin. Never forget that you cannot expect to enjoy the benefits of seeking God without first dealing with your sin. Even today people put on a front around the preacher, hoping to earn special favor from him.

As soon as Jeroboam's wife met the prophet, he confronted her with her hypocrisy, saying, *"why feignest thou thyself to be another?"* The Lord sees through every one of our facades. It is impossible to conceal the true condition of your heart when you seek His help. Notice the prophet's response to Jeroboam's wife, *"I am sent to thee with heavy tidings"* (14:6). Covering sin always leads to more trouble.

JUN. 28   WHEN THE BROOK DRIES UP   1 KINGS 16-17

"...it came to pass after a while, that the brook dried up" (1 Kings 17:7).

After Elijah pronounced God's judgment that there would be no rain, the Lord sent him to hide by the brook Cherith. There the prophet enjoyed two hearty meals flown in twice a day via "Raven Airways." Further, the Lord provided for his thirst, saying, *"thou shalt drink of the brook"* (17:4). Everything was going well. He was in a safe location with a full belly. However, *"after a while...the brook dried up."*

Imagine what went through Elijah's mind as he observed the water level dropping each day. We are not told if he worried about the depleting supply, but it is fair to say many of us would have. Do you ever get anxious about how you are going to feed your family, pay the bills, and save for your future? Will God fail to supply your needs? No!

Elijah had followed God's will for his life, but it seemed like he was going to suffer. However, when the water ceased, *"the word of the LORD came unto him"* (17:8). Though *"the brook dried up,"* God's provision for Elijah had not. The Lord had a widow, a barrel of meal, and a cruse of oil to sustain him. When you begin to worry, remember to lean upon *"the word of the LORD"* for your comfort and direction. As He had alternative means to provide for Elijah, He is able to help you too!

1 KINGS 18	**LESSONS ON PRAYER**	JUN. 29

"And Elijah said unto Ahab, Get thee up, eat and drink; for there is a sound of abundance of rain" (1 Kings 18:41).

Reading books about prayer can be helpful, but the best teachers are those who have proven results. Elijah's prayer on Mt. Carmel provides an example of power in prayer. Effective prayer is:

Confident – Even before Elijah began his prayer time, he envisioned an answer. Though the skies were clear, he told Ahab, *"there is a sound of abundance of rain."* How could he be so confident? His prayer was based on a promise from God, Who had said, *"I will send rain"* (18:1). Even when no sign of an answer is in sight, rely on God's promises.

Humble – Elijah *"cast himself down upon the earth, and put his face between his knees"* (18:42). This reminds us that God gives *"grace to the humble"* (1 Peter 5:5). Utter dependence on God gets His attention.

Expectant – After a season of prayer, Elijah instructed his servant, *"look"* (18:43). When you pray, expect to see something happen.

Persistent – When the servant responded, *"There is nothing,"* Elijah kept praying. Learn to pray until God gives an answer. Don't give up!

Blessed – After continued prayer, God sent *"a great rain"* (18:45). When you pray like Elijah, you can expect results. God answers prayer.

1 KINGS 19-20	**DISRUPTING A PITY PARTY**	JUN. 30

"But he himself went a day's journey into the wilderness, and came and sat down under a juniper tree: and he requested...that he might die; and said, It is enough; now, O LORD, take away my life" (1 Kings 19:4).

Even the most faithful of God's servants can become discouraged. Though Elijah had prayed down fire and rain, he reacted wrongly to his next trial and indulged in a pity party. Consider what transpired.

Notice his *sorrow*—*"he requested for himself that he might die."* Elijah thought he was the only one who remained faithful to the Lord. Can you see him pout as he said, *"I, even I only, am left"* (19:10)? Focusing on self in times of difficulty usually leads to discouragement.

Next we notice his *strength*. God mercifully sent an angel to redirect the prophet's attention. He said, *"Arise and eat; because the journey is too great for thee"* (19:7). What he needed was strength, not self-pity. He did as he was commanded and received supernatural strength. This provides a picture of God's Word, which has the power to sustain us for life's journey. When sorrowful, learn to feast on the Bible.

See also his *service*. Though Elijah was ready to quit, God had more work for him to do. The Lord commanded, *"Go, return"* (19:15). When feeling down, get busy for God. Allow service to dispel your sorrow.

JUL. 1 — THE POWER OF GOD'S MESSAGE — 1 KINGS 21

"...when Ahab heard those words...he rent his clothes...and fasted, and lay in sackcloth, and went softly" (1 Kings 21:27).

Following the murder of Naboth, God sent Elijah to pronounce judgment upon Ahab and Jezebel. As a result, Ahab humbled himself in such a way that the Lord took notice. We can learn much about God's dealing with sinners from this account. Consider a few lessons about witnessing to the lost.

First, God uses believers to deliver His message to the ungodly. As Elijah was commanded to *"Arise...go...speak"* (21:18-19), so we are charged with bringing the gospel to sinners.

Second, the preaching of God's judgment can get people to consider their ways. It led Ahab to change his behavior. This proud king *"rent his clothes...and fasted, and lay in sackcloth, and went softly."* Never sugarcoat the gospel by leaving out God's judgment upon sin. If we compassionately warn others of coming judgment, we can help them.

Third, God's mercy extends to the vilest people. Ahab was wicked, but when God saw his humility, He said, *"I will not bring the evil in his days"* (21:29). Even the most unlikely may humble themselves. Therefore, don't neglect to share the gospel with really bad people.

JUL. 2 — THE COST OF SERVICE — 1 KINGS 22

"Thus saith the king, Put this fellow in the prison, and feed him with bread of affliction and with water of affliction" (1 Kings 22:27).

Serving God is always exciting, but it is not always glamorous. At times, it can be quite costly. The prophet Micaiah faithfully served God despite continued mistreatment. Consider his trials.

First, he was hated. King Ahab plainly stated, *"I hate him"* (22:8). Don't expect to be liked by everyone just because you serve God.

Second, he was pressured to compromise. The false prophets gave a good message concerning Ahab, and a messenger sent to Micaiah told him to agree with them, saying, *"let thy word...be like the word of one of them, and speak that which is good"* (22:13). When we are tempted to water down our message, we must respond as Micaiah, *"what the LORD saith unto me, that will I speak"* (22:14). Don't be swayed by the crowd.

Third, he was assaulted. A false prophet *"smote Micaiah on the cheek"* (22:24), injuring and humiliating him in the presence of two kings. Serving God may lead to attacks on your body and/or reputation.

Fourth, he was imprisoned and given a meager diet. Like Micaiah, we must not waver or fear to stand for God. Remember Jesus' promise to the persecuted, *"great is your reward in heaven"* (Matthew 5:12).

| 2 KINGS 1-2 | GETTING GOD'S POWER | JUL. 3 |

"Elijah said unto Elisha, Ask what I shall do for thee, before I be taken away from thee. And Elisha said, I pray thee, let a double portion of thy spirit be upon me" (2 Kings 2:9).

Elisha wanted what he saw in Elijah. In fact, he was so enthralled with the power of God that he requested a *"double portion."* How interested are you in God's power? Let's see how Elisha received it.

Notice his *determination*. He knew that Elijah would soon be taken to heaven and would not be dissuaded from leaving him. The prophet seemed to test Elisha, saying, *"Tarry here;"* however, Elisha responded, *"I will not leave thee"* (2:2). We must be dedicated to learn as much as we can from those we aspire to be like. Spend time with godly people.

Next we see his *direction*. Elisha knew exactly what he wanted—*"a double portion."* Too often we get distracted by less important things and get our eyes off our goal of serving God. Stay focused!

Finally, we observe his *dependence*. When Elisha picked up the prophet's mantle, he cried, *"Where is the LORD God of Elijah?"* (2:14). Though he admired Elijah, he did not imitate the man's methods to gain his power; he looked to God for it. Never allow your admiration of men cause you to miss the reason for their greatness. Keep your eyes on God!

| 2 KINGS 3-4 | DEBT RELIEF | JUL. 4 |

"...thou knowest that thy servant did fear the LORD: and the creditor is come to take...my two sons to be bondmen" (2 Kings 4:1).

The above words were spoken by a widow whose husband was a prophet. Her two sons were soon to be taken away to serve as bondmen by a creditor because of an outstanding debt. She sought help from Elisha, and his plan tested her faith. Let's observe a few lessons.

First, good people are not exempt from trouble. The widow's husband feared the Lord, but despite his service and sacrifice, trouble still visited their home. However, you should not fear because *"God is not unrighteous to forget your work and labour of love"* (Hebrews 6:10).

Second, we are responsible to pay our bills. Before assisting the widow, Elisha asked if she had anything of value to help pay the debt. If we have debt, we cannot expect God to intervene until we do our part.

Third, we must not underestimate God. Though the widow had a pot of oil, she said that she had *"not any thing"* (4:2). Little is much when placed in God's hands! Trust God and make the most of what you have.

Fourth, we are often blessed in proportion to our obedience. The widow was told to borrow many empty vessels. If she had only gathered a few, she would have lacked enough oil to sell to meet her needs.

JUL. 5 — OPENED EYES — 2 KINGS 5-6

"Fear not: for they that be with us are more than they that be with them" (2 Kings 6:16).

The Lord fought for Israel by giving Elisha wisdom to know Syria's battle plans. Being frustrated, the king of Syria sought to stop Elisha. So, he sent *"horses, and chariots, and a great host: and they came by night, and compassed the city about"* (6:14).

When Elisha's servant saw the mighty army, he cried out in fear, *"Alas, my master! how shall we do?"* (6:15). In the face of danger, Elisha remained calm. Why? He saw what the servant failed to see. The Lord had sent a heavenly host of *"horses and chariots of fire round about Elisha"* (6:17). In an effort to reassure his servant, he asked the Lord, *"open his eyes, that he may see"* (6:17).

What do you see when you face trouble? Are you focused on the circumstances, or do you by faith realize that God will fend for you? The solution to our fear is to see God's deliverance by the eye of faith. In other words, we need our eyes opened. Allow the exhortation given to the servant to reassure you—*"Fear not: for they that be with us are more than they that be with them."* The angelic beings sent by God to protect us outnumber the demons appointed by the devil to harm us. We're safe!

JUL. 6 — SPREAD THE GOOD NEWS — 2 KINGS 7-8

"Then they said one to another, We do not well: this day is a day of good tidings, and we hold our peace" (2 Kings 7:9).

The Syrian army besieged Samaria, and *"there was a great famine"* in the land (6:25). The situation was so desperate that four lepers, facing certain death from starvation, chose to seek mercy from the host of Syria. When they got to the camp, they found that it had been abandoned in haste because of the Lord's intervention. The Syrians had fled so quickly that they left everything behind. The lepers ate to their hearts' content and began gathering treasures for themselves.

Realizing that the rest of the city was starving and that there were plenty of provisions in the camp of Syria, they said, *"We do not well."* They felt guilty for keeping the good news to themselves. Therefore, they returned to the city and told of God's deliverance.

This story reminds us of our obligation to witness to the lost. We, too, have been delivered from death and have a duty to proclaim the *"good tidings"* of salvation to others. Have we been guilty of keeping the good news to ourselves? If so, we ought to confess, *"We do not well"* because *"we hold our peace."* Let's resolve to *"preach the gospel of peace, and bring glad tidings of good things!"* (Romans 10:15).

KEEPING BAD COMPANY
2 Kings 9 — Jul. 7

"But when Ahaziah the king of Judah saw this, he fled...And Jehu followed after him, and said, Smite him also" (2 Kings 9:27).

Ahaziah was in the wrong place at the wrong time with the wrong people, and it cost him his life. He had gone to visit his friend, Joram, who was recovering from a wound he suffered in battle. Meanwhile, the Lord had chosen Jehu to execute judgment on the house of Ahab. Wasting no time, Jehu traveled to Jezreel to confront and kill Joram, the son of Ahab. When he arrived, he killed both Joram and Ahaziah. Before you start feeling sorry for Ahaziah, consider his life.

As king of Judah, Ahaziah represented the godly line of David, but rather than living for God, *"he walked in the way of the house of Ahab, and did evil in the sight of the LORD, as did the house of Ahab"* (8:27). Instead of reproving the king of Israel, he was just like him and enjoyed his company. His friendship with an evil man and his love for wickedness led to his premature death.

Let this be a warning to all who seek the company of those who oppose God. The Lord expects His people to be different. Too many of God's children seek companionship among the ungodly. If you partake in your friends' sin, you cannot expect to avoid judgment.

SELECTIVE OBEDIENCE
2 Kings 10 — Jul. 8

"But Jehu took no heed to walk in the law of the LORD God of Israel with all his heart: for he departed not from the sins of Jeroboam, which made Israel to sin" (2 Kings 10:31).

In chapter ten, Jehu continued to execute judgment upon the house of Ahab as the Lord had commanded him. On his way to slay Ahab's remaining descendants, he said to his friend, *"Come with me, and see my zeal for the LORD"* (10:16). He was proud of his service for God, and it seems that he took great pleasure in punishing those who offended God. He even *"destroyed Baal out of Israel"* (10:28). However, we should not think that his zeal in one area of life made him a good man.

Unfortunately, Jehu only followed God when it pleased him. We read that he *"took no heed to walk in the law of the LORD God of Israel with all his heart."* This shows that he served God with half a heart. The other half was devoted to sin—*"he departed not from the sins of Jeroboam."* It is possible to be deceived about our relationship with the Lord, thinking we are serving Him when we are not.

Perhaps you think you are zealous for God, focusing only on all the things you do right. Don't forget to take inventory of your adherence to the rest of God's commands. He expects you to serve with all your heart.

JUL. 9 — OFFSETTING A BAD HOME — 2 KINGS 11-12

"And Jehoash did that which was right in the sight of the LORD all his days wherein Jehoiada the priest instructed him" (2 Kings 12:2).

Joash did not have a godly heritage. As we saw two days ago, his father, Ahaziah, *"did evil in the sight of the LORD"* (8:27) and died prematurely because of it. His evil grandmother, Athaliah, murdered his brethren and usurped the throne. How could Joash rise above such negative circumstances and do *"that which was right in the sight of the LORD"*? Consider three things that made a difference.

First, someone intervened on his behalf. Jehosheba stepped in and rescued him from Athaliah. She invested six years of her life into Joash, and it paid off. Compassion and commitment can help people from troubled homes overcome negative influences. Is there someone in a bad situation who the Lord wants you to help?

Second, he spent time in God's house. Notice that *"he was with her hid in the house of the LORD six years"* (11:3). A great way to assist someone is to make church an integral part of his life.

Third, he was taught God's Word. Joash did right *"all his days wherein Jehoiada the priest instructed him."* Godly counsel and instruction can help overcome a bad home life.

JUL. 10 — TOO PROUD TO LISTEN — 2 KINGS 13-14

"Amaziah would not hear" (2 Kings 14:11).

Amaziah was a good king—*"he did that which was right in the sight of the LORD"* (14:3). However, he was not perfect. The Lord was sure to mention that he was *"not like David"* (14:3), indicating that there are varying degrees of righteous men. You may be good in one area but deficient in another. One of Amaziah's downfalls was pride.

After defeating Edom in battle, his ego was inflated. Soon, he challenged the king of Israel, saying, *"Come, let us look one another in the face"* (14:8). The king of Israel gave him some wise advice. He warned, *"Thou hast indeed smitten Edom, and thine heart hath lifted thee up: glory of this, and tarry at home: for why shouldest thou meddle to thy hurt...?"* (14:10). Unfortunately, *"Amaziah would not hear"* and suffered a great defeat in battle. The haughty man was humiliated.

At times, we overestimate our abilities because of a few small successes. Confidence is not a problem, but arrogance is. Be careful not to get so proud of your accomplishments that you feel invincible. Never fail to listen to sound advice, even if it comes from an unlikely source as in Amaziah's case. When we become too proud to listen, we will make fools of ourselves. *"Pride goeth before destruction"* (Proverbs 16:18).

2 KINGS 15 — NOT GOOD ENOUGH — JUL. 11

"In those days the LORD began to send against Judah Rezin the king of Syria, and Pekah the son of Remaliah" (2 Kings 15:37).

While the kings of Israel were a steady stream of evildoers, Judah had a series of kings who did what was right in God's sight. In fact, the combined reigns of Joash, Amaziah, Uzziah, and Jotham provided Judah with 137 continuous years of good kings. It seems surprising that God sent two kings against Judah. Why did He do it?

Although the four kings mentioned above *"did that which was right in the sight of the LORD"* (15:34), each of them shared a common failure. They were good but not good enough. God expected more from them. None of them had removed the high places where *"the people sacrificed and burned incense"* (15:35), and the Lord was not pleased. They should have eliminated all worship that was not pleasing to God.

Each king made the same mistake. It is common for some to repeat the mistakes of others. Even good people tend to justify their actions after witnessing other good men act the same way. However, our deeds should be guided by God's Word, not by what others get away with.

Let it not be said of us that we did right except in some very important area. One day, failing to do as we should will catch up to us.

2 KINGS 16-17 — REMOVE THE HIGH PLACES — JUL. 12

"And the children of Israel did secretly those things that were not right against the LORD their God" (2 Kings 17:9).

Yesterday we saw God's displeasure with the high places remaining in Judah. Today we see the wickedness associated with them. Ahaz was so evil that he *"made his son to pass through the fire, according to the abominations of the heathen...And he sacrificed and burnt incense in the high places"* (16:3-4). In Israel, the people set up idols *"and wrought wicked things"* in the high places (17:10-11).

The high places gave people a place to practice wickedness in private. Note that *"Israel did secretly those things that were not right."* They knew what was right and wrong, but they chose sin. The conviction in their consciences drove them to hide their evil deeds.

Do you have any high places that remain in your life—areas which you secretly practice sin? It might be a place you visit in person or online. Perhaps it is a vice you pursue behind closed doors. What might be a secret to others is known by God, and as He judged Israel after repeated warnings to repent, He will surely sentence you. Listen to God's warning before it is too late—*"Turn ye from your evil ways, and keep my commandments"* (17:13). Failure to hearken can ruin your life.

| JUL. 13 | FAITHFULNESS REWARDED | 2 KINGS 18 |

"He trusted in the LORD God of Israel; so that after him was none like him among all the kings of Judah, nor any that were before him"
(2 Kings 18:5).

The reign of Hezekiah was like a breath of fresh air. Though his father was an evil man, he chose to follow the Lord. Let's consider Hezekiah's character and the blessings which resulted from it.

His character is admirable. Notice his *disgust* for sin. He did not tolerate the wickedness that the previous kings failed to address—*"He removed the high places, and brake the images, and cut down the groves"* (18:4). Next we see his *dependence*—*"He trusted in the LORD God."* He did not rely on his own strength to fight against the evil of his day. We must seek help from the Lord to battle sin. Consider also his *determination*—*"he clave to the LORD, and departed not from following him"* (18:6). Never give up doing right if you wish to be blessed.

Let's briefly observe some of his blessings. He enjoyed God's *presence*—*"the LORD was with him"* (18:7). He had *prosperity*—*"he prospered whithersoever he went forth"* (18:7). Finally, he had *power*—*"He smote the Philistines"* (18:8). If we are faithful like Hezekiah, God will be with us, grant us success, and strengthen us for spiritual warfare.

| JUL. 14 | WHEN TROUBLE COMES | 2 KINGS 19-20 |

"And it came to pass, when king Hezekiah heard it, that he rent his clothes, and covered himself with sackcloth, and went into the house of the LORD" (2 Kings 19:1).

Following God does not exempt us from trouble. Though Hezekiah was faithful to the Lord, he experienced an overwhelming trial. After the fierce king of Assyria invaded Judah and received a large portion of treasures from Hezekiah, he sent his army to threaten Jerusalem. By observing Hezekiah's response, we can learn how to handle our own troubles when they come.

Notice that he humbled himself—*"he rent his clothes, and covered himself with sackcloth."* God allows problems to come our way to get our attention. Business cannot continue as usual when the tempest snarls at us. We must set aside time to look within for sin and look up for help.

Next we see that he *"went into the house of the LORD."* Never let trouble keep you out of church. When problems arise, you need to seek the Lord more, not less!

Finally, Hezekiah sought help from the man of God. He sent men to Isaiah the prophet looking for a message from the Lord. God gave an answer of peace—*"Be not afraid"* (19:6). He will do the same for you!

2 KINGS 21-22   WORSE THAN THE HEATHEN   JUL. 15

"Manasseh seduced them to do more evil than did the nations whom the LORD destroyed before the children of Israel" (2 Kings 21:9).

Hezekiah was a good king, but he was a terrible father. His son Manasseh was extremely evil. Not only did he do *"as did Ahab"* (21:3), he followed *"the abominations of the heathen, whom the LORD cast out before the children of Israel"* (21:2). What can we learn?

First, regardless of how important your job is, you must not neglect your family. Manasseh reigned almost twice as long as Hezekiah and made a bigger impact on Judah than his father. Imagine how things would have been different had Hezekiah instructed him in the ways of the Lord. There is no greater responsibility than your family.

Second, sin progressively gets worse. Manasseh *"built up again the high places which Hezekiah his father had destroyed"* (21:3). However, he did not stop there. He made a grove, worshipped strange gods, defiled God's temple, and practiced witchcraft. In the end, he seduced Israel *"to do more evil than did the nations whom the LORD destroyed before the children of Israel."* When God's people start down the path of sin, they can become worse than the heathen. The result is God's judgment. If He promised to turn Jerusalem upside down, will He spare you? Fear sin!

2 KINGS 23   A BRIGHT LIGHT IN DARK DAYS   JUL. 16

"And like unto him was there no king before him, that turned to the LORD with all his heart, and with all his soul, and with all his might, according to all the law of Moses" (2 Kings 23:25).

Under the reign of Manasseh, Judah became more evil than the heathen who inhabited the land before them. Manasseh's son continued in rebellion, but then Josiah began to rule. He was a bright light in dark days. We, too, are living in evil times and can learn how to shine for the Lord as Josiah did in his day. Consider what is needed.

Contriteness – When Josiah heard God's Word, it broke his heart. Because he listened to God, the Lord spared him. This teaches us that it is possible to delay God's judgment upon a nation. We need brokenness!

Commitment – Josiah was committed to what he heard. In fact, he gathered all the people, *"and he read in their ears all the words of the book of the covenant"* (23:2). We must share what we learn with others.

Cleansing – Josiah did everything in his power to stamp out the evil in his realm. In like manner, we must cleanse our hearts and homes.

Compliance – Josiah led Judah to observe the Passover, which had been neglected. In evil times, we should challenge others to follow God.

As Josiah shined in Judah's darkest days, so must we in evil times.

JUL. 17   A BETTER KING   2 KINGS 24-25

"And his allowance was a continual allowance given him of the king, a daily rate for every day, all the days of his life" (2 Kings 25:30).

How sad to see the defeat of Judah and the destruction of Jerusalem! All of God's warnings to His people came to pass. Though the final chapters record a sobering reminder of the penalty for sin, the last few verses provide a glimmer of hope for those who are judged.

King Jehoiachin had been taken captive and brought to Babylon, but after 37 years of imprisonment, mercy was extended to him by Evil-merodach. If a heathen king treated him so well, could we think that the King of kings would treat us with less favor? Certainly not!

Consider what we can expect from our great King. First, He will bring us *"out of prison"* (25:27) and set us free from sin's shackles. Next, as Evil-merodach *"spake kindly"* to Jehoiachin (25:28), God has spoken gracious words to us in the Bible. Further, our King has *"changed"* our *"prison garments"* (25:29) and suited us with His righteousness. Let's keep ourselves *"unspotted from the world"* (James 1:27). Lastly, God provides for us a *"continual allowance...a daily rate for every day."* Has He not promised us our daily bread? Thank Him today for His deliverance, kindness, and provision. Praise our King!

JUL. 18   NO FREE PASSES   1 CHRON. 1-2

"And the sons of Zeruiah; Abishai, and Joab, and Asahel, three" (1 Chronicles 2:16).

The sons of Zeruiah were mighty men in David's army. In the book of 2 Samuel, the phrase *"sons of Zeruiah"* is mentioned four times, but on three of those occasions it is used negatively by David. When *"Joab and Abishai his brother slew Abner"* (2 Samuel 3:30), David exclaimed, *"the sons of Zeruiah be too hard for me"* (2 Samuel 3:39). Though he found fault with them, he did not discipline them for their crime. Later, Joab disobeyed David's command and killed Absalom in battle. Why did David let these men literally get away with murder? The answer may be found in the genealogies of today's reading.

Zeruiah was David's sister, which meant that her sons were his nephews. Could it be that David was lenient on them because of family ties? Without the genealogies, we may have missed this important connection and the lesson that follows.

We must not allow family relationships to blur our vision of right and wrong. Too often people turn a blind eye to the sins of their relatives. Family members must never be given a free pass to get away with sin. Strive to be more faithful to God's Word than to your relatives.

1 CHRON. 3-4	**BLESSED SORROW**	JUL. 19

"And Jabez called on the God of Israel, saying, Oh that thou wouldest bless me indeed...And God granted him that which he requested" (1 Chronicles 4:10).

The short account of Jabez is another gem nestled in the genealogies. His name means "sorrowful" and was given to him by his mother because she *"bare him with sorrow"* (4:9). His life is a reminder that blessings often follow grief. Consider what we know about Jabez.

First, we see his *respect*—he *"was more honourable than his brethren"* (4:9). Why was he respected so much? It may have been due to his piety in prayer or his perseverance in problems. We know he was a man of prayer. It is also possible that the sorrow at his birth involved a physical impairment that led to greater dependence upon God throughout his life. Always see trouble as an opportunity to draw closer to God.

Next, observe his *request*. It was balanced. The types of blessings he sought were material—*"enlarge my coast,"* physical—*"be with me,"* and spiritual—*"keep me from evil, that it may not grieve me!"* (4:10).

Finally, we see his *reward*—*"God granted him that which he requested."* If sin grieves you, you can confidently pray for deliverance and know that God will grant your request. Holiness is always rewarded!

1 CHRON. 5	**GOD'S PURPOSE IN WAR**	JUL. 20

"For there fell down many slain, because the war was of God. And they dwelt in their steads until the captivity" (1 Chronicles 5:22).

We all enjoy peace and prosperity, but there are times when God intends for us to engage in battle. Nevertheless, we should never dread entering the fray because the result of the battle often leads to the very peace and prosperity we seek. Thus was the case for God's people in days of old, and so it will be for us.

The sons of Reuben, Gad, and the half tribe of Manasseh *"made war with the Hagarites"* (5:19). Notice that *"they were helped"* because *"they cried to God in the battle"* and *"put their trust in him"* (5:20). When God chooses battles for us to fight, we must respond in like manner. Let us not respond with cowardice or complaint but exercise fearless faith. When the next conflict arises, trust the mighty God to deliver you without injury and bless you beyond measure.

Notice that *"the war was of God."* He had purposed to use it to bless His people. When the battle against the Hagarites was over, the two and a half tribes captured land and wealth. When war is of God, we can trust Him to defeat our enemies and greatly enrich our lives. Let us learn to see our battles as part of God's plan to bless us.

JUL. 21 — CHANGE OF DUTIES — 1 CHRON. 6

"And these are they whom David set over the service of song in the house of the LORD, after that the ark had rest" (1 Chronicles 6:31).

As we learned previously, the sons of Gershom, Kohath, and Merari were charged with the care and transport of the tabernacle. After the tabernacle was permanently set up and *"the ark had rest,"* David directed some of these men to a new ministry. He set them *"over the service of song in the house of the LORD."* Consider a couple of lessons.

Be flexible when your services are needed in a new area of ministry. Heman, Asaph, and Ethan, along with their children, were chosen to serve with music. Whatever their former duties were we are not told, but they had to change their focus. It can be difficult at times to assume new responsibilities, but we must always put God's will ahead of our own. For example, a young man who is content being a Sunday School teacher must be willing to train for the mission field if God calls him. Are you open to the challenge of a new role?

The next lesson we see is that music plays a vital role in the house of God. Notice that some people were *"set over the service of song"* and *"ministered...with singing"* (6:31-32). Always remember that music in the church is about serving God, not entertaining a crowd.

JUL. 22 — FIT FOR BATTLE — 1 CHRON. 7-8

"...mighty men of valour...fit to go out for war and battle" (1 Chronicles 7:11).

The descendants of Jediael were mighty men of valor. What made them so successful? Preparation. Notice that they were *"fit to go out for war and battle."* If you want to be useful in the Lord's army, you must be fit. What will prepare us for spiritual warfare?

Exercise – Paul instructed Timothy, *"exercise thyself...unto godliness"* (1 Timothy 4:7). Since God's blessing is upon the righteous, we must put great effort into Bible study, prayer, and self-denial.

Strength – By exercise, we gain strength for the battle. However, self-determination is not the basis of our power. We must seek God for spiritual vigor. Consider another charge to Timothy, *"be strong in the grace that is in Christ Jesus"* (2 Timothy 2:1). Ask God for His grace.

Endurance – We are told to *"endure hardness, as a good soldier of Jesus Christ"* (2 Timothy 2:3). Frequent exposure to hardships, though unpleasant, develops stamina and spiritual grit. Never quit on God!

Focus – *"No man that warreth entangleth himself with the affairs of this life"* (2 Timothy 2:4). Fix your attention on the will of God, not worldly pursuits. The battle will come; are you prepared for it?

1 CHRON. 9-10	**GETTING CARRIED AWAY**	**JUL. 23**

"...they were...carried away to Babylon for their transgression"
(1 Chronicles 9:1).

God's people were taken to Babylon because of their rebellion— they were *"carried away...for their transgression."* Despite repeated warnings, they thought they could live like the heathen and go unpunished. Finally, God's promise of judgment came to pass. Though His counsel often goes unheeded, His correction cannot be impeded.

Those who get carried away with sin will also be carried away from God's blessings. Israel lost their homes, fields, and freedom. The benefits of the Promised Land were forfeited for the temporary enjoyment of sin. Too often we fail to realize what we will lose by clinging to our wicked ways. Satan is a master at getting us to focus on earthly pleasures in order to rob us of heavenly blessings. In the end, we may get what we want, but we will lose what we have.

Sin always leads to captivity. In a distant land Israel considered their losses and mourned. Listen to their testimony—*"By the rivers of Babylon, there we sat down, yea, we wept, when we remembered Zion"* (Psalm 137:1). All who neglect God's warnings will one day weep when they reflect on lost blessings. Don't get carried away!

1 CHRON. 11	**THE REASON FOR SUCCESS**	**JUL. 24**

*"So David waxed greater and greater: for the LORD of hosts
was with him"* (1 Chronicles 11:9).

The secret of David's success was not his courage, skill, or wisdom. Neither can his mighty men be credited for his great victories. Our text for today is tucked between the exploits of David and the deeds of his men of valor, reminding us that accomplishments are dependent upon God. Notice that *"David waxed* [grew] *greater and greater"* because *"the LORD of hosts was with him."* It had little to do with his men.

Too often we marvel at the spectacular feats of David's mighty men but ignore the Mighty God Who made their success possible. Though God uses men to accomplish His work, we must remember that only He is to be praised. David's host of soldiers, as strong as they were, pale in comparison to the heavenly army at God's disposal. David would have been a failure without the Lord. Dependence must be on God, not man.

Never think your achievements are the result of your savvy, strength, or strategies. If you have been successful in a particular venture, take a moment and acknowledge *"the LORD of hosts"* for His might and mercy in the matter. Only when He is with you, can you expect to get *"greater and greater"* in your service for Him. God blesses those who trust Him.

JUL. 25   HALF RIGHT   1 CHRON. 12-13

"And they carried the ark of God in a new cart" (1 Chronicles 13:7).

At times we are convinced that what we are doing is right and wonder why things fail to work out as we planned. This is what happened to David. He did the right thing without realizing that he did it the wrong way. Let's see what happened.

Consider his *desire—"let us bring again the ark of our God to us"* (13:3). The ark had been in Kirjathjearim for over forty years after the Philistines returned it, and David wanted to bring it to Jerusalem. This was commendable, but he ignored God's directions for handling the ark.

Notice his *disobedience—"they carried the ark of God in a new cart."* God had made it clear to Moses that the Levites were to carry the ark on their shoulders with poles, but a different method was chosen. Let us remember that God's work must be done God's way.

Next we see God's *discipline*. When Uzza touched the ark as it teetered, *"the anger of the LORD was kindled against Uzza, and he smote him"* (13:10). Though sincere, the people had disobeyed God.

Last, we see David's *displeasure*. He was angry because God killed Uzza. Are you prone to get upset when God corrects you? Be careful not to be only half right in your service, or you won't like the outcome.

JUL. 26   RIGHTING A WRONG   1 CHRON. 14-15

"God helped the Levites that bare the ark of the covenant of the LORD" (1 Chronicles 15:26).

Yesterday, we saw that David had a good motive but a bad method for transporting the ark to Jerusalem. Today, we see that he corrected his error and instructed the Levites to carry the ark as God had commanded. What was the result? *"God helped."* It is comforting to know that the Lord often gives second chances and is willing to help us when we follow His principles.

Have you, like David, ignored God's instructions in a particular matter? Perhaps you are presently reaping because of disobedience to the Lord. Why not confess your sin and determine to do things His way? That is what David did, and our text is a wonderful reminder that God graciously extends mercy to those who amend their ways.

What made David a man after God's own heart was not his failure but his willingness to admit his faults and pursue God's will. If you have failed in your service to the Lord, determine to right your wrongs.

Let us end with a sobering thought. Though the nation of Israel had a fresh opportunity to make things right, their disobedience led to Uzza's destruction. Never forget the awful price others may pay for your sin.

| 1 CHRON. 16 | TELL ALL NATIONS | JUL. 27 |

"Declare his glory among the heathen; his marvellous works among all nations" (1 Chronicles 16:24).

After the ark was brought to Jerusalem, David delivered a psalm to the Levites *"to thank the LORD"* (16:7). In the psalm, he reminded Israel of God's great covenant with them. Then, he charged them to publish the goodness and glory of God to every nation. God's heart for the heathen was evident even before Christ came to earth!

Jesus gave a similar charge to His disciples—*"Go ye therefore, and teach all nations"* (Matthew 28:19). If Jehovah was to be declared to *"all nations"* in David's day, how much more should we endeavor to proclaim His name in this day of grace? Has every tribe and tongue heard the good news yet? No. Millions presently sit in darkness with no gospel witness. Paul asked, *"how shall they hear without a preacher?"* (Romans 10:14). Is there not a need for more missionaries? The lost across the street and across the world must hear of Christ's goodness, sacrifice, and love. Without it, they will perish in everlasting fire.

Let us not forget that spreading the glory of our God is not merely a suggestion. We are commanded, *"Go...and teach all nations."* Have you been actively witnessing for Jesus lately? Will you today?

| 1 CHRON. 17-18 | PLEADING GOD'S PROMISES | JUL. 28 |

"Therefore now, LORD, let the thing that thou hast spoken concerning thy servant and concerning his house be established for ever, and do as thou hast said" (1 Chronicles 17:23).

David's prayer may have been bold, but it was not presumptuous. God had promised, *"I will subdue all thine enemies. Furthermore I tell thee that the LORD will build thee an house"* (17:10). It was David's faith that led him to plead, *"do as thou hast said."* We do not have to read much farther to see that God kept His promise and answered David's request. He defeated the Syrians and *"the LORD preserved David whithersoever he went"* (18:6). Moreover, his throne was blessed.

When God speaks, He is bound by His Word. Let us, therefore, be quick to seize the blessings He has promised to give. Has the Spirit of God impressed upon your heart a particular passage of Scripture to cheer you? Since He cannot fail, do not neglect to rehearse His Words in His ears. The God of creation cannot deny His own promises.

The psalmist expressed his dependence upon the Lord with these heartfelt words: *"Remember the word unto thy servant, upon which thou hast caused me to hope"* (Psalm 119:49). Whisper that prayer to the Lord right now and patiently wait for the answer to come. Have hope!

JUL. 29   RETURNING TO GOD   1 CHRON. 19-21

"And David said unto Gad, I am in a great strait: let me fall now into the hand of the LORD; for very great are his mercies" (1 Chronicles 21:13).

After great victories, David's heart was lifted up with pride, and he numbered his armies to revel in his might. However, *"God was displeased with this thing; therefore he smote Israel"* (21:7). David's response provides guidance for all who seek to restore their walk with God after sinning.

It started with *confession*—*"David said unto God, I have sinned greatly...for I have done very foolishly"* (21:8). Like David, we must learn to admit the true nature of our deeds. Never sugarcoat your sin.

Next we see *confidence*. Though David was forgiven, he had to reap the consequences of his actions. When given three choices of punishment, he cast himself upon the mercy of God, saying, *"let me fall now into the hand of the LORD; for very great are his mercies."* When reaping from sin, we must trust God to know when our punishment *"is enough"* (21:15). Patiently wait for His refining fires to burn your dross.

Finally, we observe the *cost*. When renewing his consecration, David refused to *"offer burnt offerings without cost"* (21:24). Be willing to express your love and thankfulness to God by personal sacrifice.

JUL. 30   GO TO WORK   1 CHRON. 22-23

"Arise therefore, and be doing, and the LORD be with thee"
(1 Chronicles 22:16).

It was David's desire that God's house would be *"exceeding magnifical, of fame and of glory"* (22:5). Therefore, he *"prepared abundantly"* to ensure Solomon had the necessary supplies for the project (22:5). Instead of having a pity party because he could not build the temple, David did what he could. He was so determined to contribute to God's work that he refused to let affliction stop him. Notice his testimony: *"Now, behold, in my trouble I have prepared for the house of the LORD"* (22:14). He provided a great example of diligence to his son.

When it came time to pass the baton to Solomon, David charged him, *"Arise therefore, and be doing, and the LORD be with thee."* It was time for Solomon to show the same dedication to the task that his father had displayed. David was anxious for his son to build the temple of God. All of the preparation had been made; it was now time to get to work.

Is there a task which is ready to be started that you have not yet begun? Allow today's text to prompt you to get busy. After preparation has been made, only one thing remains—*"Arise...and be doing."* Once you get to work, rest assured that *"the LORD"* will *"be with thee."*

| 1 CHRON. 24-25 | **HUMBLE SERVICE** | JUL. 31 |

"And they cast lots, ward against ward, as well the small as the great, the teacher as the scholar" (1 Chronicles 25:8).

David had appointed the sons of Asaph, Heman, and Jeduthun to minister in music. When it came time to divide the men into twenty-four groups, they cast lots to determine their order. No special preference was given to those who were prominent. The selection treated everyone the same—*"as well the small as the great."* This provides us with an important reminder that, regardless of our position, we must not become enamored with our own importance. God did not allow these men to "pull rank" on others to make it more convenient for themselves. At times, people rise to leadership roles and begin to think they are exempt from service. Position shouldn't shelter us from service.

Pride makes a man think he deserves preferential treatment. Let us remember the words of Jesus, *"But he that is greatest among you shall be your servant"* (Matthew 23:11). The greater our position, the greater our service should be. Never elevate yourself above others or think that a task is beneath you. Despite our titles, we must maintain the right attitude. Paul wrote, *"For I say…to every man that is among you, not to think of himself more highly than he ought to think"* (Romans 12:3).

| 1 CHRON. 26-27 | **A BLESSED FAMILY** | AUG. 1 |

"Obededom…God blessed him" (1 Chronicles 26:4-5).

The Lord rewarded Obededom because he cared for the ark of God (2 Samuel 6:11). What a privilege to be blessed, especially when God does the blessing! We are not told of all the ways the Lord showed favor to Obededom, but one area is recorded for us. God blessed his family. What could be better than that? Notice the qualities of his sons—*"able men for strength for the service"* (26:8).

They were *skilled*—*"able men."* The Lord equips people with talents and abilities, and when individuals exceed their peers with special skills, the glory should be given to God. Next, they were *strong*—*"able men for strength."* When God's hand of blessing is upon a man, he will be empowered for His work. He enables some to be stronger mentally, physically, and emotionally than others. Last, they were *serving*. Notice that the strength they received was *"for the service"* of God. The Lord's blessings upon our lives should be used for His business, not for selfish pursuits. What has the Lord given to you that can be used for Him?

May we seek God's blessing on our homes today. Would it not be wonderful to have children who are skilled, strong, and serving? We can if we are faithful to the Lord as Obededom was.

| AUG. 2 | FATHERLY ADVICE | 1 CHRON. 28-29 |

"And thou, Solomon my son, know thou the God of thy father, and serve him with a perfect heart and with a willing mind" (1 Chronicles 28:9).

Not all of David's sons served the Lord. When charging Solomon to build the temple, David's heart was burdened for him. Our text provides insight to some good fatherly advice.

Notice David's *recommendation*—*"know thou the God of thy father."* Every father should do all that he can to help his children develop a relationship with God. David also charged his son to be real, saying, *"serve him* [God] *with a perfect heart and with a willing mind."* Too many second generation Christians only pretend to walk with God.

Next, David provided his son with a *reason* to be genuine—*"the LORD searcheth all hearts"* (28:9). He reminded him that God knows everything and any hint of hypocrisy would be detected. Those who pretend at religion ultimately find it harder to act holy than to be holy.

Solomon had to choose whether he would follow or forsake God. David mentioned the *results* that would follow each choice—*"if thou seek him, he will be found of thee; but if thou forsake him, he will cast thee off"* (28:9). Every parent must make the consequences clear to their kids. Are you properly guiding your children to know and serve God?

| AUG. 3 | MEETING GOD | 2 CHRON. 1-2 |

"In that night did God appear unto Solomon, and said unto him, Ask what I shall give thee" (2 Chronicles 1:7).

Imagine how Solomon must have felt when the Lord appeared to him. Surely, he was overwhelmed with awe, thrilled with excitement, and filled with gratitude. His humble response indicates that he was ready for the meeting. Instead of asking for riches and fame, he requested wisdom to serve others. Perhaps the condition of his heart is the precise reason the Lord appeared to him. Is your heart prepared for such a visitation?

Experiencing God's presence should not be a rare event for the Christian. Neither should it be considered a mystical encounter that happens by chance. On the contrary, the Lord has provided a simple plan to follow in order to experience His presence—*"Draw nigh to God, and he will draw nigh to you"* (James 4:8). This is exactly what Solomon had done. Before we read, *"that night did God appear,"* we first see that *"Solomon went up thither to the brasen altar before the LORD...and offered a thousand burnt offerings upon it"* (1:6). God appeared to him because he had worshipped Him. We, too, can expect a meeting with the Lord when we seek Him with all of our hearts.

2 CHRON. 3-5 — A FRUITFUL FOCUS — AUG. 4

"...they lifted up their voice with the trumpets and cymbals and instruments of musick, and praised the LORD, saying, For he is good; for his mercy endureth for ever" (2 Chronicles 5:13).

The temple construction involved great detail, craftsmanship, and expense. Finally, it was complete, and all the furniture was in place. When the priests exited the holy place, the Levites began to worship the Lord in song. Let's consider some characteristics of true praise.

The *focus* of our praise must be God. Notice that the people *"praised the LORD."* Much of what is considered praise in our modern age gives more glory to man than to God. Musicians are admired for their talent, applauded for their performances, and emulated by their fans. Rather than focusing on man's abilities, we ought to acknowledge God's attributes. The Levites proclaimed, *"For he is good; for his mercy endureth for ever."* When praising God, be sure that you address Him directly and adore Him more than the musicians behind the music.

When praise is correct, *fruit* will accompany it. In the case of the Levites, the temple was *"filled with a cloud"* (5:13), which indicated God's presence. When your praise focuses on the Lord, His glory will be manifested in your life. With that said, strike a chord of praise right now.

2 CHRON. 6 — GOD KNOWS YOUR HEART — AUG. 5

"Then hear thou from heaven thy dwelling place, and forgive, and render unto every man according unto all his ways, whose heart thou knowest; (for thou only knowest the hearts of the children of men:)"
(2 Chronicles 6:30).

When Solomon prayed at the dedication of the temple, he acknowledged that Israel would be subject to God's chastening if they sinned. As he prayed, he asked the Lord to forgive all who would turn to Him in true repentance. Included in his request for forgiveness was a soul-searching phrase—*"whose heart thou knowest."* All who heard it were reminded that God knows everyone's heart, and this served as a warning to any who would superficially seek Him.

At times, we are quick to make a half-hearted confession of sin in order to get out of trouble that we have created for ourselves. We must not be deceived into thinking that God is pleased with such self-serving requests. What gets His attention is brokenness over sin. David testified, *"The sacrifices of God are a broken spirit: a broken and a contrite heart, O God, thou wilt not despise"* (Psalm 51:17). Remember that God knows your heart. If you seek forgiveness, it must be on His terms. He expects godly sorrow, not careless confession. How do you confess sin?

AUG. 6   PRAYING DOWN FIRE   2 CHRON. 7-8

"Now when Solomon had made an end of praying, the fire came down from heaven, and consumed the burnt offering and the sacrifices; and the glory of the LORD filled the house" (2 Chronicles 7:1).

Solomon dedicated the temple by making sacrifices and offering prayer. At the conclusion of his prayer, God sent His fire of acceptance, and His glory flooded every inch of the temple. What was the result? The people worshipped and praised the Lord (7:3).

Today, *"the most High dwelleth not in temples made with hands"* (Acts 7:48). Instead, He lives in another sort of temple—the heart of man. Speaking to Christians, Paul said, *"your body is the temple of the Holy Ghost"* (1 Corinthians 6:19). As Solomon dedicated the temple in Jerusalem to God, we must commit our lives to the Lord through prayer and the sacrifice of our personal ambitions. We are told, *"present your bodies a living sacrifice, holy, acceptable unto God"* (Romans 12:1).

Though you may not pray down literal fire from heaven, your life can burn brightly as a testimony to the Lord. When we are emptied of self and filled with God's Spirit, *"the glory of the LORD"* will radiate through all that we do and say. Take a moment and present yourself unreservedly to God. A glorious day awaits those who do!

AUG. 7   TOO GOOD TO BE TRUE?   2 CHRON. 9-10

"And when the queen of Sheba heard of the fame of Solomon, she came to prove Solomon with hard questions at Jerusalem" (2 Chronicles 9:1).

The Lord made Solomon to exceed *"all the kings of the earth in riches and wisdom"* (9:22). When the queen of Sheba heard of his fame, she thought it was too good to be true. So, she *"came to prove Solomon with hard questions."* To test his savvy, she brought the trickiest and most puzzling questions she could imagine. Whether she realized it or not, she not only had doubts about Solomon but also wondered if God could bless a man so richly. She was about to find out!

Solomon graciously received the queen and *"told her all her questions: and there was nothing hid from Solomon which he told her not"* (9:2). She was so overwhelmed by what she heard and saw that *"there was no more spirit in her"* (9:4). In other words, all that she witnessed literally took her breath away.

The Lord likes to do things in such a spectacular way that it leaves people speechless. Are you hungry to see a glorious manifestation of His power? Too often we limit what God will do in our lives by our unbelief. Take a moment and think about God's glory and greatness. You may be visited with a blessing that exceeds your expectations!

2 CHRON. 11-12   HUMBLE YOURSELF   AUG. 8

"And when he humbled himself, the wrath of the LORD turned from him, that he would not destroy him altogether: and also in Judah things went well" (2 Chronicles 12:12).

For three years, many of the leaders did right and *"walked in the way of David and Solomon"* (11:17). This *"strengthened the kingdom of Judah, and made Rehoboam the son of Solomon strong"* (11:17). However, after Rehoboam became strong *"he forsook the law of the LORD, and all Israel with him"* (12:1). We shall see that following God brings His blessing and forsaking Him brings His chastisement.

Because of Judah's rebellion, the Lord sent Shishak, king of Egypt, to trouble them. This got their attention, and once *"they humbled themselves,"* God said, *"I will not destroy them, but I will grant them some deliverance"* (12:7). Sin kindles the wrath of God, but repentance secures His mercy. We may not escape all of the problems resulting from our sin, but it is wonderful to know that a change of heart can provide *"some deliverance."* The purpose of God's discipline is to correct, not to destroy. Therefore, we ought to humble ourselves so that *"the wrath of the LORD"* will turn from us. As *"things went well"* for Judah after the people repented, they can go well for us too.

2 CHRON. 13-14   OUTNUMBERED   AUG. 9

"And Asa cried unto the LORD his God, and said, LORD, it is nothing with thee to help, whether with many, or with them that have no power: help us, O LORD our God; for we rest on thee" (2 Chronicles 14:11).

Judah was greatly outnumbered. An army of one million Ethiopian soldiers had invaded the land. How did God's people respond?

First, we see *courage*—*"they set the battle in array"* (14:10). When you feel like the odds are against you, it is not time to run and hide. Face your problems and enter the fray. You can never win by retreating.

Next, consider the *cry*—*"Asa cried unto the LORD his God."* Though we must engage in the conflict, we must not do so in our own strength. Seek the Lord's help with heartfelt prayer.

Another key is *confidence*. Asa prayed, *"it is nothing with thee to help, whether with many, or with them that have no power."* The king knew that victory did not depend on the size of his army. All He needed was the Lord. With God on your side, your opposition is outnumbered! *"If God be for us, who can be against us?"* (Romans 8:31).

Finally, observe *calmness*—*"we rest on thee"* (14:11). Satan wants us to be filled with fear and anxiety, but faith brings peace and comfort. How do you respond to overwhelming situations? Lean upon the Lord!

AUG. 10	LOOKING TO BLESS	2 CHRON. 15-17

"For the eyes of the LORD run to and fro throughout the whole earth, to shew himself strong in the behalf of them whose heart is perfect toward him" (2 Chronicles 16:9).

Our text for today provides wonderful encouragement that God is actively seeking people to bless. You need not worry about being overlooked because His eyes are looking *"throughout the whole earth."* No nation, race, or class of people are excluded from His search. If your *"heart is perfect toward him,"* you meet God's requirements.

Ironically, this promise was given as a reminder and a rebuke to king Asa. Though he had previously trusted God for a great victory, he sought help from a heathen king when threatened by Baasha. Had Asa sought the Lord as he had done aforetime, he would have been delivered. Instead, the Lord reproved him, saying, *"thou hast done foolishly"* (16:9). Rather than repenting, Asa *"was in a rage"* and imprisoned the prophet that God sent with His message (16:10).

Is your heart perfect toward God? The word *perfect* means "complete." God does not require us to be sinless to gain His blessing. He desires that our faith is completely in Him, not placed in man. When our confidence is in God, He can *"shew himself strong"* on our behalf.

AUG. 11	UNHOLY ALLIANCES	2 CHRON. 18-19

"Shouldest thou help the ungodly, and love them that hate the LORD? therefore is wrath upon thee from before the LORD" (2 Chronicles 19:2).

Jehoshaphat was a good king. Notice his testimony—*"he walked in the first ways of his father David...sought to the LORD God...his heart was lifted up in the ways of the LORD"* (17:3, 4, 6). Revival broke out in the land under his reign, and God blessed him greatly with *"riches and honour"* (18:1). Despite his good qualities, he lacked an important essential—separation from the ungodly.

Jehoshaphat visited king Ahab and agreed to assist him in battle against Ramoth-gilead. He said, *"I am as thou art, and my people as thy people"* (18:3). That was not true! Jehoshaphat followed Jehovah but Ahab was a wicked unbeliever. His compromise led him to remain silent when the prophet Micaiah was smitten and imprisoned for speaking the truth. Further, Jehoshaphat almost lost his life in battle because of his unholy alliance with Ahab. Thus, God sent a prophet to cry against him, saying, *"therefore is wrath upon thee from before the LORD."*

Always remember that God is angered by a lack of separation. Do what Jehoshaphat should have done—*"Enter not into the path of the wicked, and go not in the way of evil men"* (Proverbs 4:14).

2 CHRON. 20 — THE FLESH IS WEAK — AUG. 12

"And after this did Jehoshaphat king of Judah join himself with Ahaziah king of Israel, who did very wickedly" (2 Chronicles 20:35).

Though Jehoshaphat formed an unholy alliance with Ahab, he had a tender heart and repented. God said, *"there are good things found in thee"* (19:3). When the enemy came against Judah, *"Jehoshaphat feared, and set himself to seek the LORD"* (20:3). He trusted the Lord so much that he challenged his people when they faced danger, saying, *"Believe in the LORD your God, so shall ye be established; believe his prophets, so shall ye prosper"* (20:20). Jehovah provided a great victory and *"God gave him rest"* (20:30). All was going well until Jehoshaphat's weakness returned—he formed another unequal yoke.

This time it was a business venture in the shipping industry instead of a military expedition. He joined *"himself with Ahaziah king of Israel, who did very wickedly."* The prophet declared, *"Because thou hast joined thyself with Ahaziah, the LORD hath broken thy works"* (20:37). Thus, *"the ships were broken"* (20:37). Sin always leads to loss.

Learn an important lesson from this account. Though we may have a sincere heart and display great faith at times, we must guard against the frailties of our flesh. If we're not vigilant, besetting sins can return.

2 CHRON. 21-22 — LASTING CONSEQUENCES — AUG. 13

"And he walked in the way of the kings of Israel, like as did the house of Ahab: for he had the daughter of Ahab to wife: and he wrought that which was evil in the eyes of the LORD" (2 Chronicles 21:6).

Today we see a sad repercussion of Jehoshaphat's life of inconsistency. Because of his friendship with Ahab, his son Jehoram married Ahab's daughter. As a result, Jehoram *"wrought that which was evil in the eyes of the LORD."*

Decisions have consequences. Jehoshaphat's sin had a direct impact on his son. Let every parent live with that in mind. Yielding to the lusts of our flesh may make it difficult for our children to follow the Lord.

As Ahab's daughter influenced Jehoram to do evil, even so relationships developed by our children as a result of our backslidden condition can make them worldly. In the end, Jehoram died a slow, miserable death—*"after the end of two years, his bowels fell out by reason of his sickness: so he died of sore diseases"* (21:19).

When he died, nobody missed him—he *"departed without being desired"* (21:20). Is that the legacy you want for your children? If not, live a consistent life and protect them from evil influences. Though we may recover from our sin, our children may not. Be cautious.

AUG. 14	STRONG BUT WEAK	2 CHRON. 23-24

"For the army of the Syrians came with a small company of men, and the LORD delivered a very great host into their hand, because they had forsaken the LORD God of their fathers" (2 Chronicles 24:24).

Previously, we have seen how God worked great victories for His people when they were outnumbered. Today, we see the opposite— *"with a small company of men"* the Syrian army defeated *"a very great host"* of Judah. Why did God's people lose the battle when they were bigger and stronger than their enemy? It was *"because they had forsaken the LORD God."*

This account teaches an important lesson. Our natural strength means little. What counts most is our relationship with the Lord. When weak and close to God, we are mighty. When strong and distant from God, we are feeble.

Too often believers trust their own wisdom, strategies, and resources for victory. Strengthen yourself as you may, but you will soon realize that you are powerless against the enemy without God. If you renew your dedication to Him, you can depend upon His deliverance. Have you undertaken a task in your own strength? If so, do not be surprised when it fails. By leaning upon the Lord, you can be victorious.

AUG. 15	UP AND DOWN	2 CHRON. 25-26

"And he sought God...and as long as he sought the LORD, God made him to prosper" (2 Chronicles 26:5).

The way up is down, and the way down is up. When Uzziah trusted the Lord, *"God helped him"* against his enemies (26:7). However, *"when he was strong, his heart was lifted up to his destruction"* (26:16). Those who seek the Lord will find success, but let them take heed lest they forsake the One Who makes their efforts to prosper.

Though once blessed, Uzziah forsook the Lord. Unfortunately, his success led to heady pride instead of grateful humility. Emboldened by his achievements, he began to think he could do as he pleased. He even dared to violate God's order for the temple and offered incense in the priests' office. When eighty valiant priests rebuked him, *"Uzziah was wroth"* (26:19). Then God's judgment fell—*"leprosy even rose up in his forehead before the priests in the house of the LORD"* (26:19). Uzziah learned what the Lord had taught his father—*"God hath power to help, and to cast down"* (25:8). The same God who had richly blessed him smote him with a hideous disease, which caused him to live in seclusion.

Things went well for Uzziah *"as long as he sought the LORD."* Seek Him and maintain humility when He showers His goodness upon you.

2 CHRON. 27-28 — PUT GOD FIRST — AUG. 16

"So Jotham became mighty, because he prepared his ways before the LORD his God" (2 Chronicles 27:6).

King Jotham enjoyed the blessings of God on his life because he *"prepared his ways before the LORD."* He had made Jehovah *"his God"* and determined that the direction of his life would please Him. Oh, that we would seek God's approval for each path we consider! Notice the benefits which result from putting God first.

Wisdom – Jotham served God as his father had done but avoided his father's transgression. He *"entered not into the temple of the LORD"* to offer incense inappropriately as Uzziah did (27:2). It is always wise to follow a man's righteous qualities, not his rebellious ones.

Work – He did not neglect God's house; he labored to promote the work of the Lord—*"He built the high gate of the house of the LORD"* (27:3). Not only did God bless Jotham's sacred efforts but also his civil ones. He successfully constructed cities, castles, and towers. When we seek the Lord, He will establish the work of our hands.

Wealth – After defeating the enemy, Jotham received large sums of silver and sustenance. In like manner, *"seek ye first the kingdom of God...and all these things shall be added unto you"* (Matthew 6:33).

2 CHRON. 29 — CLEANSE THE TEMPLE — AUG. 17

"Hear me...sanctify now yourselves, and sanctify the house of the LORD God of your fathers, and carry forth the filthiness out of the holy place" (2 Chronicles 29:5).

Revival came to the nation during the reign of Hezekiah, and it started in the temple. Wasting no time, the king began this task during his first month on the throne. Revival is serious and must not be delayed.

Remember Paul's message to believers: *"your body is the temple of the Holy Ghost"* (1 Corinthians 6:19). If we ever hope to have revival, we must show the same sense of urgency in cleansing our temples as Hezekiah did. Let's consider how he cleansed the temple.

First, he *"opened the doors"* (29:3). Each individual must open his heart to God so that it can be cleansed and furnished with godly traits. Next, after opening the doors to the temple, Hezekiah *"repaired them"* (29:3). Doors protected the temple. We must mend the gates that guard our hearts by establishing safeguards for our eyes and ears. Finally, Hezekiah charged the priests to *"carry forth the filthiness out of the holy place."* Every evil thought, motive, and habit must be purged from your heart if you hope to enjoy revival. Will you take the necessary steps to cleanse your temple today?

AUG. 18	SOURCES OF JOY	2 CHRON. 30-31

"So there was great joy in Jerusalem" (2 Chronicles 30:26).

What brought such great joy to Jerusalem? The people kept the Passover which had been not observed in such a manner since the days of Solomon. Let's consider three sources of joy from this account.

Obedience brings joy. The Lord had commanded Israel to keep the Passover every year, but they had neglected it. When we disobey God, our lives always become miserable. If you have neglected one of God's commands, hasten to obey it so that you can experience *"great joy."* Have you forgotten how happy obeying God made you in the past?

Worship brings joy. The Passover was a reminder to Israel of God's deliverance from Egypt. If you want joy, take some time to reflect on the Savior and consider the bondage from which you have been set free. Get your eyes off the world and set your affection on things above.

Repentance brings joy. Hezekiah had sent messengers to the northern kingdom, inviting them to keep the Passover with them in Judah. Though many in Israel mocked, some returned to the Lord and traveled to Jerusalem to keep the feast. What a happy reunion! This reminds us of what Jesus said—*"there is joy...over one sinner that repenteth"* (Luke 15:10). Let's work to bring people to the Lord.

AUG. 19	ENCOURAGING WORDS	2 CHRON. 32

"Be strong and courageous, be not afraid nor dismayed for the king of Assyria, nor for all the multitude that is with him" (2 Chronicles 32:7).

Sennacherib was a fierce and formidable foe, yet Hezekiah provided steady leadership to his followers in the face of danger. The exhortation in our text, *"Be strong and courageous, be not afraid nor dismayed,"* is a message found frequently in Scripture. What makes this account unusual is that it was Hezekiah speaking, not God. The lesson is clear; those in leadership positions must provide encouragement.

Hezekiah *reassured* his people when he *"spake comfortably to them"* (32:6). Leaders should try to comfort those who are distressed. Parents must teach their children to trust in the Lord when they experience opposition. In like manner, pastors need to bolster their flock when trouble comes. Hezekiah reminded the people concerning Sennacherib, *"With him is an arm of flesh; but with us is the LORD our God to help us, and to fight our battles"* (32:8). What a promise!

Notice the *response* to Hezekiah's counsel—*"the people rested"* (32:8). When leaders point people to God, they can bring peace to troubled souls. If your faith wavers, do as Hezekiah; he *"prayed and cried to heaven"* (32:20). Who might need your encouragement today?

| 2 CHRON. 33-34 | RICH IN MERCY | AUG. 20 |

"And when he was in affliction, he besought the LORD his God, and humbled himself greatly before the God of his fathers, And prayed unto him" (2 Chronicles 33:12-13).

When tempted to think that someone is beyond redemption, remember Manasseh. Though he was more wicked than any of the kings of Judah and caused God's people *"to do worse than the heathen"* (33:9), he found mercy in God's sight. Consider the events.

First, we see *reaping*. The Lord spoke *"to Manasseh, and to his people: but they would not hearken"* (33:10). Therefore, God allowed the enemy to bind him and carry him captive to Babylon.

Next, notice the *remorse—"when he was in affliction, he besought the LORD his God, and humbled himself greatly."* It often takes much sorrow, pain, and trouble for hardened sinners to consider their ways.

Observe the *restoration*—God *"heard his supplication, and brought him again to Jerusalem"* (33:13). Truly, the Lord is *"rich in mercy"* (Ephesians 2:4). His love and forgiveness reach even the worst sinners.

Finally, we see *renewal*. Manasseh's life changed—*"he took away the strange gods, and the idol out of the house of the LORD...And he repaired the altar"* (33:15-16). God is still in the life-changing business!

| 2 CHRON. 35-36 | JUST JUDGMENT | AUG. 21 |

"...the wrath of the LORD arose against his people...there was no remedy" (2 Chronicles 36:16).

People often misunderstand the Lord, thinking He is not a God of judgment. They say, "God is a God of love and would not judge anybody." What they fail to realize is that the Lord is not only loving but also just. Because He cares for people, He offers forgiveness. Because He is holy, He punishes sin. Today's reading proves this and also shows a correlation between His love and judgment.

His love warns of judgment. Before God's wrath was kindled against His people, He first sent prophets to them. He loved them enough to plead with them to amend their ways. Notice that *"he had compassion on his people"* (36:15), indicating that love points out sin.

His love provides a season to repent. God's judgment did not fall immediately. He gave His people many opportunities to repent before sending them into captivity. How did they respond? They *"mocked the messengers of God, and despised his words, and misused his prophets"* (36:16). Those who snub God's mercy forfeit His blessings.

His love does not negate justice. Neglected love led to severe trouble—*"there was no remedy."* Receive His love and avoid judgment.

AUG. 22 — PREPARING TO BUILD — EZRA 1-2

"The LORD...hath charged me to build him an house" (Ezra 1:2).

After seventy years of captivity, the Lord set the stage for the return of His people to Jerusalem to rebuild the temple. As God sought laborers in that day, He seeks people to work in His service today.

Notice God's *providence*—*"the LORD stirred up the spirit of Cyrus king of Persia"* (1:1). God chose a king from a heathen nation to rally His people for the work. Has the Lord stirred your heart for a particular task? If so, be as willing to fulfill it as Cyrus was.

Consider God's *plan*. A call for volunteers was issued—*"Who is there among you of all his people?"* (1:3). Many of the Jews had become comfortable with their new life in Persia, but some were willing to leave their homes and return to Jerusalem. Are you willing to forsake the comforts of home for God's service? Few seem eager to do so.

Next, we see God's *power*. The promise to those who went back to Jerusalem was, *"his God be with him"* (1:3). Thankfully, we don't go on God's missions alone; He promises to be with us each step of the way!

Lastly, we see God's *provision*. Those who remained in Persia were charged to help the ones who went (1:4). World-wide missions need some to go and others to give for their support. Which are you doing?

AUG. 23 — BUILDING FOR GOD — EZRA 3-5

"Then rose up Zerubbabel the son of Shealtiel, and Jeshua the son of Jozadak, and began to build the house of God" (Ezra 5:2).

The progress on the temple brought great joy to God's people. However, not everyone in the area was happy. Satan always seems to stir up adversaries to hinder the work of the Lord. Consider what to expect when building for God.

Opposition – Notice that *"the people of the land weakened the hands of the people of Judah, and troubled them in building"* (4:4). Don't be surprised when the devil sends people to cause trouble. Though they hope to discourage us, we must remain faithful.

Setbacks – The enemy succeeded to get king Artaxerxes to issue a decree to stop the building of the temple, and *"made them to cease by force and power"* (4:23). At times, it may seem as if the devil prevails, but we know his defeat will come at last.

Assistance – The Lord sent His prophets to stir the people to restart the work. *"Then rose up"* the leaders *"and began to build the house of God."* Though they were opposed again, *"the eye of their God was upon the elders of the Jews, that they could not cause them to cease"* (5:5). The Lord helped! He always assists those who labor for Him.

EZRA 6-7 — OVERCOMING OPPOSITION — AUG. 24

"And they builded, and finished it, according to the commandment of the God of Israel" (Ezra 6:14).

Though the adversaries appealed to Darius in hopes of stopping the construction of the temple, their plot failed. Not only did the king confirm Cyrus' decree, he also ensured that nothing would hinder the work on God's house. This ought to encourage us that the Lord will soon take up our cause and turn our enemy's curse into a blessing.

Notice three benefits which resulted from Darius' intervention. First, those building the temple had *protection*. The king commanded the instigators, *"be ye far from thence: Let the work of this house of God alone"* (6:6-7). In due time, the Lord may command your opponents to leave you alone too. Second, we see *provision*. Darius authorized that *"expenses be given"* to the men building the temple (6:8). Without the opposition, they never would have received additional funds from Darius. Once again we see that God works all things for good! Finally, we see *prosperity*—*"they prospered...And they builded, and finished it"* (6:14). Since God had commanded them to build, He enabled them to finish. We can succeed in what God calls us to do. If you are presently troubled, wait on the Lord until He sends help. Victory is ahead.

EZRA 8-9 — SEEKING A RIGHT WAY — AUG. 25

"I proclaimed a fast...that we might afflict ourselves before our God, to seek of him a right way for us, and for our little ones, and for all our substance" (Ezra 8:21).

Ezra and a small group of Jews made plans to journey from Babylon to Jerusalem, carrying a large amount of silver and gold for the temple. Travel for such a feeble caravan would be dangerous without trained soldiers for safety. However, Ezra was ashamed to ask the king for a band of men because he had boasted that God would protect them.

Notice his *faith*. He said to the king, *"The hand of our God is upon all them for good that seek him"* (8:22). Ezra knew that God was more capable of protecting them than a king's army. After all, he served the King of kings. We, too, must learn to place our confidence in the Lord.

Next, came *fasting*. Without divine direction, all of the people and their precious cargo were in grave danger. He needed guidance from God and sought it through fasting. At times, we may need to afflict ourselves through fasting to seek *"a right way"* for our lives. When is the last time you deprived yourself of food to seek the Lord's direction?

Faith and fasting get results. Like Ezra, we will be able to testify, *"the hand of our God was upon us, and he delivered us"* (8:31).

AUG. 26 — A LACK OF SEPARATION — EZRA 10

"And Ezra the priest stood up, and said unto them, Ye have transgressed, and have taken strange wives, to increase the trespass of Israel" (Ezra 10:10).

This chapter records the call to the Israelites to put away strange wives (10:11). Though some may wish to use this passage to justify divorcing an unsaved spouse, it would be an improper application. The Scriptures are clear that God does not command Christians to divorce unbelieving mates. Jesus said, *"What therefore God hath joined together, let not man put asunder"* (Mark 10:9). Further, Paul exhorted, *"If any brother hath a wife that believeth not, and she be pleased to dwell with him, let him not put her away"* (1 Corinthians 7:12).

What, therefore, can we learn from our text? Like Ezra we must recognize the danger that a lack of separation poses. The Jews had *"not separated themselves from the people of the lands"* and were *"doing according to their abominations"* (9:1). We must remember that our associations will affect our behavior. Sadly, the people did not realize the seriousness of their offence. Ezra understood the end result, saying, *"we cannot stand"* (9:15). We must learn to see our sin as God sees it and take steps to rid ourselves of sinful influences in our lives.

AUG. 27 — MOVED BY AFFLICTION — NEHEMIAH 1-2

"And it came to pass, when I heard these words, that I sat down and wept, and mourned certain days, and fasted, and prayed before the God of heaven" (Nehemiah 1:4).

Nehemiah heard of the broken wall, burnt gates, and the *"great affliction and reproach"* of the remnant living in Jerusalem (1:3). With his people suffering and the holy city in disarray, he could not remain indifferent. Notice his response.

First, we see his *consideration*—he *"sat down."* The sad news affected him. When is the last time you allowed the trouble of others to cause you to pause and consider their needs? Though the misery brought on by sin may abound around us, we must not become callous and insensitive to those in adversity. Take time to think of the afflicted.

Next, we observe Nehemiah's *contrition*—he *"wept, and mourned certain days, and fasted."* Nehemiah realized that the reason for his people's troubles was sin. It caused him to reflect on his own life too and led him to pray, *"we have sinned against thee"* (1:6). Let us learn to be broken over the sin of others and our own sin too.

Finally, we see *compassion*. Love involves action. As we will see, Nehemiah did more than pray about the problems he saw. He helped.

NEHEMIAH 3-4 — FACING OPPOSITION — AUG. 28

"So built we the wall; and all the wall was joined together unto the half thereof: for the people had a mind to work" (Nehemiah 4:6).

After Nehemiah shared his vision of rebuilding the walls of Jerusalem, the people joined him in the work. So much progress was made that the enemy *"was wroth...and mocked the Jews"* (4:1). Don't be surprised when your service angers the lost. By studying the Jews' response, we see how to react when we face opposition.

First, we must *pray*. Nehemiah cried out, *"Hear, O our God; for we are despised"* (4:4). At the first sign of spiritual resistance, we must employ the help of our heavenly Father. When doing His bidding, we can expect His assistance. Next, we must *work*. After Nehemiah prayed, he records what they did next—*"So built we the wall."* The goal of the enemy is to get us to stop our work for the Lord. Therefore, we must not quit. Persevere in your labor for God, and you will be blessed. Despite opposition, the Jews made tremendous progress on the wall because *"the people had a mind to work."* Finally, we must *resist*. When trouble increased, the Jews *"set a watch against them day and night"* (4:9). With one hand they built and with the other they held a weapon. Be willing to stand *"against"* your foes. React with courage, not cowardice.

NEHEMIAH 5-6 — THE ONE-TWO PUNCH — AUG. 29

"For they all made us afraid" (Nehemiah 6:9).

If Satan cannot stop us by attacking from the outside, he will stir up conflicts within our own ranks. Some of the Jews became greedy and seized the possessions of their brethren through usury. Thankfully, Nehemiah took action and rebuked those involved, calling them to *"leave off this usury"* and *"Restore"* the property they had unfairly acquired (5:10-11). Here we see the importance of strong, Biblical leadership which led the people to repent. As a result, the people were prepared for the next conflict.

In boxing, the one-two punch consists of throwing a jab with one hand followed by a hard blow with the other. The first punch distracts an opponent, making the second one more lethal. This tactic is often used by the devil. In the case of the Jews, Satan attempted to weaken them by turning them against one another so that they would be unprepared for his next attack by Sanballat and Tobiah. By making things right in chapter five, God's people avoided the knockout punch in chapter six!

When the enemy struck fear in the hearts of the Jews, they fought back with prayer and persistence. Instead of being defeated, *"the wall was finished"* (6:15). Watch out for Satan's one-two punch!

AUG. 30 — THE BIBLE AND REVIVAL — NEHEMIAH 7-8

"So they read in the book in the law of God distinctly, and gave the sense, and caused them to understand the reading" (Nehemiah 8:8).

Though *"the wall was finished"* (6:15), work of another sort remained. The people had built the physical walls of the city; now it was time to fortify their hearts through the Word of God.

First, we see *the request for God's Word—"they spake unto Ezra the scribe to bring the book of the law of Moses"* (8:1). They asked to hear the Bible. The people had seen God at work in the midst, and they wanted more of Him. Do you long in your heart for a message from the Word of God? Those who hunger for it will be blessed by it.

Next, observe *the reception of God's Word*. Ezra read *"from the morning until midday"* (8:3). That's a long time! Further, *"the ears of all the people were attentive"* (8:3). Are you engaged when a lengthy passage of Scripture is read in church, or does your mind wander? Perhaps it's time to renew your interest in the message of the Bible.

Consider also *the reasoning of God's Word*. The men of God *"caused the people to understand"* as they *"gave the sense"* (8:7-8). When our hearts are prepared, the Lord will give us men to preach and minds to comprehend. As we obey, we'll enjoy *"great gladness"* (8:17).

AUG. 31 — READY TO FORGIVE — NEHEMIAH 9

"...thou art a God ready to pardon, gracious and merciful, slow to anger, and of great kindness" (Nehemiah 9:17).

This chapter records a brief history of Israel and their rebellion against Jehovah. While confessing their nation's sins, the people rehearsed their sinfulness and God's goodness. Let's learn from their past.

The people had *"hardened their necks, and in their rebellion appointed a captain to return to their bondage"* (9:17). Consider the foolish nature of rebellion. First, it *binds*. The end result of their defiance was bondage, not liberty. There is always a price to pay for resisting God. Second, rebellion *blinds*. The people failed to see that their decision was actually a *"return to their bondage."* When we harden our hearts toward God, we do not gain freedom; we lose it.

Despite Israel's rebellion, the Lord repeatedly showed love to His people. Truly, He is *"a God ready to pardon, gracious and merciful, slow to anger, and of great kindness."* The Jews in Nehemiah's day sought the Lord with a right attitude. Though they had experienced God's chastening, they prayed, *"thou hast done right, but we have done wickedly"* (9:33). Have you strayed from the Lord? If so, return to Him without delay. He is ready to forgive if you are ready to confess.

NEHEMIAH 10-11 COMMITTED TO GOD'S HOUSE SEP. 1

"...we will not forsake the house of our God" (Nehemiah 10:39).

The children of Israel had made a *"a sure covenant"* to follow the Lord (9:38). They promised *"to walk in God's law...and to observe and do all the commandments of the LORD"* (10:29). The key to keeping their promise is found in our text. They determined, *"we will not forsake the house of our God."*

It is impossible to have a right relationship with the Lord if you have a wrong relationship with His house. The local church provides Christians with instruction, fellowship, and opportunities to serve. It is a place of refreshment, comfort, and joy. Church affords us with the privilege to worship, pray, and praise collectively. Further, Jesus promised, *"where two or three are gathered together in my name, there am I in the midst of them"* (Matthew 18:20). With so many benefits provided by the local church, it is a shame that many neglect it.

As the Jews in Jerusalem saw the importance of God's house, let us renew our commitment to our local churches. Has your heart grown cold or indifferent towards the services, brethren, or ministries of your church? Our motto should be: *"Not forsaking the assembling of ourselves together, as the manner of some is"* (Hebrews 10:25).

NEHEMIAH 12 PAUSING AT THE PRISON GATE SEP. 2

"...they stood still in the prison gate" (Nehemiah 12:39).

The Levites were gathered to Jerusalem to celebrate the dedication of the city wall. It was a joyous occasion marked by *"thanksgivings, and with singing"* (12:27). The people divided into two groups and praised God upon the walls as they went. Nehemiah's group passed several gates, but *"they stood still in the prison gate."*

We are not told why the procession paused at the prison gate, but it is quite symbolic. The Jews had recently returned to the holy city after seventy years in exile. It could be that the prison gate reminded them of their release from captivity. What cannot be disputed is that they were free and rejoicing. Is this not a picture of a happy Christian who has been released from sin's shackles?

Have you been set free from the bondage of sin? If so, is there not a song of thanksgiving you could render to your gracious Lord for His great deliverance? How soon we forget His sacrifice and tender mercies! Take a moment and pause at the *"prison gate"* to remember the *"so great salvation"* which Jesus has provided (Hebrews 2:3). If you are still held captive by sin, repent and trust Jesus for forgiveness. *"If the Son therefore shall make you free, ye shall be free indeed"* (John 8:36).

SEP. 3 — REMEMBER ME — NEHEMIAH 13

"Remember me, O my God, for good" (Nehemiah 13:31).

On Nehemiah's second visit to Jerusalem, he found many people in a backslidden condition. His zeal for God, concern for the people, and position as a leader compelled him to confront those who had strayed from the Lord. As in Nehemiah's day, few are willing to rise to the occasion and plead for righteousness, but those who do are blessed. Consider how bold service secures God's favor.

Nehemiah addressed three areas of concern: the neglect of God's house, disobedience to the Law, and corrupting influences in families. It was after he corrected the people in all three areas that he prayed, *"Remember me, O my God"* (13:14, 22, 31). Because he attended to matters that were important to the Lord, he expected God would remember his needs. We, too, can have confidence in prayer if we zealously follow the Lord.

Many times we get focused on what's meaningful to us and neglect God's will. We cry, "Remember me," but cannot expect His intervention until we first remember what is important to Him. Solomon reminds us, *"In the fear of the LORD is strong confidence"* (Proverbs 14:26). To be confident of God's blessing, we must fear Him as Nehemiah did.

SEP. 4 — GOD AT WORK — ESTHER 1-3

"And Mordecai walked every day before the court of the women's house, to know how Esther did, and what should become of her" (Esther 2:11).

Though the name of God is not mentioned in the book of Esther, His presence, providence, protection, and provision are clearly evident. For instance, today's reading records how Esther *"obtained favour"* (2:15) and was chosen to be queen, which enabled her to save her people.

Another sign that God was at work among His people is seen in the testimony of Mordecai. His godly character reflected his relationship with the Lord. First, he was *compassionate*. After Esther's parents passed away, he raised her as *"his own daughter"* (2:7). When she was taken to be considered as the future queen, he *"walked every day before the court of the women's house, to know how Esther did."* Truly, he loved her as his own. Second, he was *committed*. Mordecai foiled a plot to assassinate the king, which indicated he was submissive to his God-given authority. Third, he was *courageous*. Though respectful of authority, he honored God above man. When commanded to bow before the evil Haman, *"Mordecai bowed not, nor did him reverence"* (3:2).

How does your life compare to Mordecai? Does your testimony and character reveal that God is presently at work in your life?

ESTHER 4-7 — RESPONDING TO SATAN'S THREATS — SEP. 5

"So they hanged Haman on the gallows that he had prepared for Mordecai" (Esther 7:10).

Today's reading contains one of the most exciting stories in the Bible. Though Mordecai had a godly testimony, it did not exempt him from trouble. In fact, Satan used Haman to devise a plot to extinguish all of the Jews in the kingdom. What followed were acts of faith, heroism, and divine intervention.

First, we see *faith*. In great sorrow, Mordecai and Esther sought the Lord's help by spending three days in fasting and prayer. When troubles rise, so should our prayers! Take your problems directly to God.

Next, we see *heroism*. Nobody was allowed into the king's presence without being called, including Esther, but since her people were in danger, she risked her life to intercede for them. Her sacrificial spirit is seen in her heroic words, *"if I perish, I perish"* (4:16).

Finally, we observe God's *intervention*. Esther did not perish, but Haman did. He was hanged on the very gallows he had prepared for Mordecai. The Lord can turn the tables on your enemies too.

Satan may oppose us, but when we respond with faith and courage, we'll see God's divine deliverance. How do you react to Satan's threats?

ESTHER 8-10 — FROM SORROW TO JOY — SEP. 6

"The Jews had light, and gladness, and joy, and honour" (Esther 8:16).

Though the Jews faced certain annihilation, the Lord completely reversed their plight. Mordecai took Haman's place as ruler, and a new decree was issued to give the Jews victory over their enemies. God turned their *"sorrow to joy"* and their *"mourning into a good day"* (9:22). When you begin to feel discouraged, remember how quickly God can alter your present circumstances. Prayer changes things! Allow today's text to cheer your heart as you consider what the Lord can do.

God gives *hope*. Notice that the *"Jews had light."* Light dispels darkness and brings hope. When all is dismal and discouragement sets in, look for God's light. David was assured of God's intervention in his times of sorrow. He prayed, *"For thou wilt light my candle: the LORD my God will enlighten my darkness"* (Psalm 18:28).

God gives *happiness*. In addition to light, the Lord gave the Jews *"gladness, and joy."* God can change your trouble in a moment. Wait for Him to turn your sorrow and sadness to pleasantness and peace.

God gives *honor*. The Jews had been despised and persecuted, but God lifted them up. Since the word *honor* speaks of value and dignity, we know that we are prized by God! We should never feel worthless.

| SEP. 7 | COMING JUDGMENT | ISAIAH 1-2 |

"And I will turn my hand upon thee…afterward thou shalt be called, The city of righteousness" (Isaiah 1:25-26).

Isaiah prophesied to Judah over many decades. His message foretold of God's judgment and their eventual restoration. As we read the book of Isaiah in the days ahead, we will observe many rebellious acts of Israel, but sprinkled through the pages are precious promises for God's beloved people. This reminds us that though God hates sin, He loves His children. Today's reading contains highlights of the book's theme.

First, we see God's *purpose* for judgment. The people were backslidden—they were a *"sinful nation, a people laden with iniquity"* who had *"forsaken the* LORD*"* (1:4). God had pleaded with them, *"Come now, and let us reason together"* (1:18); but they refused His offer of forgiveness. Indifference to God's message leads to trouble.

Next, we observe God's *promise* of judgment—*"I will turn my hand upon thee."* It is far better to have God's hand upon us for good! However, those who refuse to repent will not avoid the Lord's correction.

Finally, we see God's *plan* for judgment—*"afterward thou shalt be called, The city of righteousness."* The Lord had their best interest in mind. His goal in chastening is to purify. Let us yield to Him today.

| SEP. 8 | CONFUSING GOOD AND EVIL | ISAIAH 3-5 |

"Woe unto them that call evil good, and good evil…!" (Isaiah 5:20).

In Isaiah's day, the moral fiber of society had drastically decayed. It was not that people struggled to identify right and wrong. The problem was far worse. They had redefined good and evil.

Consider that the *practice* of the day was to *"call evil good, and good evil."* Does that not describe our culture? Much of what the Bible describes as good is belittled by our society. Wickedness is now more acceptable than righteousness. For instance, God says that sexual activity outside of marriage is wrong, but our nation has glamorized and normalized it. Further, a modestly dressed lady is often ridiculed while a woman in sensual attire is uplifted. Such examples are countless.

Notice the *people* who were guilty of calling evil good. Isaiah was not speaking about the heathen; it was God's people who were so terrible! It is no wonder that *"the anger of the* LORD*"* was *"kindled against his people"* (5:25). Today, many Christians think worldly dress, speech, and entertainment are good instead of evil. Is not God angry?

Finally, we consider God's *pronouncement*—*"Woe…!"* The word *woe* is a strong exclamation used here to describe coming misery. Those who love evil and despise what God deems as good will be judged.

| ISAIAH 6-8 | WILLING TO SERVE | SEP. 9 |

"Also I heard the voice of the Lord, saying, Whom shall I send, and who will go for us? Then said I, Here am I; send me" (Isaiah 6:8).

The account of Isaiah's commission provides insight for every aspiring servant of God. Like the prophet, we can receive divine direction for our lives and service.

It begins by getting a proper *view* of God. Isaiah *"saw...the Lord"* (6:1). We, too, must see God as *"high and lifted up"* (6:1). Once we behold His holiness, it will cause us to see our sinfulness. The prophet cried, *"Woe is me! for I am undone; because I am a man of unclean lips"* (6:5). Spending the necessary time to behold our Lord's righteous character in Scripture will lead us to confess our wretchedness.

After we deal with our sin, we can expect to hear the *voice* of God. Isaiah heard the Lord say, *"Whom shall I send, and who will go for us?"* God reveals opportunities for service to those who are in tune with Him. Are you listening for His voice? Has He shown you a need to meet?

What remains? You must be willing to become a *volunteer* for God. Respond as Isaiah did, saying, *"Here am I; send me."* This shows your availability and desire to meet the need presented by God. Be willing to wait until He says, *"Go"* (6:9). Then, throw yourself into His service.

| ISAIAH 9-10 | A GREAT LIGHT | SEP. 10 |

"The people that walked in darkness have seen a great light: they that dwell in the land of the shadow of death, upon them hath the light shined" (Isaiah 9:2).

Israel was to be judged for their rebellion and fall under the rule of the heathen. Truly, they *"walked in darkness."* However, our text speaks of hope! Isaiah prophesied of a coming day, when God would send Messiah to deliver His people from bondage—*"The people...have seen a great light."* The book of Matthew makes it clear that Jesus was the fulfillment of Isaiah's prophecy. He was the *"great light"* and the long-awaited Messiah (Matthew 4:12-17).

Notice Christ's message to the people who were sitting in darkness: *"Repent: for the kingdom of heaven is at hand"* (Matthew 4:17). Since sin brings darkness, the only hope for those dwelling in *"the land of the shadow of death"* is to repent and come to the Light.

Is this word for you today? Do the clouds of sin hover over your head, obscuring the sunlight of heaven? If so, confess any known sin and ask the Savior to shed His beams of mercy upon your soul. Then you will be able to exclaim, *"light is sprung up"* (Matthew 4:16)! If you have found the Light, share the news of Christ with those in darkness.

SEP. 11	WELLS OF SALVATION	ISAIAH 11-13

"Therefore with joy shall ye draw water out of the wells of salvation"
(Isaiah 12:3).

This will be the privilege of Israel when Messiah delivers His people. Thankfully, those who have been redeemed by the Lamb do not have to wait to enjoy such blessings. Notice three key words in our text that relate to our salvation: joy, water, and wells.

First, we observe *"joy."* Why will Israel be so happy? Her praise to God reveals the answer—*"though thou wast angry with me, thine anger is turned away, and thou comfortedst me"* (12:1). We who are saved have not only experienced God's forgiveness but also His comfort.

Next, we see *"water."* Does this not speak of cleansing and refreshment given by the Spirit of God? Salvation quenches our inner thirst and satisfies our souls. There is no need to remain dry and withered. Jesus promised, *"He that believeth on me, as the scripture hath said, out of his belly shall flow rivers of living water"* (John 7:38).

Lastly, we consider the *"wells."* Water in a well must be drawn out. Each time we meditate in the Bible, we lower a bucket into the cool, refreshing waters that will revive our souls. Are you rejoicing in God's salvation today? If not, grab a bucket and douse your despondency!

SEP. 12	GOD'S PROMISED REST	ISAIAH 14-16

"And it shall come to pass in the day that the LORD shall give thee rest from thy sorrow, and from thy fear, and from the hard bondage wherein thou wast made to serve" (Isaiah 14:3).

The Lord promised Israel that one day they would *"rule over their oppressors"* (14:2). They would finally be granted rest from sorrow, fear, and hard bondage. This is a beautiful picture of salvation.

When people are without Christ, Satan abuses and oppresses them terribly. However, salvation changes everything. God gives His people the spiritual blessings mentioned in our text. Jesus replaces sorrow with joy, fear with faith, and bondage with liberty. Although Satan has *"made the earth to tremble"* (14:16) and refuses to open *"the house of his prisoners"* (14:17), One mightier than he has set us free!

Unfortunately, Satan still seeks to wear us out. Have you grown weary in the battle? Remember the rest that Jesus has secured for every believer—*"Take my yoke upon you, and learn of me; for I am meek and lowly in heart: and ye shall find rest unto your souls"* (Matthew 11:29).

Don't allow sorrow, fear, or bondage to steal your strength. You have a defeated foe. When we reach heaven, we will be able to exclaim, *"How hath the oppressor ceased!"* (14:4). Until then, rest in Jesus.

ISAIAH 17-20 — HURTING AND HEALING — SEP. 13

"And the LORD shall smite Egypt: he shall smite and heal it: and they shall return even to the LORD, and he shall be intreated of them, and shall heal them" (Isaiah 19:22).

Isaiah spoke of the end times when Israel's rival would become their friend. Egypt has been no lover of Jehovah throughout history, but God promised their smiting would work repentance. Though the Lord has a right to exact justice upon the wayward, He also delights in healing them. His affliction of Egypt will persuade them to *"return even to the LORD."* After their return, He will hear their cry and *"heal them."*

If the Lord promised to be so gracious to a heathen nation, will He not extend similar mercies to His children? The same pattern seen in our text is often used by the Lord with Christians. When we go astray, our loving God will at times afflict us, hoping to get our attention. He knows the path on which we are traveling leads to a bitter end. Therefore, He smites us out of love—*"For whom the Lord loveth he chasteneth, and scourgeth every son whom he receiveth"* (Hebrews 12:6).

When we *"return even to the LORD,"* He will accept us once again into His fellowship. He smites in order that He might heal. Are you presently wounded? The One Who hurt also has power to heal. Return!

ISAIAH 21-23 — CONCERN FOR THE LOST — SEP. 14

"Therefore are my loins filled with pain...I was bowed down at the hearing of it; I was dismayed at the seeing of it" (Isaiah 21:3).

Our text records Isaiah's reaction to the judgment pronounced upon Babylon. At this point in history, the Babylonians were not enemies of Judah, but they would be. Therefore, God planned to use the Medes and Persians to execute His wrath upon them.

The prophet witnessed terrible scenes of destruction in a vision and was moved with heartfelt compassion. Notice the pity that Isaiah expressed for the plight of those who would be punished. He was *"filled with pain"* and his *"heart panted"* when he heard of the doom awaiting Babylon (21:4). Should this not challenge us to be concerned about the torments that await those who are without the Savior?

Like Isaiah, we have been told of the awful punishment awaiting others. Jude encourages us to do something to prevent them from perishing eternally—*"And of some have compassion, making a difference: And others save with fear, pulling them out of the fire"* (Jude 22-23). The prophet testified, *"the night of my pleasure hath he turned into fear"* (21:4). Rather than living for pleasure, we should allow ourselves to be disturbed about the pending judgment of the lost.

SEP. 15   PEACE OR PLACEBO?   ISAIAH 24-26

"Thou wilt keep him in perfect peace, whose mind is stayed on thee: because he trusteth in thee" (Isaiah 26:3).

Israel will one day have peace. Our text is part of a song which the redeemed Jews will sing during the millennial reign of Christ. How sweet it will be for them to experience the peace that their once-rejected Messiah will give! Thankfully, we do not have to wait to enjoy such peace. God presently offers it to all who trust Him (Philippians 4:6-7).

Since Isaiah's day, it has been recorded that Messiah is *"The Prince of Peace"* (Isaiah 9:6). It is sad to think that the Jews have been missing His promised peace for so long. However, as believers in Christ, we can testify that Jesus is *"our peace"* (Ephesians 2:14). He said, *"Peace I leave with you, my peace I give unto you"* (John 14:27). With so many searching for inner tranquility in this chaotic world, it is heartbreaking that multitudes have either not discovered Christ or chosen to reject Him.

God promises *"perfect peace"* to those whose minds are *"stayed"* on Him. The word *stay* means "to lean upon." While the world frantically searches for peace through medication, entertainment, and/or relationships, only those who lean upon Jesus find it. Are you focused on Jesus, or have you become distracted by the world's placebos?

SEP. 16   A SHORT BED AND A SMALL BLANKET   ISAIAH 27-29

"For the bed is shorter than that a man can stretch himself on it: and the covering narrower than that he can wrap himself in it" (Isaiah 28:20).

In today's reading, God described the judgment of the northern kingdom by Assyria. He wanted it to serve as a warning to Judah for their waywardness (28:14). However, the people in Judah thought they would avoid trouble. They said, *"it shall not come unto us"* (28:15). Sin makes people blind to reality. Therefore, God reiterated to them, *"ye shall be trodden down"* (28:18). The Lord also used a simple illustration of a bed and a blanket to explain that problems were unavoidable.

On a short bed, a man is not able to *"stretch himself"* and get comfortable. Judah thought they were cozy, but Jehovah reminded them that the night would get long and they would soon find their situation quite unpleasant. In the same manner, every child of God will be disturbed and restless in his night of sin. God does not allow His children to get comfortable in sin. Are you presently on a short bed?

Another necessity of a good night's sleep on a cool evening is a blanket. When we resist God, He ensures that our blanket is too small. You may try to cover your sin but will find yourself exposed in God's sight. It is better to repent than to reap the misery and shame of sin.

ISAIAH 30-32	RELIGIOUS REBELS	SEP. 17

"Prophesy not unto us right things, speak unto us smooth things, prophesy deceits" (Isaiah 30:10).

Isaiah warned Judah against making an alliance with Egypt to resist the armies of Assyria. Because they were *"rebellious children,"* they were prone to trust the arm of flesh rather than God (30:1-2). Rebellion is, therefore, a rejection of God and dependence upon the flesh.

A rebel always *turns* from God. He does not want to hear *"right things."* He despises God's Word so much that he would rather be told a lie than to hear the truth. Even in our day, we have people who want to hear *"smooth things."* When describing the attitude of people in the end times, Paul said, *"they will not endure sound doctrine; but after their own lusts shall they heap to themselves teachers, having itching ears"* (2 Timothy 4:3). Churches today are filled with such religious rebels.

A rebel *trusts* the flesh. As Judah trusted worldly means and methods, so do many churches today. Music, standards, and teaching that appeal to the flesh are prevalent in many congregations. We cannot fight spiritual battles with carnal weapons. God's work done man's way may seem promising, but God warns, *"Woe to them that go down to Egypt for help"* (31:1). In the end, pragmatism is not very pragmatic.

ISAIAH 33-35	COMING BLESSINGS	SEP. 18

"Say to them that are of a fearful heart, Be strong, fear not: behold, your God will come with vengeance, even God with a recompence; he will come and save you" (Isaiah 35:4).

The days will come when Messiah will set up His kingdom and rule upon earth. Israel will then know that Jesus is their great Deliverer. Though Isaiah wrote of coming judgment, he also encouraged Israel with the blessings of the future reign of Christ. They were promised healing (35:5-6), holiness (35:8), and happiness (35:10).

To the Christian, salvation provides a foretaste of each of those blessings. First, we have been healed spiritually. Though we were once blind to the ways of God, our eyes have been opened. Next, the Lord has furnished a *"way of holiness"* for us (35:8). Thankfully, we can have victory over sin. Finally, God has made us happy; we have obtained *"joy and gladness"* (35:10). Let us claim the promise that *"sorrow and sighing shall flee away"* (35:10). What a victorious salvation we have!

The future will be brighter for Israel once Messiah reigns. Likewise, Christians will one day enjoy their salvation to the fullest. In the meantime, let us follow the advice of our text—*"Be strong."* Our Lord promised to *"come and save"* us from all sin and suffering. Hallelujah!

SEP. 19   SPREAD IT BEFORE THE LORD   ISAIAH 36-37

"Hezekiah received the letter...and read it: and Hezekiah went up unto the house of the LORD, and spread it before the LORD" (Isaiah 37:14).

Hezekiah had a real problem. The most formidable army upon earth was threatening his kingdom. They had successfully conquered many nations, and Judah was next on their list. Hezekiah, however, was persuaded that Jehovah was not like the false gods of the fallen nations.

Are you facing a fierce foe today? If so, allow Hezekiah's example to provide direction for your dilemma and hope for your heart. The Lord is well aware of your situation and is able to intervene on your behalf, but you must first seek Him. As Hezekiah went to prayer, he took the letter he had received and *"spread it before the LORD."* In times of distress, we must make our matters known to God.

Consider the content of Hezekiah's prayer. First, Hezekiah offered *praise—"thou art the God, even thou alone, of all the kingdoms of the earth"* (37:16). Be sure to acknowledge God's Person and power when you pray. Next, the king rehearsed the *problem.* Share the concerns of your heart. He is *"touched with the feeling of our infirmities"* (Hebrews 4:15). Finally, Hezekiah made his *petition—"save us"* (37:20). As the Lord delivered Judah, He will help you too. Seek Him at once!

SEP. 20   "GOOD FOR ME"   ISAIAH 38-40

"Good is the word of the LORD which thou hast spoken...For there shall be peace and truth in my days" (Isaiah 39:8).

When Hezekiah received word that his sickness would end in death, he *"prayed unto the LORD"* (38:2). God, in His mercy, healed Hezekiah and extended his life by fifteen years. Unfortunately, he did not show his appreciation to the Lord by his actions. We read, *"Hezekiah rendered not again according to the benefit done unto him; for his heart was lifted up"* (2 Chronicles 32:25).

The king of Babylon sent a delegation to Hezekiah with a letter and presents. Hezekiah foolishly showed all of his treasures to the visitors, not realizing they would later return with an army for the spoils. When he was humble he had spread the letter from the king of Assyria before the Lord and sought God's counsel. He would have been wise to have done the same thing when he received the letter from Babylon's king.

Consider Hezekiah's response when he heard that God's judgment would fall in his sons' time. *"Good is the word of the LORD...For there shall be peace and truth in my days."* Though his children would suffer, he was more concerned about himself. Pride leads to self-centeredness. Beware of only accepting God's Word when it benefits you.

ISAIAH 41-42	HEAVENLY HELP	SEP. 21

"Fear thou not; for I am with thee: be not dismayed; for I am thy God: I will strengthen thee; yea, I will help thee; yea, I will uphold thee with the right hand of my righteousness" (Isaiah 41:10).

Jehovah reassured His people of assistance. Though the nations would afflict them, God's people would one day be victorious. He promised, *"Thou art my servant; I have chosen thee, and not cast thee away"* (41:9). Consider the blessings promised in our text.

Courage – Fear is the enemy of our souls, and the Lord gives plenty of reason to cast it off. How can we fear when He assures, *"I am with thee"*? His presence ensures His power. Let the enemy fear, not us!

Competence – Since fear weakens and faith empowers, we can boldly claim God's next promise—*"I will strengthen thee."* It is wise to acknowledge our frailty but foolish to remain weak, especially when supernatural power is available. Strength is available for every trial.

Cooperation – Three times in this chapter God promised, *"I will help thee."* When we do our part, Omnipotence will always do His. Look for the Lord's helping hand in your spiritual battles today.

Comfort – How can we fall when God pledges, *"I will uphold thee"*? His right hand of power will bolster us through every storm.

ISAIAH 43-44	TIRED OF GOD?	SEP. 22

"But thou hast not called upon me, O Jacob; but thou hast been weary of me, O Israel" (Isaiah 43:22).

The Lord reminded Israel why He created them—*"This people have I formed for myself; they shall shew forth my praise"* (43:21). Their duty was to please and praise God, but instead they were more concerned with their own lives. Unfortunately, that describes many believers today.

The people were tired of God. Consider the Lord's indictment—*"thou hast been weary of me."* Their weariness was revealed by their prayerlessness. God pinpointed the problem, telling Israel, *"thou hast not called upon me."* Failing to pray demonstrates fatigue, not faith. We may not like to admit that we are tired of God and His ways, but what does it say when we neglect prayer? Have you grown weary of the Lord and not realized it? If so, rekindle your prayer life at once!

Those who are tired of God have forgotten that He is tired of their sin. The Lord told His people, *"thou hast wearied me with thine iniquities"* (43:24). If you have drifted away from close fellowship with your Savior, seek Him today. Thankfully, He promises forgiveness—*"I, even I, am he that blotteth out thy transgressions"* (43:25). Once restored, remember that your purpose is to please Him, not self.

SEP. 23   TREASURES OF DARKNESS   ISAIAH 45-47

"And I will give thee the treasures of darkness, and hidden riches of secret places, that thou mayest know that I, the LORD, which call thee by thy name, am the God of Israel" (Isaiah 45:3).

The Lord intended to prove Himself to Cyrus, king of Persia. To compensate him for assisting Israel, God promised a rich reward—*"the treasures of darkness, and hidden riches of secret places."* What those blessings were, we are not told. However, our text indicates that though they were obscured by darkness, they would one day be discovered. Is this not a wonderful lesson for us too?

Perhaps shades of night have fallen upon your soul and you wonder why you must be subjected to grief and agony. Rest assured that, though trouble blurs the blessing, hidden riches of grace are just beyond your night of heartache. Cheer up. The blackness of midnight should not prevent us from looking for God's gemstones in the darkness.

By the eye of faith, you can look for the sun to rise on the horizon. Soon, the rays of morning light will cause a jewel or two to sparkle. Once you see the dazzling treasure, you will quickly forget your short-lived sorrow. May the Lord help us to patiently wait for His promised *"treasures of darkness."* Let problems lead to your provision.

SEP. 24   HOW TO PROSPER   ISAIAH 48-49

"O that thou hadst hearkened to my commandments! then had thy peace been as a river, and thy righteousness as the waves of the sea" (Isaiah 48:18).

The Lord wanted Israel to prosper, but they chose to rebel by doing *"very treacherously"* (48:8). In love, God did not destroy them but instead purged them with fiery trials. He said, *"I have refined thee, but not with silver; I have chosen thee in the furnace of affliction"* (48:10).

God deals much the same way with Christians. Consider Jehovah's plan—*"O that thou hadst hearkened to my commandments!"* He would rather bless us than bruise us and expresses regret when we hinder His intentions. We must remember that God's blessings are tied to our obedience. Those who wish to fare well must follow well.

Notice God's *promises* to those who submit to His will. First, He gives *"peace...as a river."* Are you filled with trouble and care? God's paths lead beside still waters and calm the soul. Second, He provides *"righteousness as the waves of the sea."* Waves have great power, and so does righteous living. Little remains unmoved by the ocean's mighty billows. In like manner, holy living influences people around us. God wants to use your life to send ripples of His goodness to many.

ISAIAH 50-52	LOSING GOD'S COMFORT	SEP. 25

"I, even I, am he that comforteth you: who art thou, that thou shouldest be afraid of a man that shall die...?" (Isaiah 51:12).

Though Israel would go into captivity due to their sins, God promised that He would bring them back to Zion. He said, *"they shall obtain gladness and joy; and sorrow and mourning shall flee away"* (51:11). When God determines to bless us with peace, no foe can prevent it. However, if we are not quick to believe God, we can forfeit the comfort He has pledged. Notice three culprits to guard against.

Forgetfulness – God promised, *"I, even I, am he that comforteth you."* Of Israel it was said, *"thou...forgettest the LORD thy maker"* (51:12-13). Too often we lose the blessings that God intended to give us simply because we fail to remember His Word. If He promises us comfort, comfort we shall have.

Fear – Israel *"feared continually every day"* (51:13). Do you tend to borrow trouble? Why embrace fear when God offers peace?

Fury – The rage of our enemies is often the source of fear and disturbs our comfort. However, fear tends to create problems that don't exist. God asked, *"where is the fury of the oppressor?"* (51:13). It was only in their minds. Don't imagine worst-case scenarios. Trust God.

ISAIAH 53-56	THE SUFFERING SAVIOR	SEP. 26

"All we like sheep have gone astray... and the LORD hath laid on him the iniquity of us all" (Isaiah 53:6).

A great tragedy concerning Israel is that they misunderstood the ministry of their promised Messiah. Though He was to conquer their enemies and reign as Sovereign, He first had to suffer for the sins of His people to offer forgiveness. Isaiah's prophecy portrays the suffering Savior. Sadly, even after Jesus fulfilled this prophecy in every detail, the majority of Jews still fail to accept Him as Messiah. Let's consider Him.

Notice His *suffering*—*"He is despised and rejected of men; a man of sorrows, and acquainted with grief"* (53:3). Though Jesus helped and healed many, He was shamefully treated and delivered to die. What was His crime? He rightfully claimed to be the Messiah. Truly, the apostle was correct in saying, *"He came unto his own, and his own received him not"* (John 1:11). Not much has changed today. Christ is still rejected by many of His own people and is belittled by the heathen.

Consider His *substitution*—*"the LORD hath laid on him the iniquity of us all."* Since Jesus is Immanuel, meaning "God with us," He was sinless and able to bear our sins. Those who trust Him for forgiveness will not be punished for their sins. Thank You, Lord, for Your sacrifice!

Sep. 27   Restoring Fellowship   Isaiah 57-59

"Behold, the LORD'S hand is not shortened, that it cannot save; neither his ear heavy, that it cannot hear" (Isaiah 59:1).

Has it ever seemed as though God's hand was not upon your life or that He did not hear your prayers? Rest assured it is no fault of God when that happens. The Bible makes it clear that we are to blame when fellowship is severed. Today's reading provides hope for restoration.

First, recognize the *hindrance—"your iniquities have separated between you and your God"* (59:2). Sin drives a wedge between you and the Lord. Have you allowed a wrong desire or attitude to isolate you from God? Acknowledge your faults without delay.

Next, we see *humility*. Isaiah confessed, *"our transgressions are multiplied before thee, and our sins testify against us"* (59:12). Only those who are honest about their true condition can experience the cleansing they desperately need. Confess each sin you are aware of.

Finally, the Lord offers *healing—"the Redeemer shall come...unto them that turn from transgression"* (59:20). We must take the first step in mending our relationship with God by turning from our sin and seeking the Lord. When we do, our Redeemer will move to meet us. *"Draw nigh to God, and he will draw nigh to you"* (James 4:8).

Sep. 28   God's Exchange Program   Isaiah 60-62

"To appoint unto them that mourn in Zion, to give unto them beauty for ashes, the oil of joy for mourning, the garment of praise for the spirit of heaviness" (Isaiah 61:3).

The verses which precede our text speak of the two advents of Christ. He came first to *"preach good tidings"* and will come again to execute judgment in *"the day of vengeance"* (61:1-2). After this Jesus will establish His kingdom on earth. Though many Jews will face terrible persecution during the Tribulation, they will later be comforted.

Today's text reveals the help God promises to His people. He will replace their burdens with blessings. Notice that they will receive *"beauty for ashes."* Ashes represent loss and languishing, but Christ can make life lovely. Jesus also gives *"joy for mourning."* One day He will turn sorrow into smiles. Finally, we see that God swaps *"praise for the spirit of heaviness."* The tongue that is bound in the dungeon of discouragement will one day be loosed to sing the Savior's praises.

Has not experience already proven that God's exchange program is able to transform us? At salvation, Christ replaced our sin with His righteousness, and He will not stop there. He is willing to comfort all who mourn. Let those who are downhearted request grace for their grief.

ISAIAH 63-64 — PRAYER OF THE AFFLICTED — SEP. 29

"Oh that thou wouldest rend the heavens, that thou wouldest come down, that the mountains might flow down at thy presence" (Isaiah 64:1).

Isaiah recorded the prayer that the redeemed of Israel will utter in the Tribulation times. In great affliction, they will cry to Jehovah for deliverance. We can glean some wonderful lessons about prayer from this passage.

First, we see *desperation*—*"...that thou wouldest come down...!"* In times of trouble, a divine visitation should be of utmost importance to us. Do you long for God's presence? Ask Him to *"come down."*

Second, we notice *expectation*—*"men have not heard...neither hath the eye seen, what he* [God] *hath prepared for him that waiteth for him"* (64:4). We ought to anticipate the indescribable blessings of God.

Third, we consider their *confession*—*"we are all as an unclean thing...and our iniquities, like the wind, have taken us away"* (64:6). We must confess the defilement that sin brings and admit when we have been carried away with our sin. Repentance always gets God's attention.

Lastly, we see *submission*—*"O LORD, thou art our father; we are the clay, and thou our potter"* (64:8). As a good child obeys his father and a lump of clay yields to the will of the potter, so we must submit to God.

ISAIAH 65-66 — TROUBLED OR BLESSED — SEP. 30

"Thus saith the LORD...to this man will I look, even to him that is poor and of a contrite spirit, and trembleth at my word" (Isaiah 66:1-2).

In our journey through the book of Isaiah, we have read of God's displeasure with the rebels and seen promises made to the remnant yet to be restored. The closing chapters follow the same theme. The Lord will judge the wicked and bless the righteous.

Trouble awaits the transgressor. Judah was *"a rebellious people, which"* walked *"in a way that was not good, after their own thoughts"* (65:2). They were self-righteous, saying, *"I am holier than thou"* (65:5). Such attitudes irritate the Lord. He responded to their pride by saying, *"These are a smoke in my nose"* (65:5). Thus, God promised, *"I also will choose their delusions, and will bring their fears upon them"* (66:4). Ultimately, the lost will be destroyed—*"the LORD will come with fire...to render his anger with fury, and his rebuke with flames of fire"* (66:15).

God will treat the humble in a different manner. He pledges to consider the needs of those who have *"a contrite spirit"* and tremble at His Word. Such people will enjoy heavenly blessings and answered prayer. God promised, *"And it shall come to pass, that before they call, I will answer; and while they are yet speaking, I will hear"* (65:24).

Oct. 1   CALLED AND CONFIDENT   JEREMIAH 1-2

"Be not afraid of their faces: for I am with thee to deliver thee, saith the LORD" (Jeremiah 1:8).

Jeremiah was called to be God's spokesman. What an honor it is to represent the Lord! As a prophet to Judah, he was commissioned to warn of the pending captivity they would experience because of their disobedience. Knowing Jeremiah would face opposition, God charged him, *"Be not afraid of their faces"* and exhorted, *"I am with thee to deliver thee."* This gave him confidence for his calling.

The Lord has *"formed thee"* and *"ordained thee"* for a particular task too (1:5). Like Jeremiah, you may feel inadequate. Consider his response to God when he was called, *"Ah, Lord GOD! behold, I cannot speak: for I am a child"* (1:6). Of course, the Lord had a solution for his deficiency and said, *"Behold, I have put my words in thy mouth"* (1:9). We can rest assured that God's divine power can enable us to overcome our weaknesses too. Don't forget that His *"strength is made perfect in weakness"* (2 Corinthians 12:9).

We may be tempted to fear, but we must believe God's comforting promise—*"I am with thee."* With His presence and power, we are confident that we will fulfill our calling like Jeremiah did.

Oct. 2   RETURN TO GOD   JEREMIAH 3-4

"Return, ye backsliding children, and I will heal your backslidings" (Jeremiah 3:22).

Judah had spiritually *"played the harlot"* by being unfaithful to the Lord and serving idols, but God offered to show mercy on those who repented. Though God had every right to be angry, He pleaded with tender tones, saying, *"Return, ye backsliding children."* The Lord's desire is to restore His erring children, not cast them away. Have you strayed from God? If so, you can return to Him.

Notice the Lord's *plea*—*"Return."* This requires a change of direction. To get back to God, one must turn from his sin. Turning to God must not be shallow and superficial as it was for many in Josiah's day. Though Josiah had genuine revival, the majority in Judah did not turn with the *"whole heart, but feignedly"* (3:10). Repentance must be sincere and honest, not a façade. There are too many pretenders! God commands the backslider, *"acknowledge thine iniquity"* (3:13).

Next, we see God's *promise*—*"I will heal your backslidings."* Sin is unhealthy for the soul, but the Savior offers to heal our hearts and give us victory over sin. Any backslider can seek and find refreshment and restoration if they meet the Lord's condition—*"Return."*

JEREMIAH 5-6 — A REBELLIOUS HEART — OCT. 3

"But this people hath a revolting and a rebellious heart"
(Jeremiah 5:23).

Rebellion is a matter of the heart. It is a refusal to listen and obey. Yesterday we read of God's call to Judah to return to Him. Today we see that they *"refused to return"* (5:3) because they had *"a revolting and rebellious heart."* Revolt means "to turn away." In other words, the people did the exact opposite of what they were told.

Consider the *traits* of rebellion. First, we see disobedience. Their response to God's offer of a restful path was, *"We will not walk therein"* (6:16). Next we see disinterest. When it came to God's Word, they had *"no delight in it"* (6:10). Be careful when your interest in the Bible begins to wane. Though the Lord pleaded with them to listen to His warnings of judgment, they said, *"We will not hearken"* (6:17).

When we refuse to listen and obey, we are heading for *trouble*. Because of Judah's rebellion, God declared, *"I will bring evil* [trouble] *upon this people"* (6:19). Rebellion promises pleasure but produces problems. Further, our stubbornness can cause us to lose blessings. Perhaps *"your sins have withholden good things from you"* (5:25). If so, return to God and obey. Rebellion, even in small matters, brings trouble.

JEREMIAH 7-8 — WHICH WAY ARE YOU HEADING? — OCT. 4

"But they hearkened not...but walked in the counsels...of their evil heart, and went backward, and not forward" (Jeremiah 7:24).

Though judgment was pending, the Lord called on His people to repent, saying, *"Amend your ways and your doings"* (7:3). Sadly, His efforts to restore Judah had been rejected repeatedly. He testified, *"I called you, but ye answered not"* (7:13). Unfortunately, this stubborn attitude had become engrained in their nation from one generation to another. Jehovah reminded them that their forefathers had treated Him the same way—*"But they hearkened not...and went backward, and not forward."* Judah had become guilty of *"a perpetual backsliding"* (8:5). Consider what can happen when you fail to amend your ways.

First, your actions will affect your children. In Judah's case, they not only learned to act like their fathers but *"did worse than their fathers"* (7:26). Parents reading these lines must realize that their example is either leading their children toward God or away from Him.

Next, when you fail to listen to God, you can only move in one direction—*"backward...not forward."* Following your heart will cause you to backslide. All forward movement stops in the Christian life when you disobey God. If you are presently going backward, turn around!

| Oct. 5 | THE HEART OF A SERVANT | JEREMIAH 9-10 |

"Oh that my head were waters, and mine eyes a fountain of tears, that I might weep day and night for...my people!" (Jeremiah 9:1).

Today's reading reveals the tender heart of Jeremiah. Though he was called to condemn the sins of the people, he maintained compassion toward them. Too often we are quick to judge sinners but slow to care for them. Evaluate yourself as we consider Jeremiah's heart.

He had a *sorrowful* heart. He wept until he had no more tears to shed. The judgment of his people brought deep pain. How much does your soul anguish for the lost who will one day suffer eternal torment?

Jeremiah also had a *separated* heart. Though he loved his people, he hated their sin and wished he could dwell in the wilderness and *"go from them!"* (9:2). How comfortable are you around sin? It should grieve us.

The prophet had a *submitted* heart. Even though it hurt him to stay with his people, he understood God wanted him to remain with them as His spokesman. He put God's will ahead of his own and said, *"Truly this is a grief, and I must bear it"* (10:19). Are you that submitted?

Finally, we see a *supplicating* heart. He brought his grief and frailties to the Lord, saying, *"O LORD, correct me"* (10:24). Prayer has the power to mend your heart and correct a sour attitude.

| Oct. 6 | TAKE IT TO THE LORD | JEREMIAH 11-12 |

"Righteous art thou, O LORD, when I plead with thee: yet let me talk with thee of thy judgments" (Jeremiah 12:1).

Judah was cursed because they had broken their covenant with God. Things got so bad that the people threatened Jeremiah, saying, *"Prophesy not in the name of the LORD, that thou die not by our hand"* (11:21). They hoped to silence God's message by killing His messenger.

How did the prophet respond? He prayed! When you experience opposition, take the matter straight to your heavenly Father. In the end, you will be able to say with the psalmist, *"In my distress I cried unto the LORD, and he heard me"* (Psalm 120:1). God does not fail His servants.

Jeremiah began his prayer as we should—he acknowledged that God was holy and just in His ways. When trouble comes, learn to pray, *"Righteous art thou, O LORD."* The prophet then poured out his heart, saying, *"let me talk with thee of thy judgments."* Though we must not find fault with God's will, we can share our heart with Him. Jeremiah had genuine concerns and brought them immediately to the throne.

Because Jeremiah leaned on God, he was open to His answer. The Lord warned that things would get worse before getting better (12:5-6). Though trouble may persist for a season, we can cheerfully await relief.

JEREMIAH 13-14   GOOD FOR NOTHING   OCT. 7

"This evil people, which refuse to hear my words...shall even be as this girdle, which is good for nothing" (Jeremiah 13:10).

Jehovah provided His people with an object lesson using a linen girdle. A girdle was a belt or sash tied about the waist. Soldiers wore girdles to fasten weapons to their sides, and servants used them to gather up their long robes to make work easier. Leather girdles were more durable, and linen ones were typically decorative. God seems to have chosen a linen girdle for Jeremiah to wear as a representation of His glory seen through His people. Unfortunately, Judah's sinfulness cast a bad light on God and led to their rejection. Because it was soiled by sin, *"the girdle was marred"* and *"profitable for nothing"* (13:7). Sin reduces our value.

Like *"the girdle cleaveth to the loins of a man"* (13:11), the Lord has chosen each of us to be close to Him. However, when we are marred by sin, God does not want us close to Him. It was the sin of arrogance that led Judah to rebel against God and *"walk in the imagination of their heart"* (13:10). When God displays His power through you, be careful not to be filled with pride. As the Lord promised to *"mar the pride of Judah,"* He will do the same to all who exalt themselves (13:9). In the end, the proud *"shall even be as this girdle, which is good for nothing."*

JEREMIAH 15-16   THE COST OF CONTINUED SIN   OCT. 8

"I have taken away my peace from this people, saith the LORD, even lovingkindness and mercies" (Jeremiah 16:5).

The Lord's anger was kindled because of the wickedness of Judah and their refusal to repent. He said, *"I will destroy my people, since they return not from their ways"* (15:7). Though He had patiently sent prophets to them year after year, they *"walked after other gods"* (16:11).

Have you repeatedly resisted any of God's commands? At some point, His judgment will fall. Though He has extended mercy to you, it may end quickly. With Judah, He got tired of giving them additional chances. Eventually, He said, *"I am weary with repenting"* (15:6).

Continuing in sin can be quite costly. Judah lost God's peace, lovingkindness, and mercies. They exchanged spiritual blessings for temporary gratification and quickly discovered that it was a bad deal. Were they not warned by Isaiah who said, *"There is no peace, saith my God, to the wicked"* (Isaiah 57:21)? Though we may be tempted by sin, we must never forfeit the peace of God for the pleasures of the world.

It is sad to see miserable Christians. Why are some so troubled? God answered that question in our text, saying, *"I have taken away my peace."* If you have strayed from the Lord, return soon or pay the price.

| Oct. 9 | THE POTTER'S PLAN | JEREMIAH 17-18 |

"And the vessel that he made of clay was marred in the hand of the potter: so he made it again another vessel" (Jeremiah 18:4).

God sent Jeremiah to the potter's house for another visual lesson. As the prophet watched the craftsman, he noticed that the vessel on the wheel was marred and that the potter had to start over again. This was a picture of Israel. Like the clay, God's people had a serious flaw, and it prevented the Lord from fashioning them as He desired. Jehovah's message was clear—*"Behold, as the clay is in the potter's hand, so are ye in mine hand, O house of Israel"* (18:6). Thus, His judgment had to fall on Judah so He could remake them. Despite their rebellion, He still called them to repentance (18:8). Let's apply this to us as individuals.

God has a plan for our lives. We are like clay that He is forming *"on the wheels"* (18:3). The wheels speak of activity. As we get busy for the Lord, He shapes us. For instance, God molds us into better soulwinners as we go out and witness. While the wheel is moving, the potter adds water to the clay to smooth out rough spots. In Scripture, water is an emblem of the Word of God. To remain pliable, we need the Bible sprinkled on our hearts each day. When we fail to yield to God's plan for our lives, we will be marred in His hand. Don't ruin His work!

| Oct. 10 | DOWN AND DISCOURAGED | JEREMIAH 19-20 |

"I will not make mention of him, nor speak any more in his name. But his word was in mine heart as a burning fire shut up in my bones, and I was weary with forbearing, and I could not stay" (Jeremiah 20:9).

It is easy to get discouraged when we see no positive results come from our labors for the Lord. This was the case of Jeremiah. When you are feeling a bit down, consider his bout with discouragement.

His *difficulty* started after he faithfully delivered the Lord's message. Pashur, one of the temple leaders, *"smote Jeremiah the prophet, and put him in the stocks"* (20:2). His service was rewarded with pain and shame. Further, he was abused verbally; he cried, *"I am in derision daily, every one mocketh me"* (20:7). Are your troubles that bad?

Jeremiah's *discouragement* was so overwhelming that he decided to quit preaching. In fact, he wished he had never been born (20:14). Thankfully, God's Word worked in his heart *"as a burning fire."* When you get down, allow the Scriptures to warm your heart and convict you.

His *decision* was to look up, not down. He said, *"I could not stay."* With new confidence he proclaimed, *"the LORD is with me...therefore my persecutors shall stumble"* (20:11). Once we decide to stop feeling sorry for ourselves, God will renew our strength.

| JEREMIAH 21-22 | **IS IT WELL?** | OCT. 11 |

"He judged the cause of the poor and needy; then it was well with him: was not this to know me? saith the LORD" (Jeremiah 22:16).

In the midst of God's condemnation of the latter kings of Judah, He singled out Josiah as a good example. Josiah's testimony was a rebuke to those who had forsaken the Lord. Because he sought to know God, *"it was well with him."* Is it well with you today? If not, learn from Josiah.

Consider his *righteousness—"He judged the cause of the poor and needy."* He used his position to serve others, not to abuse them.

Notice the *reason* he did right. He wanted to know the Lord better. His purpose in helping the unfortunate was not to make a name for himself. He wished to please God and follow His commands. This should challenge us to maintain pure motives in our works of charity.

Finally, think about his *reward—"it was well with him."* Would you like things to go well in your life? Zedekiah wanted things to go well when Nebuchadnezzar made war with him. However, instead of receiving a message of hope from God, he got the opposite (21:4-5). What was the difference between Josiah and Zedekiah? One sought to know the Lord and the other only wanted His blessings. When you do right, have proper motives, and seek God, you can expect to be rewarded.

| JEREMIAH 23 | **SHEPHERDS NEEDED** | OCT. 12 |

"Ye have scattered my flock, and driven them away, and have not visited them: behold, I will visit upon you the evil of your doings, saith the LORD" (Jeremiah 23:2).

God's concern for His sheep is evident. Though the spiritual leaders in Judah did little to help the sheep, the Lord promised that Messiah would deliver them one day (23:5-6). He also expressed displeasure with those charged with caring for the sheep. In addition to condemning the pastors, He said, *"I am against the prophets"* (23:30).

If you are responsible to feed, protect, or guide any of God's sheep, be faithful in your duties. Could God say that you *"have not visited them"*? Perhaps someone under your watch-care needs a visit. God might need you to help a lost sheep or a struggling believer.

When you speak for God, make sure you represent Him properly. The prophets in Jeremiah's day spoke *"a vision of their own heart, and not out of the mouth of the LORD"* (23:16). What people need is the Word of God, not man's ideas. The Bible is able to melt cold hearts and break hard ones—*"Is not my word like as a fire? saith the LORD; and like a hammer that breaketh the rock in pieces?"* (23:29). Look for an opportunity to share His Word with someone today.

OCT. 13   FOR YOUR GOOD   JEREMIAH 24-25

"Like these good figs, so will I acknowledge them that are carried away captive of Judah, whom I have sent out of this place into the land of the Chaldeans for their good" (Jeremiah 24:5).

Two baskets of figs described two groups in Judah. The first basket had good figs and represented the people who had already been carried captive to Babylon. God promised to restore them to the land and indicated that He had sent them out *"for their good."* It is reassuring to know that the chastening of the Lord is meant to help us, not hurt us. Truly, the seventy years of captivity caused some to seek the Lord. Men such as Daniel, Nehemiah, and Ezra were products of the captivity. Though your season of correction may seem grievous, *"afterward it yieldeth the peaceable fruit of righteousness"* (Hebrews 12:11).

The second basket of figs was *"very naughty"* (24:2). The bad figs represented the people who followed Zedekiah's rebellion against God. Because they refused correction, they would be scattered among the nations. Unlike the first group, their trouble would be *"for their hurt"* (24:9), not *"for their good."* Be careful not to resist God's correction!

Correction may not be pleasant, but God uses it for our good. When we resist Him, problems will result in our hurt. The choice is yours.

OCT. 14   AGAINST GOD'S MAN   JEREMIAH 26-27

"And all the people were gathered against Jeremiah in the house of the LORD" (Jeremiah 26:9).

Jeremiah was not popular with the religious crowd. After he spoke God's message in the temple, *"the priests and the prophets and all the people took him, saying, Thou shalt surely die"* (26:8). It is odd that the man of God preaching the Word of God in the house of God would be rejected by a group claiming to be the people of God.

Unfortunately, God's messengers have been mistreated throughout history. Were not Moses, Jesus, and Paul hated? During the Dark Ages countless Christians were put to death by Catholic leaders. Today, self-righteous church goers are quick to criticize and condemn their pastors.

Let us consider four important lessons. First, do not reject God's message to you. Second, never lash out at God's appointed man for telling you the truth. Third, people will oppose you when you speak the truth. Fourth, do not water down your message when people attack you because of the truth. Jeremiah stood firm when he was threatened. Instead of wavering, he thundered, *"Therefore now amend your ways and your doings"* (26:13). He bravely faced danger, saying to the angry crowd, *"do with me as seemeth good and meet unto you"* (26:14).

| JEREMIAH 28-29 | A MESSAGE TO THE AFFLICTED | OCT. 15 |

"For I know the thoughts that I think toward you…thoughts of peace, and not of evil, to give you an expected end" (Jeremiah 29:11).

The Lord cared deeply for His people who were carried to Babylon. Though they were under discipline for their rebellion, He had not cast them away. Consider His message to them in Jeremiah's letter.

First, He provided direction for their present predicament. He told them to build houses, plant gardens, marry, and multiply. God desired that they would *"be increased there, and not diminished"* (29:6). When we are chastened, God wants us to move forward, not backward. Learn to make the best of your situation, even when reaping from sin.

Second, God gave hope for a future deliverance. Though they needed to be in the refiner's fire, they would not remain there a moment longer than necessary. God set the period of captivity at seventy years to give them *"an expected end."* He offers you hope of deliverance too.

Is God trying to get your attention through tribulation? His dealings are motivated by *"thoughts of peace."* God's primary purpose in chastening you is the same as it was for Judah. He longs for you to return to Him. That's His goal. He said, *"And ye shall seek me, and find me, when ye shall search for me with all your heart"* (29:13).

| JEREMIAH 30-31 | FAITHFUL LIGHT | OCT. 16 |

"…the LORD…giveth the sun for a light by day, and the ordinances of the moon and of the stars for a light by night" (Jeremiah 31:35).

Our text was given as a proof of God's faithfulness to Israel. As long as the sun, moon, and stars hung in the sky, the Lord would not cast away His people. We, too, can be assured of His constant love and faithfulness. As an individual, you can claim what God promised Israel as a nation—*"I have loved thee with an everlasting love"* (31:3).

Now that we have seen the setting of the text, let's make another application. God promised *"a light by day"* and *"a light by night."* How comforting to know that His light cannot be extinguished. Even in our seasons of darkness, God provides at least a little light to guide and cheer us. When a storm cloud of affliction obscures His promised night light, we will not fret. Knowing that the light is still there, we will wait for the cloud to pass and rejoice at the first glimpse of His faithful light.

If darkness lingers longer than expected, continue to maintain hope because morning light is on the horizon. All will be bright soon! God is faithful. Allow Jehovah's words to Israel to console your heart today—*"I will turn their mourning into joy, and will comfort them, and make them rejoice from their sorrow"* (31:13). His light brings gladness!

Oct. 17 — Stretching Your Faith — Jeremiah 32

"Behold, I am the LORD, the God of all flesh: is there any thing too hard for me?" (Jeremiah 32:27).

The life of faith can be difficult. Sometimes we will suffer for doing what is right, and at other times we will be challenged to abandon human reasoning to follow God. Jeremiah's faith was stretched in both manners at the same time, teaching us how to respond to our own trials.

First, trust God with your *person*. Jeremiah was *"shut up in the court of the prison"* by the king for preaching God's Word, but he did not change his message to get out of his affliction (32:2). Are you ever tempted to compromise your convictions to make things easier for yourself? Learn to commit the safekeeping of your life into God's hands.

Next, trust God for your *provision*. The Lord told Jeremiah to buy a field in Anathoth. Knowing that Babylon would soon conquer the land, this may have seemed like an unwise investment. However, God promised that Israel would return to the land after seventy years. By faith, Jeremiah had to part with a large sum of money that he may have needed in the coming days of adversity. At times, God leads us to make financial decisions that stretch our faith. When you have doubts, remember His words, *"is there any thing too hard for me?"*

Oct. 18 — Blessings in Dark Times — Jeremiah 33-34

"Moreover the word of the LORD came unto Jeremiah the second time, while he was yet shut up in the court of the prison" (Jeremiah 33:1).

The destruction of Jerusalem was looming and Jeremiah was in prison. All was bleak, or was it? Some of our brightest blessings come in our darkest hours. Notice what Jeremiah experienced in prison.

First, we see the *presence* of God—*"the word of the LORD came unto Jeremiah."* God does not leave us alone in our affliction; He has a message in His Word to comfort and strengthen us. When trouble arises, run to the Bible and seek Him. He will be found!

Second, consider the *promise* of God—*"Call unto me, and I will answer thee, and shew thee great and mighty things, which thou knowest not"* (33:3). What a promise! We would not have this golden gem in the Bible if Jeremiah had not suffered in prison. Good things certainly come out of bad situations when God is involved! If you call, He will answer.

Third, we see the *plan* of God. The Lord spoke of Israel's return, their forgiveness, and the coming Messiah in the verses that followed. Though problems prevailed at the moment for Jeremiah, all would be well in due season. We, too, can rest in hope of God's intervention on our behalf and anticipate *"great and mighty things"* on the horizon.

JEREMIAH 35-36 — BE CAREFUL WITH THE BOOK — OCT. 19

"Take thee again another roll, and write in it all the former words that were in the first roll, which Jehoiakim the king of Judah hath burned" (Jeremiah 36:28).

Baruch *"wrote from the mouth of Jeremiah all the words of the LORD...upon a roll of a book"* (36:4). After reading it to the people of Judah, Baruch was summoned to read it to the princes. Foolishly, the king took the roll and *"cut it with the penknife, and cast it into the fire"* (36:23). Consider three lessons from this event.

First, the Word of God cannot be destroyed. Though the first copy of the roll was burned, Jeremiah and Baruch made another one with the same words. In fact, God added *"many like words"* to the message that the king sought to diminish. His Word stands even when it is rejected.

Second, man cannot disannul the Word of God. Though the king did not like the message, he could not reverse God's plans or escape His judgment. Perhaps we may not be so bold to burn pages of our Bibles, but we may be guilty of ignoring parts that either convict or challenge us.

Third, resisting God's message is a serious offence. At times, God suffers long with our disobedience, but rebellion will be judged. Will He have to say of you as He did of Jehoiakim, *"I will punish him"* (36:31)?

JEREMIAH 37-38 — SAVED FROM SINKING — OCT. 20

"And in the dungeon there was no water, but mire: so Jeremiah sunk in the mire" (Jeremiah 38:6).

Jeremiah was falsely accused of treason and confined to a dungeon. After many days, the king took him out and asked, *"Is there any word from the LORD?"* (37:17). This was the prophet's chance to get on the king's good side by telling him what he wanted to hear. However, the prophet did not waver in his message. Despite giving the king bad news, Jeremiah was not sent back to the dungeon. As God rewarded him for his refusal to compromise, He will certainly bless your integrity too.

Eventually, the princes of Judah cast Jeremiah into another dungeon, hoping to kill him through starvation and dehydration. At the bottom of the pit, *"Jeremiah sunk in the mire."* There was no way out of the dark and damp dungeon. Have you ever felt like you were sinking in a pit of despair? At times we may feel like we are stuck in unpleasant circumstances, but like the prophet, we have hope. As God used Ebed-melech to intercede with the king for Jeremiah, He has One far greater pleading for us. Jesus is *"at the right hand of God"* and *"maketh intercession for us"* (Romans 8:34). Are you in a pit today? Believe that Christ's petitions will one day bring you *"out of the dungeon"* (38:10).

OCT. 21   BOUND OR DELIVERED?   JEREMIAH 39-40

"For I will surely deliver thee...because thou hast put thy trust in me, saith the LORD" (Jeremiah 39:18).

Jerusalem had fallen to the Babylonians, and King Zedekiah payed dearly for not heeding God's warnings. His sons were executed before him, and then his eyes were put out. Blind and bound, he was carried to Babylon. What a picture of the terrible effects of sin!

Those who follow the Lord can expect a different end. God worked upon the heart of Babylon's king to consider Jeremiah's plight. Nebuchadnezzar commanded his captain, *"Take him [Jeremiah], and look well to him, and do him no harm"* (39:12). Thus, God's servant was loosed from his chains and set free. What a contrast to the fate of Zedekiah! Satan binds, but Jehovah liberates. Let us be careful which master we follow.

The Lord also remembered the faith of Ebed-melech, the one who helped Jeremiah. He promised, *"I will surely deliver thee...because thou hast put thy trust in me."* Trouble may surround us, but we must remember that God cares for His own. If you follow the Lord, He will deliver you, but if you rebel like Zedekiah, you will needlessly suffer spiritual bondage. Will you choose to be bound or delivered?

OCT. 22   ASK AND ACCEPT   JEREMIAH 41-42

"Be not afraid of the king of Babylon, of whom ye are afraid...saith the LORD: for I am with you to save you" (Jeremiah 42:11).

The captains of Judah were afraid because Ishmael killed Gedaliah, *"whom the king of Babylon made governor in the land"* (41:18). Their plan was to flee to Egypt to escape the wrath of the king, but before they fled, they asked Jeremiah to pray for them. They said, *"pray for us...that the LORD thy God may shew us the way wherein we may walk, and the thing that we may do"* (42:2-3). Consider three lessons.

First, God answers prayer—*"And it came to pass after ten days, that the word of the LORD came unto Jeremiah"* (42:7). Do you need direction in life? Ask God to show you *"the way"* to go.

Second, God answers prayer on His timetable. Notice that His response came *"after ten days."* We must learn to be patient and wait upon the Lord. Do not be in a hurry. In due time, He will answer.

Third, we should accept God's answers. Instead of running to Egypt, God wanted them to trust Him. He promised, *"I am with you to save you"* (42:11). Sadly, they rejected His counsel and heard the fateful words, *"know certainly that ye shall die"* (42:22). Too often people only accept answers that are agreeable to them, but that leads to destruction.

JEREMIAH 43-44	THE DECEITFULNESS OF SIN	OCT. 23

"But since we left off to burn incense to the queen of heaven…we have wanted all things, and have been consumed" (Jeremiah 44:18).

Sin blinds people and causes them to become delusional. Thus was the case with the remnant that fled to Egypt. They were convinced that their troubles started when they stopped praying to the queen of heaven. Jeremiah reminded them that their problems were due to their idolatry. He said, *"Because ye have burned incense, and because ye have sinned against the LORD…this evil is happened unto you"* (44:23).

Sin is so deceitful that it causes people to justify the sin that has created their trouble. It does not stop there; it will lead them to turn against those who tell them the truth. The people rebelled against Jeremiah saying, *"As for the word that thou hast spoken unto us in the name of the LORD, we will not hearken unto thee"* (44:16).

Unfortunately, we see people reacting in the same way in our day. When backsliders begin to reap from their sin, they often make foolish statements such as, "All I've had are problems since coming to this church and listening to the Bible. I'm leaving!" They fail to see that sin has caused their troubles, not God. They have been *"hardened through the deceitfulness of sin"* (Hebrews 3:13). Don't be deceived by your sin.

JEREMIAH 45-47	CHECK YOUR FOCUS	OCT. 24

"And seekest thou great things for thyself? seek them not…but thy life will I give unto thee" (Jeremiah 45:5).

Baruch was the faithful servant who penned Jeremiah's message and read it to the people in Jehoiakim's day. As discussed previously, the king had such a great disdain for God's Word that he burned it in the fire. This, however, did not sit well with Baruch.

Consider his *complaint*—*"Woe is me now! for the LORD hath added grief to my sorrow; I fainted in my sighing, and I find no rest"* (45:3). Not only was he sad about the judgment pronounced on Judah, he was also grieved that his efforts to call the people to repentance had been in vain. We must be careful not to wallow in self-pity when our labor for the Lord appears fruitless. If we fret, we will faint as Baruch did.

Notice also his *correction*. Baruch hoped for *"great things"* in return for his service, but God rebuked him, saying, *"seek them not."* We must guard against fleshly desires of fame and recognition. As Christ *"is despised and rejected of men"* (Isaiah 53:3), we must never demand better treatment. After all, *"The servant is not greater than his lord"* (John 15:20). Though Baruch would not be popular, at least his life was spared! Let us learn to focus on things that matter most.

OCT. 25	THE HUMBLING OF THE PROUD	JEREMIAH 48

"We have heard the pride of Moab, (he is exceeding proud) his loftiness, and his arrogancy, and his pride, and the haughtiness of his heart" (Jeremiah 48:29).

Many prophecies were issued against Judah in the book of Jeremiah, but in the closing chapters, the prophet turned his attention to several heathen nations. In today's reading, judgment is pronounced upon Moab. The Moabites were descendants of Abraham's nephew, Lot.

Consider their *character* and the words used to describe their sinful attitude—*pride, loftiness, arrogancy,* and *haughtiness.* The source of Moab's pride was *"his heart."* Pride is always a matter of the heart, and that is the reason we must guard our hearts. Paul warns each of us *"not to think of himself more highly than he ought to think"* (Romans 12:3). Those who exalt themselves will reap as Moab did.

Notice their *calamity*—*"And Moab shall be destroyed...because he hath magnified himself against the LORD"* (48:42). Pride is an offense to God, and those who exalt themselves will be humbled by Him. Have you allowed an attitude of pride to rise in your heart? Though you may feel high and mighty for a season, *"joy and gladness"* will be taken from you as it was from Moab (48:33). It is better to walk humbly with God.

OCT. 26	LEVELING THE LOFTY	JEREMIAH 49

"Thy terribleness hath deceived thee, and the pride of thine heart, O thou that dwellest in the clefts of the rock...I will bring thee down from thence, saith the LORD" (Jeremiah 49:16).

The Edomites were descendants of Esau and followed his ungodly example. Though they dwelt safely for many years in caves among their rugged mountains, they could not escape God's hand of judgment. It is amazing how pride can deceive people into thinking they are untouchable. We recall the fate of Pharaoh who said, *"Who is the LORD, that I should obey his voice...?"* (Exodus 5:2). His kingdom was destroyed through the series of plagues that God sent upon Egypt. He certainly found out who the Lord was! Like Edom, he was haughty.

Perhaps your heart has deceived you into thinking that you can get away with sin. You might dwell safely at the present moment, but there is no guarantee that the Lord will allow you to continue in your false sense of security. God promised Edom, *"I will bring thee down,"* and He is capable of doing the same to all who try to live above His laws.

Solomon issued a warning to the lofty: *"Pride goeth before destruction, and an haughty spirit before a fall"* (Proverbs 16:18). Let us humble ourselves and warn others about pride's destructive nature.

JEREMIAH 50	TREATED IN LIKE MANNER	OCT. 27

"Call together the archers against Babylon…recompense her according to her work; according to all that she hath done, do unto her: for she hath been proud against the LORD" (Jeremiah 50:29).

Though Babylon was used by God to judge His people, He would not allow the city to go unpunished for its wickedness and contempt toward Him. The Lord promised that forces *"out of the north"* would *"make her land desolate"* (50:3). This prophecy referred to the Medes and Persians who defied the odds and conquered Babylon.

God's pronouncement against Babylon was clear—*"according to all that she hath done, do unto her."* The Babylonians were to be treated as they had treated Judah. The lesson before us today is a reminder that our actions will catch up to us. *"Be not deceived; God is not mocked: for whatsoever a man soweth, that shall he also reap"* (Galatians 6:7). Though we may seem to prosper in our rebellion, our success will be short-lived. The seeds we sow today will determine our future harvest.

Since our treatment of others determines how we will be treated, let us follow the Golden Rule given by Jesus—*"And as ye would that men should do to you, do ye also to them likewise"* (Luke 6:31). If we have been unfair, unkind, or ungrateful towards others, let us amend our ways.

JEREMIAH 51	A TIMELY RECOMPENSE	OCT. 28

"…her mighty men are taken, every one of their bows is broken: for the LORD God of recompences shall surely requite" (Jeremiah 51:56).

Today's reading reminds us that justice will be dealt to the wicked. Jeremiah predicted that the mighty men of Babylon were going to fall into the hands of *"the LORD God of recompences."* The word *recompense* means "to repay." God promised, *"I will render unto Babylon…all their evil that they have done in Zion"* (51:24).

When mistreated by others, we are often tempted to respond by treating our offenders the same way they treat us. However, we are commanded, *"Recompense to no man evil for evil"* (Romans 12:17). The strong man is the one who restrains himself, not the one who retaliates. Allow God to do His job. To Him *"belongeth vengeance, and recompence"* (Deuteronomy 32:35). Not only does God know who needs to be recompensed, He knows best how and when to do it.

The fall of the mighty city of Babylon serves as a reminder that even our strongest foes are no match for the Lord of hosts. If you are presently oppressed, take heart. One day, your troublers will discover that *"every one of their bows is broken."* The Lord will stop their aggression, and they will find themselves defenseless against a holy God.

| OCT. 29 | IT CAME TO PASS | JEREMIAH 52 |

"And it came to pass...that Nebuchadrezzar king of Babylon came, he and all his army, against Jerusalem" (Jeremiah 52:4).

Throughout the book of Jeremiah, we have seen repeated warnings that God would judge His people for their disobedience. In the closing chapter of the book, we read that *"it came to pass."* The vessels in the temple were stolen, the temple was burned, and the walls of Jerusalem were broken. Many were slain, and *"Judah was carried away captive out of his own land"* (52:27). History records that their disobedience brought destruction. However, it could have been avoided.

If you think that executing judgment is God's primary desire, think again. He delights more in expressing His love and extending mercy. David testified, *"The LORD is gracious, and full of compassion; slow to anger, and of great mercy"* (Psalm 145:8). Jerusalem could have been spared if the people had repented, but they chose to ignore God.

Has the Lord been dealing with you about a particular matter for a while? His plan for your life is *"good, and acceptable, and perfect"* (Romans 12:2). He would much rather bless you than chasten you. Be quick to accept His will and follow His guidance. Unfortunately, those who fail to obey will one day realize that His judgment *"came to pass."*

| OCT. 30 | IS IT NOTHING TO YOU? | LAMENTATIONS 1-2 |

"Is it nothing to you, all ye that pass by? behold, and see if there be any sorrow like unto my sorrow, which is done unto me, wherewith the LORD hath afflicted me in the day of his fierce anger" (Lamentations 1:12).

The words of our text are both pathetic and prophetic. In the first case, they are the words of Jerusalem soliciting pity. Once glorious, the place had become desolate. Consider the description of the city and its people: *"no rest," "in bitterness," "afflicted," "beauty is departed," "without strength,"* and *"miseries"* (1:3-7). Though sin promises pleasure, it leaves its victims weary, bitter, unattractive, weak, and miserable! As the heathen did not pity Jerusalem, the wicked will not be sympathetic to our grief. In vain we will seek comfort from our worldly friends, asking, *"Is it nothing to you...?"* Oh, the straits of sin!

The passage also looks past Jerusalem and describes the great suffering Christ endured for our sins. Certainly, the words reveal His heart's cry as He agonized on the cross—*"behold, and see if there be any sorrow like unto my sorrow."* This reminds us of Isaiah's description of Messiah—*"Surely he hath borne our griefs, and carried our sorrows"* (Isaiah 53:4). When you consider the hardships that Jesus has endured for you, do you remain unaffected? He asks, *"Is it nothing to you...?"*

LAMENTATIONS 3   THE DUNGEON OF DESPAIR   OCT. 31

"I called upon thy name, O LORD, out of the low dungeon"
(Lamentations 3:55).

Jeremiah's heart was broken because of the destruction of Jerusalem and the chastisement of God's people. He also suffered loss due to the judgment, and for a while he focused too much on his affliction. As a result, he found himself in *"the low dungeon"* of discouragement.

Notice Jeremiah's *distress*. He cried, *"My strength and my hope is perished from the LORD"* (3:18). When he lost hope in God, his strength to continue was gone too. When you find yourself in the pit, don't stay there! What was Jeremiah's downfall? He dwelt on his *"affliction"* and *"misery"* (3:19). Be careful not to magnify your troubles.

Thankfully, the prophet made a good *decision*. He recalled the Lord's mercies and faithfulness (3:21-23). Before long, he declared, *"The LORD is good unto them that wait for him, to the soul that seeketh him"* (3:25). Set your eyes on God, not on your problems.

With hope restored, he waited for *deliverance*. When in the dungeon, pray like Jeremiah. Soon, you will praise God as he did, saying, *"I called upon thy name, O LORD...Thou hast heard my voice...Thou drewest near in the day that I called upon thee"* (3:55-57).

LAMENTATIONS 4-5   RENEWING THE SHINE   NOV. 1

"Turn thou us unto thee, O LORD, and we shall be turned; renew our days as of old" (Lamentations 5:21).

As Jeremiah lamented the destruction of Jerusalem, he exclaimed, *"How is the gold become dim!"* (4:1). Their splendor and glory was gone; they lost their luster. Oh, how sin tarnishes the character and reputation of God's people! How can we shine for the Lord once again?

First, we need *remorse*. Sometimes people will not turn to the Lord until they suffer the consequences of their sin. When chastening hurts, it tends to get our attention. Like the prophet, we must acknowledge that sin is the reason for our dullness. He said, *"The joy of our heart is ceased...woe unto us, that we have sinned!"* (5:15-16).

Second, *repentance* is necessary. Repentance is a change of mind which involves turning from sin to God. Jeremiah's prayer showed, not only a desire for change, but also dependency on God for it—*"Turn thou us unto thee, O LORD, and we shall be turned."* Are you ready to turn?

Third, God provides *renewal* when we meet the requirements. Jeremiah pleaded with God, *"renew our days as of old."* He wanted the gold to shine once again. As God will restore Israel one day after they repent, He will renew individuals who humble themselves (1 Peter 5:6).

Nov. 2 — ANGELIC LESSONS — EZEKIEL 1-2

"And the living creatures ran and returned as the appearance of a flash of lightning" (Ezekiel 1:14).

Ezekiel was a priest living in captivity in the land of the Chaldeans and ministering to fellow Jews. His first recorded vision described four angelic beings called *"living creatures."* Though the angels appear mysterious, they provide a pattern of service that we can emulate.

They *"sparkled like...brass"* (1:7). As their brightness represented the glory and holiness of God, our lives should reflect His righteousness. The Lord commands us, *"Be ye holy; for I am holy"* (1 Peter 1:16).

Next, the angels were equipped with *"the hands of a man under their wings"* (1:8). In like manner, we have hands to serve others and *"wings as eagles"* (Isaiah 40:31) to effectively carry us into the harvest fields.

Notice also that *"they went every one straight forward"* (1:12). We must also stay focused on God's will and not be distracted in our service.

Further, the angels were swift to obey—they *"ran and returned as...a flash of lightning"* (1:14). Let us also be quick to follow God.

Finally, they were energized. There was *"as it were a wheel in the middle of a wheel"* (1:16). Inner wheels often move outer ones, which is a beautiful picture of the Holy Spirit empowering the life of a believer.

Nov. 3 — PARTAKE OF THE WORD — EZEKIEL 3-4

"Son of man, eat that thou findest; eat this roll, and go speak unto the house of Israel" (Ezekiel 3:1).

God had a message for Israel, and He chose Ezekiel to deliver it. The roll was a scroll which contained God's Words. The prophet was told to eat the roll and then speak to others. Consider some lessons.

First, we must internalize the Word before we share it with others. Eating the scroll was a picture of partaking of God's Word personally. Our service is not effective when we try to encourage others to receive what we are not willing to accept ourselves.

Next, those who accept God's Word find it satisfying. Ezekiel testified, *"Then did I eat it; and it was in my mouth as honey for sweetness"* (3:3). The Bible provides nourishment to grow, strength to labor, and sweetness to enjoy. It's true comfort food! Do you hunger for God's Word? If not, *"taste and see that the LORD is good"* (Psalm 34:8).

Unfortunately, not everyone has an appetite for the Word of God. Ezekiel was sent to speak to Israel, but they did not want to listen. God even warned the prophet, *"the house of Israel will not hearken unto thee"* (3:7). Though not everyone will like the message we bring, we must be faithful to deliver it. If people resist you, *"fear them not"* (3:9).

EZEKIEL 5-6 — GOD'S HEART IS BROKEN — NOV. 4

"I am broken with their whorish heart, which hath departed from me, and with their eyes, which go a whoring after their idols" (Ezekiel 6:9).

Ezekiel echoed Jeremiah's prophecy that God would judge Jerusalem with the sword, famine, and pestilence. Further, the Lord promised, *"I will scatter a third part into all the winds"* (5:12). As we know, their plight was not unfounded. Despite repeated warnings, they refused to repent. God testified, *"they have refused my judgments and my statutes, they have not walked in them"* (5:6). Certainly, the Lord was angry with their hardheartedness, but our text reveals that He was also saddened.

Israel had a *"whorish heart."* The people committed spiritual adultery by putting their sin before God. They used *"their eyes"* to *"go a whoring after their idols."* Notice that their eyes and heart were both involved in causing them to be unfaithful to the Lord. We must guard what we look at, or we will develop a *"whorish heart"* that is consumed with fulfilling the lusts of the flesh instead of following the will of God.

God's heart is broken when we depart from Him and long after evil. After He has shown such love, kindness, and mercy toward us, He is crushed when we choose wickedness over Him. As you seek relief when you are grieving, so does the Lord. Stop grieving Him and repent today.

EZEKIEL 7-8 — SECRET CHAMBERS — NOV. 5

"Son of man, hast thou seen what the ancients of the house of Israel do in the dark, every man in the chambers of his imagery? for they say, The LORD seeth us not; the LORD hath forsaken the earth" (Ezekiel 8:12).

Today's reading reveals the depths of hypocrisy and idolatry of Judah's spiritual leaders. In a vision, God transported Ezekiel to the temple in Jerusalem and allowed him to see the great wickedness that was practiced. Hidden in secret chambers, idolatrous images were portrayed on the wall and priests offered incense to strange gods.

How sad to see God's temple used to dishonor the One it was meant to glorify! We have a similar problem today. As we know, the body of every believer is *"the temple of the Holy Ghost"* (1 Corinthians 6:19). Unfortunately, many people work diligently to make themselves appear to be holy externally, but inwardly they are full of sin. Israel's leaders committed their evil deeds *"in the dark."* We should have no secret compartments in our hearts where we hide sin.

Those who put on a good show outwardly but harbor wickedness inwardly are deceived, thinking, *"The LORD seeth us not."* Rest assured that the Maker of the temple knows exactly what transpires within every chamber. If you are practicing sin, God knows and will judge.

Nov. 6 — Spared or Judged — Ezekiel 9-10

"Slay utterly old and young...but come not near any man upon whom is the mark; and begin at my sanctuary" (Ezekiel 9:6).

Ezekiel's vision describes the destruction of Jerusalem. The destroying angels in the vision represented God's hand in the punishment of His people through the Babylonian armies. Let's consider two lessons found in our text.

First, God shows mercy to the righteous. His judgment upon Judah was not based upon age, gender, or social status. Righteousness was the deciding factor. Before the slaughter took place, the Lord commanded the angel, *"set a mark upon the foreheads of the men that sigh and that cry for all the abominations that be done"* (9:4). God remembered His faithful. People like Jeremiah, Baruch, and Ebed-melech were spared because of their faith in God and hatred of evil. Certainly, we can avoid a lot of trouble by living righteously.

Second, God holds leaders accountable. Notice what the Lord told the angels—*"begin at my sanctuary."* Why? The spiritual leaders were guilty of great abominations and had led many astray. God expects much more from people who represent Him. Examine your life to make sure that you are a good example to those under your watch-care.

Nov. 7 — No More Delays — Ezekiel 11-12

"For I am the LORD: I will speak, and the word that I shall speak shall come to pass; it shall be no more prolonged" (Ezekiel 12:25).

The Lord told Ezekiel to dig a hole in the wall and carry out his belongings on his shoulder to represent those who would go forth from Jerusalem into captivity. Despite repeated warnings, the people did not believe they would be judged. However, God reiterated, *"I shall scatter them among the nations"* (12:15). What can we learn from this?

First, God often *delays* judgment to give people time to repent. Those who refuse to change will one day discover that His warnings will *"be no more prolonged."* In other words, time to repent runs out.

Second, people tend to *doubt* God. The people in Ezekiel's day thought they had plenty of time to amend their ways saying, *"he prophesieth of the times that are far off"* (12:27). Many times we act as they did, thinking we can carry on in our sin and repent later. Our depraved nature is so deceitful that the longer God delays His judgment, the less likely we think it will ever come to pass. It is not *"far off."*

Finally, God *delivers* on His promises. Though the Jews were slow to believe, the Lord had said, *"the word...shall come to pass; it shall be no more prolonged."* Don't wait too long to get things right with God!

EZEKIEL 13-15 — IDOLS IN THE HEART — NOV. 8

"Son of man, these men have set up their idols in their heart...should I be enquired of at all by them?" (Ezekiel 14:3).

Certain of Israel's leaders met Ezekiel, hoping to ask God for a blessing through him. It seems that before they were even able to make their petition known, God had a message for them. He clearly told them not to expect anything from Him until they repented.

Notice their *pretense*. They acted as if they were godly by seeking the Lord's help through the prophet. However, God quickly pointed out that they had *"set up their idols in their heart."* God is concerned about what is in your heart. This is a reminder that God wants us to deal with our sins before we seek a blessing. If something or someone has become more important to you than your Savior, you cannot expect the Lord to hear your prayers. The psalmist realized, *"If I regard iniquity in my heart, the Lord will not hear me"* (Psalm 66:18).

Consider God's *plea*—*"Repent, and turn yourselves from your idols; and turn away your faces from all your abominations"* (14:6). If the people were serious about seeking the Lord, He expected them to turn from their sin. Are you ready to *"turn away"* from the things that God hates? If so, He is ready to hear your prayers.

EZEKIEL 16 — BANISHED BEAUTY — NOV. 9

"But thou didst trust in thine own beauty, and playedst the harlot because of thy renown" (Ezekiel 16:15).

Today's reading records the shameful behavior of God's people. The wording is highly descriptive to show the despicable nature of spiritual adultery. Jerusalem was as a discarded newborn before Jehovah took her under His wing. The Lord cleansed, covered, and cared for her. Then He arrayed her with the finest apparel and jewels. Because of her astounding beauty, she became the envy of the nations. Filled with pride, she played the harlot and was unfaithful to her Redeemer. Surely, her judgment was justified due to her sordid behavior and impenitent heart.

Consider several lessons for us. First, we see how vile fornication is in God's sight. Second, any beauty that we have comes from God (16:14). Third, we should not use God's blessings for selfish pursuits (16:15). Fourth, we must not forget our condition before God changed us (16:22). Fifth, God's hand will be against us when we are unfaithful to Him (16:27). Sixth, our sinful passions are insatiable (16:28). Seventh, yielding to sin is a sign of weakness (16:30). Eighth, those who sin will pay for it (16:33). Ninth, sin will rob us of all the beauty that God bestowed upon us (16:39). Tenth, God is merciful (16:60-63).

Nov. 10   FINDING FAULT WITH GOD   EZEKIEL 17-18

"Yet ye say, The way of the Lord is not equal. Hear now, O house of Israel; Is not my way equal? are not your ways unequal?"
(Ezekiel 18:25).

God confronted those in captivity for using a popular proverb about the fathers eating sour grapes and the children's teeth being set on edge. The Jews used this proverb to say that Israel was suffering because of the sins of their fathers, not because of their own wrongdoing. In short, they accused God of being unfair with them. How blind!

With the long record of Israel's sins, it is amazing that they would dare say they were innocent. The Lord clearly stated that only those who were guilty would be punished—*"the soul that sinneth, it shall die"* (18:4). Their trouble was not unwarranted. He also promised that all who would repent and live righteously would be spared—*"But if a man be just, and do that which is lawful and right...he shall surely live, saith the Lord GOD"* (18:5, 9). God offered mercy to those who would turn.

Too often, we act like Israel when we reap for our sin. In our hearts we are tempted to say, *"The way of the Lord is not equal,"* meaning, "It's not fair what God is doing to me!" However, we are told that the sinner is judged *"according to his ways"* (18:30). Don't blame God!

Nov. 11   A FRIGHTFUL FOCUS   EZEKIEL 19-20

"...their eyes were after their fathers' idols" (Ezekiel 20:24).

Children tend to follow their parents' example. Thus was the case with Israel. The Lord told His people, *"defile not yourselves with the idols of Egypt,"* but *"they rebelled"* (20:7-8). Later, in the wilderness, God instructed them to observe the Sabbath. What was their response? He testified, *"Israel rebelled against me"* (20:13). It is not surprising that *"the children rebelled"* too (20:21). Eventually, their offspring wanted to *"be as the heathen"* (20:32). It ought to frighten us to realize what can happen when our children mimic our sinful behavior!

As parents, we would do well to remember that the eyes of our children are watching us. While your children are young, you may seemingly get away with telling them to do as you say, not as you do. However, such hypocritical training only solidifies rebellion in their hearts. They will begin to think that such behavior is acceptable for older people, and they will long for the day when they can act like you.

Though the next generation of Jews saw God's judgment upon their fathers, they still committed the same sins. What was the problem? Our text reveals the answer—*"their eyes were after their fathers' idols."* Guard your focus because your children will follow!

EZEKIEL 21-22	MESSIAH WILL REIGN	NOV. 12

"Remove the diadem, and take off the crown...it shall be no more, until he come whose right it is; and I will give it him" (Ezekiel 21:26-27).

The skeptics who refuse to believe the Bible have obviously never seriously studied it. Today's text reveals a prophecy that continues to be fulfilled. Ezekiel accurately predicted that Zedekiah would be the last true king from the line of David to sit on the throne until Messiah reigns. Although governors reigned in the land after Zedekiah, the Davidic throne has remained vacant. It awaits the King of kings.

Though Jesus was rejected as Messiah in His first advent, He promised to come again. When He does, He will *"judge and make war...and he shall rule them with a rod of iron"* (Revelation 19:11, 15). His reign will fulfill Ezekiel's prophecy—*"the crown...shall be no more, until he come whose right it is; and I will give it him."* It is His throne!

Consider a few lessons for us. First, Jesus will come again, and we must be prepared. Second, God's promises are always fulfilled. Third, those who are wicked will reap for their sin. Zedekiah was described as a *"profane wicked prince of Israel, whose day is come"* (21:25). Our day will come, too, if we continue in sin. Fourth, those who exalt themselves are brought low. God said, *"abase him that is high"* (21:26).

EZEKIEL 23	FORGETTING GOD	NOV. 13

"Because thou hast forgotten me, and cast me behind thy back, therefore bear thou also thy lewdness and thy whoredoms" (Ezekiel 23:35).

The parable of Aholah and Aholibah provides another vivid description of the lewdness of Israel's spiritual adultery. We are told that *"Samaria is Aholah, and Jerusalem Aholibah"* (23:4). As Samaria longed for the idols of Assyria and were judged by that nation, so Judah desired the idols of Chaldea and would be pillaged by them. Despite seeing the condemnation of Samaria, the people in Jerusalem were *"more corrupt...than her sister"* (23:11). How bad had they become? They *"had slain their children to their idols"* (23:39). It is no wonder that the beauty and wealth of the city would be taken away (23:6).

Our text reveals how God's people sunk so low. God said, *"thou hast forgotten me, and cast me behind thy back."* The act of forgetting in this passage was not a mere lapse of memory. It was a deliberate decision which involved casting God and His Word behind their backs. They wanted the Lord out of their way so they could pursue evil. Intentional, premeditated sin comes with a hefty price tag. God told them that their sin would be a burden—*"bear thou also thy lewdness."* If you try to push God out of your mind to enjoy sin, you will reap too.

Nov. 14   PAINFUL LOSS   EZEKIEL 24-25

"Son of man, behold, I take away from thee the desire of thine eyes with a stroke: yet neither shalt thou mourn nor weep" (Ezekiel 24:16).

Many Christians serve God only when it is convenient. This was not the case with Ezekiel. The Lord told him that He would suddenly *"take away"* the desire of his eyes, referring to the wife he loved so dearly. To make things more difficult, the prophet was to refrain from all outward expressions of grief as a sign to the people in captivity. As Ezekiel did not mourn publicly for the loss of his wife, neither would the Jews living in Chaldea display their grief when Jerusalem would fall. Now that we have considered the event, let us make some applications.

First, despite overwhelming grief, we can remain faithful to God. Ezekiel testified, *"So I spake unto the people in the morning: and at even my wife died; and I did in the morning as I was commanded"* (24:18). He did not allow his loss to hinder his service but did as he was commanded. Do you allow problems stop you from serving God? Second, emotions can be controlled. God told the prophet not to *"mourn nor weep."* Even in difficult times, it is possible to keep our grief in check. Third, what is dearest to us may be taken and used for God's glory. Don't hang on too tightly to *"the desire of thine eyes."*

Nov. 15   HAPPY NO MORE   EZEKIEL 26-27

"And I will cause the noise of thy songs to cease; and the sound of thy harps shall be no more heard" (Ezekiel 26:13).

Ezekiel prophesied against some of the heathen nations. Today, we consider the downfall of Tyre, also known as Tyrus. Tyre was a wealthy coastal city. Merchants from many lands traded their wares in this worldly center of commerce. When Jerusalem was destroyed, Tyre rejoiced, saying, *"Aha, she is broken"* (26:2). Jerusalem was also an economic power, and with it laid waste, Tyre hoped to gain from their competitor's demise. Wishing to benefit from another's downfall is selfish and despicable. For this attitude, Tyre would not go unpunished.

This serves as a lesson to us. It is wrong to rejoice when others suffer loss. Solomon said, *"Rejoice not when thine enemy falleth, and let not thine heart be glad when he stumbleth"* (Proverbs 24:17). How do you react when your enemy or competitor suffers a setback? It may be human nature to rejoice, but such an attitude displeases the Lord.

Because Tyre rejoiced at Israel's calamity, they would lose their happiness. God promised, *"I will cause the noise of thy songs to cease."* The Lord knows how to put His finger on the very thing that seems to mean most to us. He can turn our inappropriate laughter to sorrow.

| EZEKIEL 28-29 | PROUD AND POWERFUL | NOV. 16 |

"Thou hast been in Eden the garden of God; every precious stone was thy covering...the workmanship of thy tabrets and of thy pipes was prepared in thee in the day that thou wast created" (Ezekiel 28:13).

The chapter where this text is found speaks of the judgment of the proud king of Tyre. However, it is obvious that the Lord used this occasion to address one even more arrogant—Satan. The devil, not the king of Tyre, was in *"Eden the garden of God."* He was *"the anointed cherub"* that covered the throne of God (28:14). So great was his beauty that he is described as being arrayed with *"every precious stone."* He was apparently fitted with pipes and tabrets to make majestic music as he flew above Jehovah's throne. He was *"perfect...till iniquity was found in"* him (28:15). Rather than humbling himself in God's presence, his heart was exalted. His fate was to be cast out of heaven (Luke 10:18).

Clearly, Lucifer was a beautiful, talented, and powerful angel. Since his fall, he uses those attributes to promote his wicked agenda. He is not an ugly-faced creature with a pointed tail. He is beautiful—*"Satan himself is transformed into an angel of light"* (2 Corinthians 11:14), and he does his best to make sin look attractive. Instead of making spiritual music, his skills are at work producing fleshly, sensual music. Beware!

| EZEKIEL 30-31 | BROKEN ARMS | NOV. 17 |

"And I will strengthen the arms of the king of Babylon, and put my sword in his hand: but I will break Pharaoh's arms" (Ezekiel 30:24).

The time had come for Jehovah to declare judgment upon Egypt. Pharaoh had become so proud that he claimed to be the Creator, saying, *"My river is mine own, and I have made it for myself"* (29:3). Despite boasting that he had great power, he could not defend Judah when they relied upon him. In fact, God called Egypt *"a staff of reed"* that was so weak that it broke when Judah leaned upon it (29:6-7). God had begun to humble him, and it was only going to get worse.

The Lord promised that He would *"strengthen the arms of the king of Babylon"* and *"break Pharaoh's arms."* Had God only broken one of his arms, Pharaoh could have still fought, but injuring both arms made him defenseless. Nebuchadnezzar easily defeated him.

The Lord is the Almighty, and those who exalt themselves against Him will discover how frail they are. Let us remember God's warning to the proud, *"Pride goeth before destruction, and an haughty spirit before a fall"* (Proverbs 16:18). As Pharaoh fell, so can we be humbled.

Pride likes to take credit for things God has done. Let us beware not to exalt ourselves, knowing that God can break our arms too.

Nov. 18 — FAITHFUL WATCHMEN — EZEKIEL 32-33

"I have set thee a watchman unto the house of Israel...thou shalt hear the word at my mouth, and warn them from me" (Ezekiel 33:7).

God provided an illustration of a watchman whose job it was to *"blow the trumpet"* and *"warn the people"* when the land was invaded (33:3). After giving this example, the Lord made it clear that Ezekiel had been appointed as a watchman to Israel. It was the prophet's duty to *"hear the word"* and *"warn"* the people of God's pending judgment. If they did not repent, they would be judged, but he would clear himself. If he held his peace when a warning should have been issued, they would die in their sin, but God would hold him accountable.

The application is clear to every Christian. We have been commanded to *"preach the gospel to every creature"* (Mark 16:15). In a sense, we are watchmen who are told to share the good news of salvation with others who are lost in sin. When we fail to *"blow the trumpet"* and *"warn the people,"* we have sinned against them and God.

Never rationalize your disobedience by saying, "It's not my fault if sinners are punished." Remember that the Lord has *"no pleasure in the death of the wicked; but that the wicked turn from his way and live"* (33:11). Let us long for and work for the conversion of the lost.

Nov. 19 — CARE FOR THE SHEEP — EZEKIEL 34-35

"I will feed my flock, and I will cause them to lie down, saith the Lord GOD" (Ezekiel 34:15).

In this passage, the sheep are the children of Israel who were *"scattered upon all the face of the earth"* (34:6). Though His people were judged for their sin, Jehovah promised, *"I will...gather them from the countries, and will bring them to their own land, and feed them"* (34:13). This speaks of Messiah as the Good Shepherd Who will bring the Jews back to Israel after the Tribulation. He will feed them and *"cause them to lie down"* in safety during the Millennium. Finally, Israel will have peace.

The leaders of Israel in Ezekiel's day had failed as shepherds. The Lord said, *"neither did my shepherds search for my flock, but the shepherds fed themselves, and fed not my flock"* (34:8). Therefore, He pronounced, *"I am against the shepherds"* (34:10). Let all of us responsible for leading others attend to their needs as God expects us to.

The Lord's care for His sheep provides an example for us to follow. Notice His determination to help them—*"I <u>will seek</u> that which was lost...<u>will bind up</u> that which was broken, and <u>will strengthen</u> that which was sick"* (34:16). Let us seek lost souls, give them the healing message of salvation, and strengthen them through discipleship efforts.

EZEKIEL 36-37 REVIVING THE DEAD BONES NOV. 20

"Thus saith the Lord GOD unto these bones; Behold, I will cause breath to enter into you, and ye shall live" (Ezekiel 37:5).

The vision of the dry bones is a prophecy of a future event. The children of Israel are pictured as dry bones which had been scattered due to their disobedience. Though they were dead, the Lord promised them, *"ye shall live."* As the bones came together and received new life, so Israel will be fully restored as a nation after the Tribulation.

This story serves as a great object lesson for those who seek new life. Whether a lost soul needs salvation or a believer needs revival, a couple of things are necessary.

God's Word – The first thing needed to get new life is the Word of God. Notice Ezekiel's message—*"O ye dry bones, hear the word of the LORD"* (37:4). The Bible is life-giving. No transformation can occur in our lives without hearing and heeding *"the word of the LORD."*

The Holy Spirit – The prophet was told to prophesy unto the wind, saying, *"...breathe upon these slain, that they may live"* (37:9). The wind is a picture of the Spirit of God. Like the dead bones, we cannot fix our spiritual problems. Notice the necessity of the Spirit: *"my spirit in you...ye shall live"* (37:14). Ask God to renew you by His Spirit today.

EZEKIEL 38-39 GOD'S PROTECTION NOV. 21

"And it shall come to pass at the same time when Gog shall come against the land of Israel...my fury shall come up in my face" (Ezekiel 38:18).

Today's reading describes a coalition of armies which will attack Israel during the Tribulation. This confederacy will be headed up by Gog, who will apparently be a Russian leader. Several of his future allies are currently Muslim nations, who have great animosity toward the Jews. The stage seems to be set for this prophecy to unfold in the days ahead. When it happens, the Lord said, *"my fury shall come up in my face."*

Despite having a great multitude descend upon it, the tiny nation of Israel will not be defeated. As God delivered His people from formidable world powers in the past, He will do so again. God stated His purpose for defending Israel—*"So will I make my holy name known in the midst of my people"* (39:7). God's protection of Israel will cause them to realize that Jehovah is still their God, and it may be the turning point that leads many Jews to return to Him. God's defense of Israel will bring glory to Himself as His holy name is exalted in their midst.

The lesson for us is that God will work in our midst too. When we face seemingly insurmountable opposition, He is able to protect us as He will Israel. We must remember that one plus God is always a majority!

Nov. 22 — Behold and Hear — Ezekiel 40

"Son of man, behold with thine eyes, and hear with thine ears, and set thine heart upon all that I shall shew thee" (Ezekiel 40:4).

The final vision of Ezekiel has challenged theologians for centuries, leaving many to admit that they do not have all of the answers. Therefore, we must be satisfied with gleaning what we can and trust God to clarify the rest in due time to the people who will live through it.

Since the temple in Jerusalem had already been destroyed, we understand that the remaining chapters of the book of Ezekiel refer to a future temple. If we take the dimensions of the new temple structures literally, great changes in the topography of Jerusalem will have to occur. Because the Tribulation accounts for such changes, we deduce that this passage refers to the millennial temple. This poses difficulty for some scholars because of the reference to animal sacrifices (40:39). However, such sacrifices will only serve as a reflection of Christ's finished work on the cross, similar to our observance of the Lord's Supper.

Now, let's consider something practical from the above text. As the prophet was charged to *"behold"* and *"hear,"* so should we be attentive to all that the Lord teaches us. If you *"set thine heart upon all"* that He has for you, you will be blessed and be able to teach others also.

Nov. 23 — Walls of Separation — Ezekiel 41-42

"He measured it by the four sides: it had a wall round about, five hundred reeds long, and five hundred broad, to make a separation between the sanctuary and the profane place" (Ezekiel 42:20).

The wall around the sanctuary will be longer and wider than the walls that surrounded the previous temples. Apparently, the walls will create a huge court that will accommodate large numbers of worshippers. Truly, the nation of Israel will not only accept the Messiah but will also visit the temple in large numbers to honor Him with their sacrifices. Finally, Jehovah will have their hearts, not only their offerings!

Notice that *"a wall round about"* will *"make a separation between the sanctuary and the profane place."* God has always drawn clear lines of distinction for His people concerning what is holy and common. It is our duty to *"judge righteous judgment"* (John 7:24) and avoid sin.

Walls are meant to protect. In the millennial kingdom, though Christ will rule, not everyone upon earth will be righteous. We know that many will follow Satan when he is released from the pit at the end of the Millennium (Revelation 20:7-9). Obviously, the Lord will want to keep the holy temple from being defiled by sinners. We, too, must erect walls of separation to guard our hearts from sin. Let's keep our temples holy.

EZEKIEL 43-44	THE GLORY OF GOD	NOV. 24

"I looked, and, behold, the glory of the LORD filled the house of the LORD: and I fell upon my face" (Ezekiel 44:4).

Earlier, in chapter ten, Ezekiel described the departure of God's glory from the temple (10:18-19). His presence would not remain there because Jerusalem was soon to be judged for the great wickedness of the people. The glory of the Lord will not return until Israel accepts Jesus as Messiah and the millennial temple is established. God's mighty glory will enter through the eastern gate (43:4), which is the same gate reserved for Messiah (44:1-3). It is interesting to note that the Muslims are aware of Ezekiel's prophecy that Messiah will enter the eastern gate. In an attempt to prevent His glorious return, they have sealed the gate with bricks. How vain are man's attempts to prevent God's purposes!

Now, let us turn our attention to God's splendid glory. When Ezekiel saw the future vision, he said, *"his voice was like a noise of many waters: and the earth shined with his glory"* (43:2). As God will fill the future temple with His power and light, so He desires to fill every believer with His Spirit. Notice Ezekiel's reaction when the glory filled the house. He said, *"I fell upon my face."* May we have the same attitude when God shines through us in a glorious manner in our service!

EZEKIEL 45-46	JUSTICE IN THE LAND	NOV. 25

"Let it suffice you, O princes of Israel: remove violence and spoil, and execute judgment and justice, take away your exactions from my people, saith the Lord GOD" (Ezekiel 45:9).

The description of the millennial reign of Christ continues in today's reading. Instructions for civil and spiritual leaders are given to ensure government and worship will follow God's guidelines. The Jews living in exile were the first recipients of this revelation, and the news of a future kingdom headed by Messiah must have reassured them that Jehovah had not forgotten His people. This teaches us that, even in our times of chastening, God gives us promises upon which we can hope!

The millennium will consist of people who are still prone to sin. Therefore, the princes will be commanded to *"execute judgment and justice."* As Messiah will ensure that His rulers are honest and fair, so He expects us to be just in all of our business dealings. Human nature often leads us to favor ourselves more than others. Our tendency is to try to get as much as we can for ourselves, even at the expense of others. Such practices will not be tolerated in the millennium, and we know that the Lord frowns upon them now too. All will be well if we remember this command, *"Thou shalt love thy neighbour as thyself"* (Mark 12:31).

Nov. 26   LIFE-GIVING WATER   EZEKIEL 47-48

"...every thing shall live whither the river cometh" (Ezekiel 47:9).

Ezekiel saw a river proceed from under the threshold of the millennial temple, flowing eastward. It will bring forth life and abundance as it winds east and then south towards what is apparently the Dead Sea. Along the banks of the river, trees will produce fruit for food and leaves for medicine. When the river reaches the lifeless Dead Sea, *"the waters shall be healed"* (47:8). Though nothing currently can survive in the Dead Sea, it will one day abound with fish of many kinds. Clearly, the river will bring nourishment and healing to the land.

It is important to remember the source of the river. It will flow from the temple where the glory of God will reside. Messiah is the One Who will give such abundant life. Has not Jesus already made life available to us? In addition to eternal life, He offers abundant life to all who trust Him for it. He said, *"I am come that they might have life, and that they might have it more abundantly"* (John 10:10). Jesus is Life. Seek Him.

Further, Jesus promised, *"He that believeth on me, as the scripture hath said, out of his belly shall flow rivers of living water"* (John 7:38). His life-giving waters not only flow to us but through us. Ask the Lord to thoroughly cleanse, refresh, and revive you by His Holy Spirit.

Nov. 27   DETERMINATION   DANIEL 1

"But Daniel purposed in his heart that he would not defile himself"
(Daniel 1:8).

When Nebuchadnezzar initially besieged Jerusalem, he brought a group of wise young men to Babylon to be trained to serve in his kingdom. Daniel, Hananiah, Mishael, and Azariah were part of this first captivity and provide an example of godly character for all to follow.

Consider their *trouble*. Though they were taken from their homeland, they refused to be bitter but made the best of their situation.

Notice also their *testing*. Part of the king's instructions was to feed them with food and drink that was not holy for a Jew. Would they be loyal to a heathen king or to the King of heaven? As we know, *"Daniel purposed in his heart that he would not defile himself."* The word *purposed* means "determined." He simply made up his mind to do right!

This led to favorable *treatment*. God brought Daniel into favor with the man in charge of caring for them, and their diet was changed. This teaches us that when we determine to do right, God will assist us!

Finally, their faithfulness secured a good *testimony*. They were *"ten times better"* than everyone else in the kingdom (1:20). Truly, it pays to follow the Lord. Will you determine to do right and trust God to help?

DANIEL 2	PRAYER AND PROPHECY	NOV. 28

"...there is a God in heaven that revealeth secrets" (Daniel 2:28).

Today's reading is both prophetic and practical. God gave a dream to Nebuchadnezzar which provided a detailed course of world powers from his day until the reign of Christ. Daniel's interpretation of the dream revealed four empires that would rule. The empires of Babylon, Media-Persia, Greece, and Rome are clearly described. The final part of the prophecy is in the future. Ten confederate kings will reign and give rise to the antichrist. The stone that will break the image in pieces is Christ Who will come and set up His own kingdom.

The practical lessons from Daniel's life are numerous. First, we see his *prayer*. When his life was in danger, he and his three friends asked *"mercies of the God of heaven"* (2:18). Always take your problems directly to the Lord and seek His help. Second, his *praise* was evident. After his prayer was answered, *"Daniel blessed the God of heaven"* (2:19). When God intervenes on our behalf, we should say as Daniel, *"I thank thee, and praise thee, O thou God"* (2:23). Third, notice his *proclamation*—*"there is a God in heaven that revealeth secrets."* Daniel gave all the credit to the Lord for the interpretation of the dream. Last, we see his *promotion*—*"the king made Daniel a great man"* (2:48).

DANIEL 3	TRIED BY FIRE	NOV. 29

"...our God whom we serve is able to deliver us from the burning fiery furnace, and he will deliver us out of thine hand, O king" (Daniel 3:17).

Nebuchadnezzar built a golden idol nearly ninety feet high and threatened to throw anyone who refused to worship it into a fiery furnace. This posed a problem for Daniel's three friends who were confronted by the angry king. Their faithfulness to Jehovah was about to get them into trouble, but, thankfully, it would also get them out of it.

Consider their *daring*. When facing the wrath of the king, they were not *"careful to answer"* (3:16), showing that they did not have to think twice about their convictions. They refused to compromise and frankly stated, *"we will not serve thy gods"* (3:18). How courageous are you?

Notice their *dependence*. They boldly proclaimed, *"our God whom we serve is able to deliver us."* They were fully persuaded that since they served the Lord, He would help them. Will He do any less for you?

Their faith in God led to their *deliverance*. Amazingly, *"three men bound"* turned into *"four men loose"* (3:24-25). Their afflictions brought fellowship with the Son of God and led to their freedom! Like them, we may experience a *"fiery trial"* (1 Peter 4:12), but we have no need to fear. God will bless us with His presence and grant deliverance.

Nov. 30 — Walking in Pride? — Daniel 4

"Now I Nebuchadnezzar praise and extol and honour the King of heaven...and those that walk in pride he is able to abase" (Daniel 4:37).

This chapter provides Nebuchadnezzar's testimony of how he was humbled by Jehovah. As the king enjoyed a prosperous reign, the Lord gave him a dream which troubled him greatly. A large, flourishing tree was cut down, and the stump was bound and left in a field. The dream pictured the king, who would be cut down like a tree, and he would wander like an animal in the field with the wild beasts. Due to his pride, he was to lose his mind and his throne, but after seven years he would regain them. He had to learn that *"the most High ruleth"* (4:17).

After Daniel interpreted the dream, he encouraged the king to repent of his pride, but the king did not heed the warning. A year later, Nebuchadnezzar boasted, *"Is not this great Babylon, that I have built for the house of the kingdom by the might of my power...?"* (4:30), but *"While the word was in the king's mouth,"* God's judgment fell (4:31).

Like Nebuchadnezzar, we are prone to take credit for many of the blessings God gives to us. If we are not careful, we will also discover how swiftly the Lord can humble us. Let us remember the king's solemn warning—*"those that walk in pride he* [God] *is able to abase."*

Dec. 1 — Defeated or Delivered — Daniel 5-6

"Thy God whom thou servest continually, he will deliver thee" (Daniel 6:16).

Today's reading provides a contrast between Belshazzar and Daniel. While Belshazzar partied with the golden vessels taken from the temple, he saw the handwriting on the wall, and *"his thoughts troubled him"* (5:6). When the prophet was called to interpret the message from God, he reminded the king how Nebuchadnezzar was humbled because of his pride. Then he said to Belshazzar, *"And thou his son...hast not humbled thine heart, though thou knewest all this"* (5:22). Despite knowing what God did to Nebuchadnezzar, Belshazzar still lifted up his heart against God. As a result, he not only lost his throne but also his life. This reminds us that God deals harshly with presumptuous sin.

As Belshazzar's life teaches that God disciplines the foolish, Daniel's life shows that the Lord delivers the faithful. When Darius made the law prohibiting prayer to anyone but himself, Daniel refused to dishonor God. When he *"knew that the writing was signed, he went into his house...and prayed, and gave thanks before his God, as he did aforetime"* (6:10). Though cast into a den of lions, he was delivered because of his faithfulness. If you are faithful, God will help you too.

DANIEL 7-8 LOOKING FORWARD TO THE KINGDOM DEC. 2

"But the saints of the most High shall take the kingdom, and possess the kingdom for ever, even for ever and ever" (Daniel 7:18).

Daniel's dream in chapter seven mentions four beasts which describe the same four kingdoms in Nebuchadnezzar's dream in chapter two. The fourth beast represents the Roman era which includes today. The ten horns seem to indicate a confederacy of ten kings who will reign before the little horn rises to power. The little horn is obviously the antichrist who will conquer three of the ten kings and rule during the Tribulation.

Though many will be saved during the Tribulation, it will be a difficult time for them. The antichrist will oppose God and His people—*"he shall speak great words against the most High, and shall wear out the saints of the most High"* (7:25). During the last three and a half years of the Tribulation, the antichrist will prove to be exceedingly vicious.

These prophecies are primarily meant to encourage those who will live through the Tribulation to focus on the future reign of Christ. Jesus will consume the antichrist *"with the spirit of his mouth, and shall destroy with the brightness of his coming"* (2 Thess. 2:8). When we are troubled by the evil around us, we can find comfort, too, by looking forward to being with Christ in His kingdom forever!

DANIEL 9-10 A PIVOTAL PROPHECY DEC. 3

"...understand the matter, and consider the vision" (Daniel 9:23).

Chapter nine contains a detailed prophecy known as Daniel's Seventy Weeks. After Daniel prayed intensely, God sent the angel Gabriel to explain the vision to him. The seventy weeks focus on the Jews and Jerusalem—*"Seventy weeks are determined upon thy people and upon thy holy city"* (9:24). Each week represents a group of seven years.

The first seven weeks appear to describe Jerusalem's restoration under Nehemiah—*"the street shall be built again, and the wall, even in troublous times"* (9:25). The next sixty-two weeks lead up to Christ's crucifixion for our sins—*"Messiah [shall] be cut off, but not for himself"* (9:26). Since the prophecy is about Israel, the seventieth week will begin when the church age ends at the Rapture. The seventieth week clearly describes the future events of the Tribulation, including the cessation of Jewish sacrifices *"in the midst of the week"* (9:27) by the antichrist who will sit in the temple and claim to be God (2 Thess. 2:4).

Why is this so important to us? Seeing the fulfillment of the first sixty-nine weeks builds our confidence in the Word of God and provides assurance that future events will happen as prophesied. The chapter also contains many lessons about prayer such as confession and intercession.

DEC. 4   HOW BRIGHT WILL YOU BE?   DANIEL 11-12

"And they that be wise shall shine as the brightness of the firmament; and they that turn many to righteousness as the stars for ever and ever" (Daniel 12:3).

The book of Daniel concludes with more prophecies. The events in chapter eleven are divided into two categories. The prophecies found in verses 1-35 have been fulfilled, and the ones contained in the rest of the chapter deal with future events associated with the antichrist. Chapter twelve discusses the Tribulation, the resurrections, and rewards.

Notice *who* will be rewarded—*"they that be wise."* This reminds us of Proverbs 11:30, *"The fruit of the righteous is a tree of life; and he that winneth souls is wise."* Wise people realize the importance of sharing the gospel with others. What does that say about those who don't?

Observe *why* they will be rewarded—*"they...turn many to righteousness."* Our goal in evangelization is not merely to increase our church attendance. We must seek to see lives changed through salvation.

Consider *how* they will be rewarded—*"they...shall shine as the brightness of the firmament; and...as the stars for ever and ever."* It appears that a person's labor in spreading the gospel will affect how they will shine in God's kingdom. How bright will you be?

DEC. 5   IT'S BETTER WITH GOD   HOSEA 1-2

"I will go and return to my first husband; for then was it better with me than now" (Hosea 2:7).

Hosea was a prophet to the northern kingdom during the days of Isaiah. He rebuked the people for their wickedness, warned of judgment, and foretold the restoration of Israel. The first part of the book compares Israel to Hosea's adulteress wife. Though Israel had been unfaithful to Jehovah, He promised to *"speak comfortably unto her"* and restore her to favor once again in the future (2:14).

The words of our text remind us of the futility of seeking happiness apart from the Lord. Israel tried to satisfy their longings with the idols of the heathen and the pleasures of the world, but they discovered that such things only left them empty and unfulfilled. In the end, they will one day declare, *"I will go and return to my first husband* [Jehovah]*; for then was it better with me than now."* Their return will finally occur after they experience severe hardships during the Tribulation and accept Messiah.

Like Israel, many Christians stray from the Lord, seeking pleasure from the world. Though Israel sought happiness, they lost it. Because of their unfaithfulness, God said, *"I will also cause all her mirth to cease"* (2:11). If you have lost your joy due to sin, return to God—it's *"better."*

HOSEA 3-5	SEEKING WITHOUT FINDING	DEC. 6

"They shall go with their flocks and with their herds to seek the LORD; but they shall not find him; he hath withdrawn himself from them" (Hosea 5:6).

Our text may appear harsh if taken by itself. It would seem that people who *"seek the LORD"* should find Him. Did He not promise, *"And ye shall seek me, and find me, when ye shall search for me with all your heart"* (Jeremiah 29:13)? It is important to notice that only those who seek God with all of the heart will find Him. Judah would not find the Lord because their worship was half-hearted at best. They loved sin.

Hosea brought an indictment against Israel because of their great wickedness. There was *"no truth, nor mercy, nor knowledge of God in the land"* (4:1). They were guilty of *"swearing, and lying, and killing, and stealing, and committing adultery"* (4:2). *"Whoredom and wine"* had taken away their hearts (4:11). Though this described Israel, it is apparent that Judah followed in their footsteps (5:5). The point is that those who engage in evil cannot expect to enjoy God's presence.

The people in our text were like many of today's Christians—they wanted the pleasures of sin and the blessings of God at the same time. It has never worked that way. If you cling to sin, you *"shall not find him."*

HOSEA 6-8	HEAVENLY CHASTENING	DEC. 7

"Come, and let us return unto the LORD: for he hath torn, and he will heal us; he hath smitten, and he will bind us up" (Hosea 6:1).

God's purpose in chastening Israel was to cause them to return to Him. He knew that trouble would get their attention. He said, *"in their affliction they will seek me early"* (5:15). During the second half of the Tribulation, the antichrist will turn against the Jews and persecute them. After that occurs, many Jews will accept Jesus as Messiah. Truly, they will seek Him early *"in their affliction."* Today's text has an application for us too. Consider what is involved in God's chastening.

First, we see *discipline*. In the last days, Israel will admit that God *"hath torn"* and *"hath smitten."* When we stubbornly refuse to follow the Lord, He has no choice but to inflict ample suffering to get our attention. Thankfully, His purpose is to correct us, not destroy us.

Next, we notice a *decision*—*"Come, and let us return unto the LORD."* This is what God ultimately wants. The sooner we return to Him, the less grief we will have to experience. Be quick to return!

Finally, we notice *doctoring*. Like Israel, we can be assured that the Great Physician *"will heal us"* when we repent. Has the heavenly rod of discipline smitten you? Return to God, and He will mend your wounds!

DEC. 8   WHO GETS THE FRUIT?   HOSEA 9-11

"Israel is an empty vine, he bringeth forth fruit unto himself: according to the multitude of his fruit he hath increased the altars" (Hosea 10:1).

In today's reading, God continued His case against Israel. With tender care, He had planted them as a vine, hoping they would be fruitful for Him. However, instead of bearing a harvest for God, they focused on producing for themselves. Notice some characteristics of selfishness.

First, selfishness disregards God's will. The Lord has a purpose for our lives, and we must live to please Him, not self. When we live for self, we show contempt for God's plan for our lives. We must remember that *"all things were created by him, and for him"* (Colossians 1:16). You were not created to please self. Paul reminded us *"that we should bring forth fruit unto God"* (Romans 7:4). Is your fruit for God or self?

Second, selfishness leads to an empty life. Though Israel brought *"forth fruit unto himself,"* God considered him *"an empty vine."* All of our selfish pursuits are vanity and will leave us empty-handed in eternity.

Third, selfishness leads to other sins. Notice how Israel used their gains—*"he hath increased the altars."* Instead of living for God, he built more idolatrous altars. The same is true today. The more we live for self, the more we indulge in worldliness. Where is your treasure?

DEC. 9   SELF-INFLICTED MISERY   HOSEA 12-14

"...thou hast destroyed thyself; but in me is thine help" (Hosea 13:9).

Israel had sinned *"more and more"* with their idols (13:2). The Lord testified of their ungratefulness and pride, saying, *"they were filled, and their heart was exalted; therefore have they forgotten me"* (13:6). How sad it is when we take our blessings for granted and forget God! Though the Lord had to judge His people, He also offered them hope. Our text provides both a rebuke and a remedy to every backslider.

Consider the *rebuke*—*"thou hast destroyed thyself."* Like Israel, we have nobody to blame but ourselves when judgment falls upon us. A decision to sin is a choice to suffer. Is it not true that many of our problems are self-inflicted? When we admit our faults, we can find help.

Notice the *remedy*. God said, *"in me is thine help."* The Lord longed for Israel to repent and turn to Him, and He desires the same for all of His wayward children. He exhorts, *"return unto the LORD thy God"* (14:1). Too often His pleas go unheeded. As a whole, Israel has still not returned to Him, but they will in the future. When they do, God promises, *"I will heal their backsliding, I will love them freely: for mine anger is turned away from him"* (14:4). You can have the same peace now if you will *"Take with you words, and turn to the LORD"* (14:2).

| JOEL 1-2 | HEARTFELT REPENTANCE | DEC. 10 |

"And rend your heart, and not your garments, and turn unto the LORD your God: for he is gracious and merciful, slow to anger, and of great kindness, and repenteth him of the evil" (Joel 2:13).

The book of Joel was written as a warning to God's people apparently before the fall of the northern and southern kingdoms. The *"day of the LORD"* is mentioned five times, providing details of the Tribulation and restoration of Israel during the Millennium. Joel's preaching also focused on a present plague of insects which had devoured and devastated their crops. So, Joel called upon the elders to proclaim a fast and *"cry unto the LORD"* (1:14). After describing a powerful army that would invade from the north (2:1-10), he pled with the people to repent.

God did not want a mere external show of rending the garments. He clearly advised, *"rend your heart."* When experiencing God's judgment, we must turn to the Lord with a broken heart. Once we do, we will find that He is *"gracious and merciful, slow to anger, and of great kindness."* He would rather pardon than punish. If we change our minds about our sin, He may change His mind about our punishment. In addition to withholding trouble, He may even give us a blessing—*"Who knoweth if he will return and repent, and leave a blessing behind him"* (2:14).

| JOEL 3 | DECISION TIME | DEC. 11 |

"Multitudes, multitudes in the valley of decision: for the day of the LORD is near in the valley of decision" (Joel 3:14).

The final chapter of Joel speaks of God's judgment upon the Gentile nations. The Lord said, *"I will also gather all nations, and will bring them down into the valley of Jehoshaphat"* (3:2). This valley is also known as *"the valley of decision."* It will not be the multitudes who will make decisions on that day. Jehovah will be the One deciding the fate of Israel's enemies. How reassuring to know that in God's timing He will judge the oppressors of His people! Perhaps you are presently troubled by the ungodly. Take heart and realize that, as God will judge Israel's foes, He will one day do the same to your adversaries.

The closing verses of the book describe the blessings of the kingdom that Jesus will establish. The people will be forgiven and the land will be fruitful—*"the mountains shall drop down new wine, and the hills shall flow with milk, and all the rivers of Judah shall flow with waters"* (3:18). What a beautiful picture of the peace and prosperity that await the saved!

Another lesson for each of us is to prepare for judgment day. Our decisions now will determine God's decisions then. Have you received Jesus as your Savior? If so, are you living to please Him or yourself?

DEC. 12 — HIGHLY PRIVILEGED — AMOS 1-3

"You only have I known of all the families of the earth: therefore I will punish you for all your iniquities" (Amos 3:2).

Amos was a prophet from Judah who preached to Israel in the northern kingdom. His ministry was during the reign of the wicked but prosperous Jeroboam II. Our reading provides a few lessons for us.

First, we see *purpose*. Though only a humble herdsman who tended the flock, God had a special plan for Amos. Like Amos, you may not be highly educated or come from an elite family, but that is of little concern to the Lord. He is not hindered by your limitations. As the Lord had a unique purpose for Amos, He has one for you too. Just be available!

Next, we notice *privilege*. God said to Israel, *"You only have I known of all the families of the earth."* Of all the nations, the Lord chose to bless Israel in such a special way. He delivered them from the bondage of Egypt, made a covenant with them, and established them as a mighty nation. If you are saved, you have been greatly blessed too.

Finally, we see *punishment*. Though Israel was highly privileged, they were not above God's laws. Like the heathen nations, they would be held accountable. There are no exemptions—if you become blinded by your blessings, God may say, *"I will punish you."* Remain humble.

DEC. 13 — DON'T TRY GOD'S PATIENCE — AMOS 4-6

"Woe to them that are at ease in Zion...!" (Amos 6:1).

Today's reading shows God's patience toward His people, a plea to return to Him, and promises of judgment on those who refused. Though the prophecy speaks to Israel, God treats us much the same way.

Consider the Lord's *patience*. God tried to draw Israel back to Himself through chastening, but they refused to repent. Five times He said, *"yet have ye not returned unto me."* After the fifth time, God said, *"Therefore thus will I do unto thee...prepare to meet thy God"* (4:12). Those who resist Him long enough will discover that His patience will run out. He knows what to do to get our attention if we are stubborn.

Next, we see God's *plea*—*"Seek the LORD, and ye shall live"* (5:6). Jehovah had not given up on His people. When we stray, He urges us to come back to Him. Part of returning to Him involves amending our ways—*"Hate the evil, and love the good"* (5:15). If we meet His conditions, *"it may be that the LORD...will be gracious"* to us (5:15).

Finally, we see God's *pronouncement* in our text. He promised woe to those who were *"at ease."* Feeling smug and secure in their sin, they *"put far away the evil day"* (6:3), thinking judgment was a long way off. However, they were wrong, and misery came. Don't be *"at ease"* in sin.

| AMOS 7-9 | DON'T LOSE YOUR APPETITE | DEC. 14 |

"Behold, the days come, saith the Lord GOD, that I will send a famine in the land, not a famine of bread, nor a thirst for water, but of hearing the words of the LORD" (Amos 8:11).

The Lord promised that Israel and the house of Jeroboam would be destroyed. Amaziah, the priest of the counterfeit religious system in Bethel, withstood the man of God. In addition to falsely accusing Amos to the king, Amaziah added that *"the land is not able to bear all his words"* (7:10). He basically told the prophet, "Go home and stop preaching around here." Though tidings of judgment may not be popular, it is what people need to hear. When you warn others about the wrath to come, do not be surprised that many will reject your message. Like Amos, we must not back down.

Little did Amaziah realize that his wish would eventually be granted. Since Israel did not want God's Word, the Lord warned that He would withhold it from them—*"I will send a famine...of hearing the words of the LORD."* The famine began at the closing of the Old Testament and lasted about four hundred years until John the Baptist proclaimed the coming of Messiah. We must be careful not to lose our appetite for God's Word. If we reject it, He may withhold it from us.

| OBADIAH | THE DECEITFULNESS OF PRIDE | DEC. 15 |

"For the day of the LORD is near...as thou hast done, it shall be done unto thee: thy reward shall return upon thine own head" (Obadiah 1:15).

The Edomites were Esau's descendants who mistreated their brother Israel. When Israel journeyed to the Promised Land, they peacefully requested to pass through Edom, but Edom violently responded, *"Thou shalt not pass by me, lest I come out against thee with the sword"* (Numbers 20:18). Later, when Jerusalem was destroyed and plundered by Babylon, Edom rejoiced and participated in the abuse of Israel (1:11-14). Now, God had a message for Edom, and Obadiah delivered it!

First, they were *deceived*—*"The pride of thine heart hath deceived thee"* (1:3). They dwelt in rugged strongholds, thinking they were invincible. However, God promised, *"thence will I bring thee down"* (1:4). No sinner is out of God's reach. Next, they were *despised*. They thought they were great, but they were actually insignificant. The Lord said, *"I have made thee small among the heathen: thou art greatly despised"* (1:2). When we are proud, we fail to realize how meaningless we truly are. Finally, they were *doomed*. God said, *"as thou hast done, it shall be done unto thee."* This reminds us that a time of reaping always follows a season of sowing. Don't allow pride to deceive you.

DEC. 16 — UNWILLINGNESS — JONAH 1-4

"Arise, go to Nineveh, that great city, and cry against it...But Jonah rose up to flee unto Tarshish from the presence of the LORD" (Jonah 1:2-3).

If one word could sum up Jonah's attitude it would be unwilling. He did not want to go where God wanted him to go or do what God wanted him to do. Jonah had to be persuaded through a series of severe trials to obey the Lord. Consider the results of having an unwilling heart.

First, it causes *distance*. Jonah's aversion to obeying God made him try to run *"from the presence of the LORD."* When you have no appetite for fulfilling God's will, you will not feel comfortable in His presence. Be careful, or the steps that follow will sever your fellowship with God.

Second, it leads to *disobedience*. When God said, *"go to Nineveh,"* Jonah *"rose up to flee"* in the opposite direction. He took steps to avoid doing God's will for his life. Never allow an unwilling spirit to remain in your heart, or you will become so hardened that you will openly rebel.

Finally, it brings *discipline*. As the Lord prepared a *"great wind"* (1:4), *"great tempest"* (1:12), and *"great fish"* (1:17) to get Jonah's attention, He will prepare great trouble to get yours. If you have been reluctant to obey God in a certain matter, do as the prophet did—*"Jonah prayed"* (2:1). Then, he obeyed—he *"arose, and went"* (3:3).

DEC. 17 — JUDGMENT WITHOUT MERCY — MICAH 1-3

"Then shall they cry unto the LORD, but he will not hear them: he will even hide his face from them at that time" (Micah 3:4).

Micah preached in the days of Isaiah to Samaria and Jerusalem. He enumerated their offenses and warned of God's judgment for their idolatry and great wickedness. Consider their character.

First, we see their *ambition*. God pronounced, *"Woe to them that devise iniquity, and work evil upon their beds!"* (2:1). The goal of many was to imagine ways to defraud people of their possessions. Their hearts were filled with covetousness and had no room for Jehovah. Since the people liked to *"devise iniquity,"* the Lord promised to *"devise an evil"* against them (2:3). In other words, God promised to trouble evildoers.

Next, consider their *attitude*. They rejected God's message and messengers, crying, *"Prophesy ye not"* (2:6). The Lord responded with a convicting question—*"do not my words do good to him that walketh uprightly?"* (2:7). His Words were good, but they refused His remedy.

Last, notice their *appetite*. They were known to *"hate the good, and love the evil"* (3:2). Because they chose sin and spurned correction, God promised judgment without mercy—*"Then shall they cry unto the LORD, but he will not hear them."* Be careful not to reject God's calls to you.

MICAH 4-5	THE BIRTH OF THE KING	DEC. 18

"But thou, Bethlehem Ephratah, though thou be little…yet out of thee shall he come forth unto me that is to be ruler in Israel; whose goings forth have been from of old, from everlasting" (Micah 5:2).

Over seven hundred years before the birth of Jesus, the prophet Micah predicted the event. When the wise men sought the newborn King, the chief priests and scribes were asked where Messiah would be born. They immediately referenced this passage of Scripture. The Jews in Jesus' day knew where He would be born, but they were not looking for Him. It is amazing how many people know facts about Jesus but have no interest in knowing Him personally. How well do you know Him?

This prophecy told where Messiah would be born—*"Bethlehem,"* what He would do—*"be ruler in Israel,"* and how long He has existed—*"whose goings forth have been from of old, from everlasting."* The birth of Christ not only fulfilled this prophecy but also proved His eternality and deity. Truly, Jesus is God! Despite being rejected as Ruler by Israel, He will come again and establish His kingdom in the end times.

As we contemplate Who Jesus is, let us remember that He came to *"be ruler."* Does He have full control of your life, or do you selfishly sit on the throne of your heart? Let Him be King, and you will have peace!

MICAH 6-7	MATTERS OF THE HEART	DEC. 19

"He hath shewed thee, O man, what is good; and what doth the LORD require of thee, but to do justly, and to love mercy, and to walk humbly with thy God?" (Micah 6:8).

Yesterday's reading spoke of Messiah and His future kingdom. Today we consider the third major division of Micah's writings. It includes the Lord's controversy, commands, and compassion.

God had a *controversy* with Israel (6:2). He asked why they had been unfaithful to Him, especially after He had delivered them from great bondage. Truly, our lives should show gratitude for His blessings.

Observe God's *commands*—*"do justly…love mercy…walk humbly."* These are matters of the heart that should affect daily living. Israel asked if sacrifices would bring God's favor (6:6), thinking that external acts of service might be sufficient. However, the Lord wanted a repentant heart that resulted in changed lives. Do you seek to do right, be merciful, and maintain a humble spirit? True devotion results in holy living.

Consider the Lord's *compassion*. One day Israel will finally confess, *"I have sinned"* (7:9) and will exclaim, *"He will turn again, he will have compassion upon us; he will subdue our iniquities; and thou wilt cast all their sins into the depths of the sea"* (7:19). God is merciful to forgive!

DEC. 20	GOD'S WAY	NAHUM 1-3

"...the LORD hath his way in the whirlwind and in the storm"
(Nahum 1:3).

Nahum declared judgment upon Nineveh, the capital of Assyria. This was the same city that repented at the preaching of Jonah decades earlier. However, another generation had risen who opposed God's people. During Hezekiah's reign, Assyria carried the northern kingdom of Israel away captive and later threatened Judah. In his book, Nahum recorded the great wickedness of the Assyrians and foretold their utter destruction. The coming fall of Assyria served as a comfort to Judah, and words of encouragement in the prophecy gave them hope. For instance, Nahum reminded them, *"The LORD is good, a strong hold in the day of trouble"* (1:7). Certainly, God helps in our *"day of trouble."*

Another wonderful truth is tucked away in today's text. While describing God's majesty, Nahum mentioned that *"the LORD hath his way in the whirlwind and in the storm."* His will is accomplished each time He sends a strong wind upon nature. Every tempest, hurricane, and tornado serves a divine purpose. Likewise, God's will is accomplished through the storms of life. He has a purpose for every trial we face. When we trust Him, we will eventually see that *"his way"* is right.

DEC. 21	GOD'S TIMING	HABAKKUK 1-3

"For the vision is yet for an appointed time...though it tarry, wait for it; because it will surely come, it will not tarry" (Habakkuk 2:3).

Habakkuk prophesied shortly before the invasion of Judah by the Babylonians. The book is much like a conversation between the prophet and God in which the Lord addresses Habakkuk's concerns. One helpful lesson from this book is that we must wait on God's timing.

In the first chapter, Habakkuk lamented the great wickedness he saw in Judah and wondered why the Lord seemed to let it go unpunished. He prayed that God would intervene, saying, *"O LORD, how long shall I cry, and thou wilt not hear!"* (1:2). At times, we are tempted to think God has not heard our prayers, but we must be patient. He hears quite well.

The Lord's response to Habakkuk was, *"I will work a work in your days, which ye will not believe, though it be told you"* (1:5). God was about to move in an unbelievable manner. The Babylonians would soon judge Judah, and the Lord assured Habakkuk, *"though it tarry, wait for it; because it will surely come."* God has a master plan and works on an infallible timetable. Never think that He is unaware of your cares. When it is time for Him to work, you will marvel. In the end, you will say, *"I will rejoice in the LORD, I will joy in the God of my salvation"* (3:18).

ZEPHANIAH 1-3 — FOUR FATAL DEFICIENCIES — DEC. 22

"She obeyed not the voice; she received not correction; she trusted not in the LORD; she drew not near to her God" (Zephaniah 3:2).

Zephaniah prophesied in the days of Josiah, king of Judah. The Lord had delayed His judgment upon Judah because of Josiah's personal revival, but wickedness still prevailed in the hearts of the majority. Therefore, God promised, *"I will also stretch out mine hand upon Judah"* (1:4). The book also includes a call to repentance (2:3), a description of Judah's sin (3:1-5), the judgment of the nations (3:8), and blessings for Israel during the Millennium (3:14-20).

Let's consider a practical lesson from our text, which speaks of the spiritual condition of Jerusalem. Notice four fatal deficiencies that we must avoid. First, *disobedience*—*"She obeyed not the voice."* Second, *defiance*—*"she received not correction."* Third, *disbelief*—*"she trusted not in the LORD."* Fourth, *distance*—*"she drew not near to her God."* If we fail to obey God, accept His correction, trust in Him, and draw close to Him in daily fellowship, we will drift far from Him. The end result will be similar to that of Judah—we will be judged.

The Lord would much rather bless us. All who seek and serve Him will know that the *"LORD thy God in the midst of thee is mighty"* (3:17).

HAGGAI 1-2 — CONSIDER YOUR WAYS — DEC. 23

"Is it time for you, O ye, to dwell in your cieled houses, and this house lie waste? Now therefore...Consider your ways" (Haggai 1:4-5).

After seventy years of captivity, many Jews returned to Jerusalem to rebuild the temple under Ezra's leadership. When an edict from the king caused them to stop the work, they became preoccupied with building their own homes and gathering riches. Because of their misplaced priorities, God chastened them economically and sent Haggai to point out their waywardness. Let's learn from the following points.

First, notice *coolness*. The people had lost their zeal for building the temple. While they lived in beautiful homes, God's house remained in ruins. We must be careful not to neglect the Lord's work to tend to ours.

Second, we see a *confrontation*—God said, *"Consider your ways."* When we experience troubles, it is always wise to consider our actions. If we allow wrong priorities to creep into our lives, the Lord may have to get our attention through chastisement. Take time to consider your ways.

Third, observe their *compliance*. God told them to *"build the house"* (1:8), and they *"obeyed the voice of the LORD"* (1:12). Simple!

Fourth, we see *comfort*. Because they obeyed, the Lord reassured them, saying, *"I am with you"* (1:13). Following God truly brings peace.

DEC. 24   TAKE THE FIRST STEP   ZECHARIAH 1-2

"Turn ye unto me...and I will turn unto you" (Zechariah 1:3).

Like Haggai, Zechariah's ministry was to the Jews who returned to Jerusalem in Ezra's day. The book records visions, warnings to listen to God's prophets, and promises about the future kingdom under Messiah. Today's text reminds us of our responsibility to return to the Lord when we have gone astray. What is involved in returning?

First, admit the *problem*. Why would the Lord admonish His children to turn *to* Him? Obviously, they had turned *from* Him. The words of Isaiah are so true—*"we have turned every one to his own way"* (Isaiah 53:6). The hymn writer, Robert Robinson, penned words we all can identify with—"Prone to wander, Lord, I feel it, prone to leave the God I love." Have you strayed from the Savior? Sadly, it's easy to do.

Second, obey the *precept*. The only solution for the wayward believer is to return. Jehovah clearly calls us back to Himself—*"Turn ye unto me."* Are you ready to turn from your sin and selfishness? Since we are the guilty ones, it is upon us to take the first step back to Him.

Third, claim the *promise*. If you turn to Him, He said, *"I will turn unto you."* We will be welcomed back by God with open arms as the prodigal was by his father. Don't delay your return!

DEC. 25   STRENGTH TO FINISH   ZECHARIAH 3-5

"This is the word of the LORD unto Zerubbabel, saying, Not by might, nor by power, but by my spirit, saith the LORD of hosts" (Zechariah 4:6).

The visions of Zechariah continued in today's reading. The political leader in charge of rebuilding the temple in Jerusalem was Zerubbabel. As we have already seen, the Jews had been hindered by a decree from Artaxerxes from continuing the building project. Truly, Satan was doing his best to hinder God's work (3:1). Zerubbabel had a daunting task, and he would need help. Consider the Lord's assistance.

First, He gives *encouragement*. God sent him a personal message—*"This is the word of the LORD unto Zerubbabel."* The Lord cheered His servant with a wonderful promise of assistance. Has your work for God been opposed? If so, a word of hope is waiting for you in the Bible.

Second, He provides *empowerment*. Zerubbabel was not to rely on his own strength to fight God's battles—*"Not by might, nor by power, but by my spirit, saith the LORD of hosts."* God always equips those He calls. Are you presently struggling to complete a God-given task? Do not look within for the needed strength. Ask the Holy Spirit for power.

Third, He gives *expectation*. Of Zerubbabel's work, God said, *"his hands shall also finish it."* With God's help, we can expect to finish!

ZECHARIAH 6-8   A GREAT TESTIMONY   DEC. 26

"We will go with you: for we have heard that God is with you"
(Zechariah 8:23).

During the Millennium, when Christ reigns in Jerusalem, people from many nations will seek to accompany the Jews and worship the Lord. The reason they will want to be with God's people is because He will be with them. When God manifests His glory in a believer's life, it can be used to draw others to Himself. Do the lost see Christ in you?

When the Lord turned the captivity of Zion, others took notice. God's deliverance brought great joy, and the Lord was magnified. Notice the psalmist's account, *"Then was our mouth filled with laughter, and our tongue with singing: then said they among the heathen, The LORD hath done great things for them"* (Psalm 126:2). The key was that God's people were *"filled with laughter, and...with singing."* Perhaps more of the heathen would be interested in the Savior if we radiated the joy of the Lord. Oh that the lost would say, *"We will go with you"*!

When a demon-possessed man was transformed by Jesus, he was sent to testify. We are not told of the results, but we do know that *"he went his way, and published throughout the whole city how great things Jesus had done unto him"* (Luke 8:39). Will you witness for Him today?

ZECHARIAH 9-10   PRISONERS OF HOPE   DEC. 27

"Turn you to the strong hold, ye prisoners of hope: even to day do I declare that I will render double unto thee" (Zechariah 9:12).

Though Judah had been in captivity for seventy years, the Lord did not leave them in their affliction. Many returned from Babylon to rebuild the temple in Jerusalem. God said, *"I have sent forth thy prisoners out of the pit wherein is no water"* (9:11). Truly, God delivers His people from horrible pits of sin and suffering. If you are presently in bondage of any sort, the Lord is willing to help.

Though the Jews were held captive, God called them *"prisoners of hope."* Their hope was in Messiah, and the Lord provided a detailed description so His people would recognize Him—*"behold, thy King cometh unto thee: he is just, and having salvation; lowly, and riding upon an ass, and upon a colt the foal of an ass"* (9:9). Jesus fulfilled this prophecy completely (see Matthew 21:1-9), but He has been rejected by the multitudes. Thankfully, all who turn to Him have hope.

Do you feel like a prisoner held captive by Satan? There is hope in Jesus—*"Turn you to the strong hold."* He will set you free from bondage, protect you like a fortress, and bless you with heaven. You can expect abundant blessings. He assures, *"I will render double unto thee."*

DEC. 28   SMITTEN WITH SORROW   ZECHARIAH 11-12

"...they shall look upon me whom they have pierced, and they shall mourn for him, as one mourneth for his only son" (Zechariah 12:10).

Both advents of Christ are seen in today's reading. In chapter eleven, we read of Israel's rejection of Messiah when He came the first time. The Lord said, *"So they weighed for my price thirty pieces of silver"* (11:12). This, of course, refers to the amount that the chief priests gave Judas to betray Jesus—*"And they covenanted with him for thirty pieces of silver"* (Matthew 26:15). Their rejection of Christ led to a loss of the blessings He had planned to give them. Thus, the staffs Beauty and Bands were broken, which represented the pleasantness and unity God wanted to give them. Sin always leads to sorrow and division.

When Jesus returns to earth the second time and defends Jerusalem in the Battle of Armageddon, Israel will receive Him as their King. However, they will also realize that they had rejected and crucified their Messiah many years ago. They will be devastated and will mourn *"as one mourneth for his only son."* Israel's future sorrow is compared to the pain of grieving parents who lose their only child. It will be weighty.

This leaves us with a question to consider. Are we broken over our sin like they will be? It should grieve us when we betray our Lord.

DEC. 29   A HAPPY ENDING   ZECHARIAH 13-14

"And the LORD shall be king over all the earth: in that day shall there be one LORD, and his name one" (Zechariah 14:9).

Things will get worse for Israel before they will get better, but our text reminds us that one day, all will be well. The final two chapters provide great details about the Savior's suffering, Israel's trouble during the Tribulation, and Christ's millennial kingdom. Three facts are seen.

Consider the *crucifixion*. Once again, Jehovah foretold how Messiah would suffer—*"And one shall say unto him, What are these wounds in thine hands?"* (13:6). Truly, Jesus' hands were pierced when the nails fastened Him to the cross. Shortly before His betrayal, Jesus referred to Zechariah's prophecy in Matthew 26:31—*"smite the shepherd, and the sheep shall be scattered"* (13:7). Christ's death was clearly predicted.

Notice the *chaos*. So fierce will be the Tribulation that two-thirds of the people in the land will die (13:8). All nations will be gathered against Jerusalem with horrific violence (14:1-2), but Christ will return *"and fight against those nations"* (14:3) and secure a great victory.

Observe the *calm*—*"the LORD shall be king over all the earth."* The antichrist will be destroyed and Jesus will reign as the true King. Amen! When all seems bleak, we can anticipate a happy ending with Jesus.

| MALACHI 1-2 | DON'T BE IGNORANT | DEC. 30 |

"I have loved you, saith the LORD. Yet ye say, Wherein hast thou loved us?" (Malachi 1:2).

Malachi preached to the remnant that returned to Jerusalem after the seventy years of captivity and is the last of the prophets until John the Baptist. The priests and the people had drifted away from God and had become indifferent. In the first two chapters we see that God's love was not appreciated (1:2), God was not respected (1:6), sacrifices were unacceptable (1:7-12), people were tired of serving (1:13), the priests caused others to stumble (2:8), and many had corrupted their marriages (2:11-16). Sadly, the people were ignorant of their true condition.

Several times in this book, the Lord pointed out the sin of the people only to get a response similar to, "Who, me?" Their sin was bad, but their lackadaisical attitude about it made matters worse. When God corrects us, we should quickly admit our faults and not shrug them off.

Our text provides an example of showing contempt toward God. When He said, *"I have loved you,"* the Jews responded, *"Wherein hast thou loved us?"* The fact that He had allowed them to return from captivity proved His love, but they were willfully ignorant. Too often we take our blessings for granted and doubt God's love when He corrects us.

| MALACHI 3-4 | FAITHFUL IN DARK DAYS | DEC. 31 |

"Then they that feared the LORD spake often one to another: and the LORD hearkened, and heard it, and a book of remembrance was written before him for them...that thought upon his name" (Malachi 3:16).

The Lord continued to expose the sin of His people. When He called unto them, *"Return unto me, and I will return unto you,"* they acted as if they had done nothing wrong (3:7). They responded in a similar manner when confronted about stealing from God. Further, they revealed great hardheartedness, saying, *"It is vain to serve God"* (3:14). Despite the widespread complacency among God's people, some still feared the Lord. Our text provides hope for all who are faithful to Him.

First, have the right kind of *fear*. A remnant *"feared the LORD."* This refers to showing reverence for God. Though others disregarded the Lord and His commands, they loved Him and respected His Word.

Next, maintain good *fellowship*. The faithful *"spake often one to another"* and *"thought upon his* [God's] *name."* Spend time talking about the Lord with people who love Him. You will edify one another.

Finally, expect God's *favor*—*"the LORD hearkened...and a book of remembrance was written before him for them."* We may be living in dark days, but God notices your devotion to Him and will bless you!

Concluding Thoughts

I hope that your time reading through this portion of the Old Testament was as profitable and challenging as it was to me. While we considered hundreds of practical lessons together in this book, many more are waiting to be discovered. Truly, the Word of God is inexhaustible! I am sure that you saw some things in your daily Bible reading that we never even mentioned in this devotional. Isn't it great when God shows us something special in His Word?

Whether or not this was your first time reading through the books of the Law, History, or Prophets, I trust it will not be your last. The more you read God's Word, the more you will begin to see how each portion of the Bible fits together. Further, what we learn from the Old Testament can equip us to be better Christians. Consider Paul's exhortation about the writings of the Old Testament authors, *"For whatsoever things were written aforetime were written for our learning, that we through patience and comfort of the scriptures might have hope"* (Romans 15:4). The truths found in the Old Testament bring comfort and hope! Keep searching the Scriptures daily. You will not regret it.

If you choose to use *Morning Light* again in the coming year, it may help to solidify some of the lessons you have learned over this past year. To all who are looking for a similar book to use while reading through the New Testament, I recommend my first devotional, *Daily Light*. May the Lord bless you as you continue to meditate on His Word!

DAILY BIBLE READING SCHEDULE

	JANUARY		
DAY	NEW TESTAMENT	OLD TESTAMENT (A.M.)	OLD TESTAMENT (P.M.)
1	Matthew 1	Genesis 1-2	Job 1:1-12
2	Matthew 2	Genesis 3-4	Job 1:13-22
3	Matthew 3	Genesis 5-6	Job 2
4	Matthew 4	Genesis 7-8	Job 3
5	Matthew 5:1-20	Genesis 9-10	Job 4
6	Matthew 5:21-48	Genesis 11-12	Job 5
7	Matthew 6	Genesis 13-15	Job 6
8	Matthew 7	Genesis 16-17	Job 7
9	Matthew 8	Genesis 18-19	Job 8
10	Matthew 9:1-17	Genesis 20-21	Job 9
11	Matthew 9:18-38	Genesis 22-23	Job 10
12	Matthew 10:1-20	Genesis 24	Job 11
13	Matthew 10:21-42	Genesis 25-26	Job 12
14	Matthew 11	Genesis 27	Job 13
15	Matthew 12:1-21	Genesis 28-29	Job 14
16	Matthew 12:22-50	Genesis 30	Job 15
17	Matthew 13:1-30	Genesis 31	Job 16
18	Matthew 13:31-58	Genesis 32-33	Job 17
19	Matthew 14	Genesis 34-35	Job 18
20	Matthew 15:1-20	Genesis 36	Job 19
21	Matthew 15:21-39	Genesis 37-38	Job 20
22	Matthew 16	Genesis 39-40	Job 21
23	Matthew 17	Genesis 41	Job 22
24	Matthew 18:1-19	Genesis 42-43	Job 23
25	Matthew 18:20-35	Genesis 44-45	Job 24
26	Matthew 19	Genesis 46-47	Job 25
27	Matthew 20:1-16	Genesis 48-49	Job 26
28	Matthew 20:17-34	Genesis 50	Job 27
29	Matthew 21:1-22	Exodus 1-2	Job 28
30	Matthew 21:23-46	Exodus 3	Job 29
31	Matthew 22:1-22	Exodus 4-5	Job 30

DAILY BIBLE READING SCHEDULE

	FEBRUARY		
DAY	NEW TESTAMENT	OLD TESTAMENT (A.M.)	OLD TESTAMENT (P.M.)
1	Matthew 22:23-46	Exodus 6-7	Job 31
2	Matthew 23:1-22	Exodus 8-9	Job 32
3	Matthew 23:23-39	Exodus 10-11	Job 33
4	Matthew 24:1-25	Exodus 12	Job 34
5	Matthew 24:26-51	Exodus 13-14	Job 35
6	Matthew 25:1-30	Exodus 15-16	Job 36
7	Matthew 25:31-46	Exodus 17-18	Job 37
8	Matthew 26:1-30	Exodus 19-20	Job 38
9	Matthew 26:31-56	Exodus 21-22	Job 39
10	Matthew 26:57-75	Exodus 23-24	Job 40
11	Matthew 27:1-25	Exodus 25-26	Job 41
12	Matthew 27:26-44	Exodus 27-28	Job 42
13	Matthew 27:45-66	Exodus 29	Psalm 1
14	Matthew 28	Exodus 30-31	Psalm 2
15	Mark 1:1-20	Exodus 32-33	Psalm 3
16	Mark 1:21-45	Exodus 34-35	Psalm 4
17	Mark 2	Exodus 36	Psalm 5
18	Mark 3	Exodus 37-38	Psalm 6
19	Mark 4:1-20	Exodus 39	Psalm 7
20	Mark 4:21-41	Exodus 40	Psalm 8
21	Mark 5:1-20	Leviticus 1-2	Psalm 9
22	Mark 5:21-43	Leviticus 3-4	Psalm 10
23	Mark 6:1-29	Leviticus 5-6	Psalm 11
24	Mark 6:30-56	Leviticus 7	Psalm 12
25	Mark 7:1-19	Leviticus 8	Psalm 13
26	Mark 7:20-37	Leviticus 9-10	Psalm 14
27	Mark 8:1-21	Leviticus 11-12	Psalm 15
28	Mark 8:22-38	Leviticus 13	Psalm 16
29	Read Favorite Chapters		

Daily Bible Reading Schedule

Day	New Testament	Old Testament (A.M.)	Old Testament (P.M.)
		March	
1	Mark 9:1-29	Leviticus 14	Psalm 17
2	Mark 9:30-50	Leviticus 15-16	Psalm 18:1-26
3	Mark 10:1-27	Leviticus 17-18	Psalm 18:27-50
4	Mark 10:28-52	Leviticus 19-20	Psalm 19
5	Mark 11	Leviticus 21-22	Psalm 20
6	Mark 12:1-27	Leviticus 23-24	Psalm 21
7	Mark 12:28-44	Leviticus 25	Psalm 22:1-21
8	Mark 13	Leviticus 26	Psalm 22:22-31
9	Mark 14:1-26	Leviticus 27	Psalm 23
10	Mark 14:27-50	Numbers 1	Psalm 24
11	Mark 14:51-72	Numbers 2	Psalm 25
12	Mark 15:1-24	Numbers 3	Psalm 26
13	Mark 15:25-47	Numbers 4	Psalm 27
14	Mark 16	Numbers 5-6	Psalm 28
15	Luke 1:1-25	Numbers 7	Psalm 29
16	Luke 1:26-56	Numbers 8-9	Psalm 30
17	Luke 1:57-80	Numbers 10	Psalm 31:1-13
18	Luke 2:1-24	Numbers 11	Psalm 31:14-24
19	Luke 2:25-52	Numbers 12-13	Psalm 32
20	Luke 3	Numbers 14	Psalm 33:1-11
21	Luke 4:1-30	Numbers 15	Psalm 33:12-22
22	Luke 4:31-44	Numbers 16	Psalm 34:1-10
23	Luke 5	Numbers 17-18	Psalm 34:11-22
24	Luke 6:1-26	Numbers 19-20	Psalm 35:1-16
25	Luke 6:27-49	Numbers 21	Psalm 35:17-28
26	Luke 7:1-23	Numbers 22	Psalm 36
27	Luke 7:24-50	Numbers 23-25	Psalm 37:1-20
28	Luke 8:1-25	Numbers 26	Psalm 37:21-40
29	Luke 8:26-56	Numbers 27-28	Psalm 38:1-12
30	Luke 9:1-36	Numbers 29-30	Psalm 38:13-22
31	Luke 9:37-62	Numbers 31	Psalm 39

DAILY BIBLE READING SCHEDULE

	APRIL		
DAY	NEW TESTAMENT	OLD TESTAMENT (A.M.)	OLD TESTAMENT (P.M.)
1	Luke 10:1-22	Numbers 32	Psalm 40
2	Luke 10:23-42	Numbers 33-34	Psalm 41
3	Luke 11:1-28	Numbers 35-36	Psalm 42
4	Luke 11:29-54	Deuteronomy 1	Psalm 43
5	Luke 12:1-34	Deuteronomy 2-3	Psalm 44:1-14
6	Luke 12:35-59	Deuteronomy 4	Psalm 44:15-26
7	Luke 13	Deuteronomy 5-6	Psalm 45
8	Luke 14	Deuteronomy 7-8	Psalm 46
9	Luke 15	Deuteronomy 9-10	Psalm 47
10	Luke 16	Deuteronomy 11-12	Psalm 48
11	Luke 17	Deuteronomy 13-14	Psalm 49
12	Luke 18:1-17	Deuteronomy 15-16	Psalm 50
13	Luke 18:18-43	Deuteronomy 17-18	Psalm 51
14	Luke 19:1-27	Deuteronomy 19-21	Psalm 52
15	Luke 19:28-48	Deuteronomy 22-23	Psalm 53
16	Luke 20:1-26	Deuteronomy 24-25	Psalm 54
17	Luke 20:27-47	Deuteronomy 26-27	Psalm 55:1-11
18	Luke 21	Deuteronomy 28	Psalm 55:12-23
19	Luke 22:1-23	Deuteronomy 29-30	Psalm 56
20	Luke 22:24-46	Deuteronomy 31	Psalm 57
21	Luke 22:47-71	Deuteronomy 32	Psalm 58
22	Luke 23:1-26	Deuteronomy 33-34	Psalm 59
23	Luke 23:27-56	Joshua 1-2	Psalm 60
24	Luke 24:1-27	Joshua 3-5	Psalm 61
25	Luke 24:28-53	Joshua 6-7	Psalm 62
26	John 1:1-27	Joshua 8-9	Psalm 63
27	John 1:28-51	Joshua 10	Psalm 64
28	John 2	Joshua 11-12	Psalm 65
29	John 3	Joshua 13-14	Psalm 66
30	John 4:1-26	Joshua 15-16	Psalm 67

DAILY BIBLE READING SCHEDULE

	MAY		
DAY	NEW TESTAMENT	OLD TESTAMENT (A.M.)	OLD TESTAMENT (P.M.)
1	John 4:27-54	Joshua 17-18	Psalm 68:1-18
2	John 5:1-23	Joshua 19	Psalm 68:19-35
3	John 5:24-47	Joshua 20-21	Psalm 69:1-18
4	John 6:1-21	Joshua 22-23	Psalm 69:19-36
5	John 6:22-48	Joshua 24	Psalm 70
6	John 6:49-71	Judges 1-2	Psalm 71:1-13
7	John 7:1-27	Judges 3-4	Psalm 71:14-24
8	John 7:28-53	Judges 5-6	Psalm 72
9	John 8:1-20	Judges 7-8	Psalm 73:1-15
10	John 8:21-40	Judges 9	Psalm 73:16-28
11	John 8:41-59	Judges 10-11	Psalm 74
12	John 9:1-23	Judges 12-14	Psalm 75
13	John 9:24-41	Judges 15-16	Psalm 76
14	John 10:1-21	Judges 17-18	Psalm 77
15	John 10:22-42	Judges 19	Psalm 78:1-18
16	John 11:1-29	Judges 20	Psalm 78:19-36
17	John 11:30-57	Judges 21	Psalm 78:37-54
18	John 12:1-26	Ruth 1-2	Psalm 78:55-72
19	John 12:27-50	Ruth 3-4	Psalm 79
20	John 13:1-20	I Samuel 1-2	Psalm 80
21	John 13:21-38	I Samuel 3-4	Psalm 81
22	John 14	I Samuel 5-7	Psalm 82
23	John 15	I Samuel 8-9	Psalm 83
24	John 16:1-16	I Samuel 10-11	Psalm 84
25	John 16:17-33	I Samuel 12-13	Psalm 85
26	John 17	I Samuel 14	Psalm 86
27	John 18:1-18	I Samuel 15-16	Psalm 87
28	John 18:19-40	I Samuel 17	Psalm 88
29	John 19:1-22	I Samuel 18-19	Psalm 89:1-17
30	John 19:23-42	I Samuel 20-21	Psalm 89:18-34
31	John 20	I Samuel 22-23	Psalm 89:35-52

DAILY BIBLE READING SCHEDULE

DAY	NEW TESTAMENT	OLD TESTAMENT (A.M.)	OLD TESTAMENT (P.M.)
		JUNE	
1	John 21	I Samuel 24-25	Psalm 90
2	Acts 1	I Samuel 26-27	Psalm 91
3	Acts 2:1-21	I Samuel 28-29	Psalm 92
4	Acts 2:22-47	I Samuel 30-31	Psalm 93
5	Acts 3	II Samuel 1-2	Psalm 94:1-11
6	Acts 4:1-20	II Samuel 3-4	Psalm 94:12-23
7	Acts 4:21-37	II Samuel 5-6	Psalm 95
8	Acts 5:1-20	II Samuel 7-9	Psalm 96
9	Acts 5:21-42	II Samuel 10-11	Psalm 97
10	Acts 6	II Samuel 12-13	Psalm 98
11	Acts 7:1-19	II Samuel 14-15	Psalm 99
12	Acts 7:20-40	II Samuel 16-17	Psalm 100
13	Acts 7:41-60	II Samuel 18	Psalm 101
14	Acts 8:1-25	II Samuel 19	Psalm 102:1-11
15	Acts 8:26-40	II Samuel 20-21	Psalm 102:12-28
16	Acts 9:1-21	II Samuel 22	Psalm 103:1-12
17	Acts 9:22-43	II Samuel 23-24	Psalm 103:13-22
18	Acts 10:1-22	I Kings 1	Psalm 104:1-18
19	Acts 10:23-48	I Kings 2	Psalm 104:19-35
20	Acts 11	I Kings 3-4	Psalm 105:1-15
21	Acts 12	I Kings 5-6	Psalm 105:16-30
22	Acts 13:1-25	I Kings 7	Psalm 105:31-45
23	Acts 13:26-52	I Kings 8	Psalm 106:1-15
24	Acts 14	I Kings 9-10	Psalm 106:16-31
25	Acts 15:1-21	I Kings 11	Psalm 106:32-48
26	Acts 15:22-41	I Kings 12-13	Psalm 107:1-16
27	Acts 16:1-21	I Kings 14-15	Psalm 107:17-30
28	Acts 16:22-40	I Kings 16-17	Psalm 107:31-43
29	Acts 17:1-17	I Kings 18	Psalm 108
30	Acts 17:18-34	I Kings 19-20	Psalm 109:1-16

DAILY BIBLE READING SCHEDULE

DAY	NEW TESTAMENT	OLD TESTAMENT (A.M.)	OLD TESTAMENT (P.M.)
		JULY	
1	Acts 18:1-17	I Kings 21	Psalm 109:17-31
2	Acts 18:18-28	I Kings 22	Psalm 110
3	Acts 19:1-20	II Kings 1-2	Psalm 111
4	Acts 19:21-41	II Kings 3-4	Psalm 112
5	Acts 20:1-16	II Kings 5-6	Psalm 113
6	Acts 20:17-38	II Kings 7-8	Psalm 114
7	Acts 21:1-17	II Kings 9	Psalm 115
8	Acts 21:18-40	II Kings 10	Psalm 116
9	Acts 22	II Kings 11-12	Psalm 117
10	Acts 23	II Kings 13-14	Psalm 118:1-14
11	Acts 24	II Kings 15	Psalm 118:15-29
12	Acts 25	II Kings 16-17	Psalm 119:1-8
13	Acts 26	II Kings 18	Psalm 119:9-16
14	Acts 27:1-25	II Kings 19-20	Psalm 119:17-24
15	Acts 27:26-44	II Kings 21-22	Psalm 119:25-32
16	Acts 28:1-16	II Kings 23	Psalm 119:33-40
17	Acts 28:17-31	II Kings 24-25	Psalm 119:41-48
18	Romans 1:1-17	I Chronicles 1-2	Psalm 119:49-56
19	Romans 1:18-32	I Chronicles 3-4	Psalm 119:57-64
20	Romans 2	I Chronicles 5	Psalm 119:65-72
21	Romans 3:1-18	I Chronicles 6	Psalm 119:73-80
22	Romans 3:19-31	I Chronicles 7-8	Psalm 119:81-88
23	Romans 4	I Chronicles 9-10	Psalm 119:89-96
24	Romans 5	I Chronicles 11	Psalm 119:97-104
25	Romans 6	I Chronicles 12-13	Psalm 119:105-112
26	Romans 7	I Chronicles 14-15	Psalm 119:113-120
27	Romans 8:1-18	I Chronicles 16	Psalm 119:121-128
28	Romans 8:19-39	I Chronicles 17-18	Psalm 119:129-136
29	Romans 9:1-16	I Chronicles 19-21	Psalm 119:137-144
30	Romans 9:17-33	I Chronicles 22-23	Psalm 119:145-152
31	Romans 10	I Chronicles 24-25	Psalm 119:153-160

DAILY BIBLE READING SCHEDULE

DAY	NEW TESTAMENT	OLD TESTAMENT (A.M.)	OLD TESTAMENT (P.M.)
	AUGUST		
1	Romans 11:1-16	I Chronicles 26-27	Psalm 119:161-168
2	Romans 11:17-36	I Chronicles 28-29	Psalm 119:169-176
3	Romans 12	II Chronicles 1-2	Psalm 120
4	Romans 13	II Chronicles 3-5	Psalm 121
5	Romans 14	II Chronicles 6	Psalm 122
6	Romans 15:1-16	II Chronicles 7-8	Psalm 123
7	Romans 15:17-33	II Chronicles 9-10	Psalm 124
8	Romans 16	II Chronicles 11-12	Psalm 125
9	I Corinthians 1	II Chronicles 13-14	Psalm 126
10	I Corinthians 2	II Chronicles 15-17	Psalm 127
11	I Corinthians 3	II Chronicles 18-19	Psalm 128
12	I Corinthians 4	II Chronicles 20	Psalm 129
13	I Corinthians 5	II Chronicles 21-22	Psalm 130
14	I Corinthians 6	II Chronicles 23-24	Psalm 131
15	I Corinthians 7:1-20	II Chronicles 25-26	Psalm 132
16	I Corinthians 7:21-40	II Chronicles 27-28	Psalm 133
17	I Corinthians 8	II Chronicles 29	Psalm 134
18	I Corinthians 9	II Chronicles 30-31	Psalm 135
19	I Corinthians 10:1-17	II Chronicles 32	Psalm 136
20	I Corinthians 10:18-33	II Chronicles 33-34	Psalm 137
21	I Corinthians 11:1-16	II Chronicles 35-36	Psalm 138
22	I Corinthians 11:17-34	Ezra 1-2	Psalm 139:1-13
23	I Corinthians 12:1-13	Ezra 3-5	Psalm 139:14-24
24	I Corinthians 12:14-31	Ezra 6-7	Psalm 140
25	I Corinthians 13	Ezra 8-9	Psalm 141
26	I Corinthians 14:1-20	Ezra 10	Psalm 142
27	I Corinthians 14:21-40	Nehemiah 1-2	Psalm 143
28	I Corinthians 15:1-20	Nehemiah 3-4	Psalm 144
29	I Corinthians 15:21-40	Nehemiah 5-6	Psalm 145
30	I Corinthians 15:41-58	Nehemiah 7-8	Psalm 146
31	I Corinthians 16	Nehemiah 9	Psalm 147:1-11

DAILY BIBLE READING SCHEDULE

		SEPTEMBER	
DAY	NEW TESTAMENT	OLD TESTAMENT (A.M.)	OLD TESTAMENT (P.M.)
1	II Corinthians 1	Nehemiah 10-11	Psalm 147:12-20
2	II Corinthians 2	Nehemiah 12	Psalm 148
3	II Corinthians 3	Nehemiah 13	Psalm 149
4	II Corinthians 4	Esther 1-3	Psalm 150
5	II Corinthians 5	Esther 4-7	Proverbs 1:1-9
6	II Corinthians 6	Esther 8-10	Proverbs 1:10-19
7	II Corinthians 7	Isaiah 1-2	Proverbs 1:20-33
8	II Corinthians 8	Isaiah 3-5	Proverbs 2:1-11
9	II Corinthians 9	Isaiah 6-8	Proverbs 2:12-22
10	II Corinthians 10	Isaiah 9-10	Proverbs 3:1-10
11	II Corinthians 11:1-15	Isaiah 11-13	Proverbs 3:11-24
12	II Corinthians 11:16-33	Isaiah 14-16	Proverbs 3:25-35
13	II Corinthians 12	Isaiah 17-20	Proverbs 4:1-13
14	II Corinthians 13	Isaiah 21-23	Proverbs 4:14-27
15	Galatians 1	Isaiah 24-26	Proverbs 5:1-14
16	Galatians 2	Isaiah 27-29	Proverbs 5:15-23
17	Galatians 3	Isaiah 30-32	Proverbs 6:1-11
18	Galatians 4:1-16	Isaiah 33-35	Proverbs 6:12-22
19	Galatians 4:17-31	Isaiah 36-37	Proverbs 6:23-35
20	Galatians 5	Isaiah 38-40	Proverbs 7:1-12
21	Galatians 6	Isaiah 41-42	Proverbs 7:13-27
22	Ephesians 1	Isaiah 43-44	Proverbs 8:1-18
23	Ephesians 2	Isaiah 45-47	Proverbs 8:19-36
24	Ephesians 3	Isaiah 48-49	Proverbs 9:1-9
25	Ephesians 4:1-16	Isaiah 50-52	Proverbs 9:10-18
26	Ephesians 4:17-32	Isaiah 53-56	Proverbs 10:1-11
27	Ephesians 5:1-17	Isaiah 57-59	Proverbs 10:12-22
28	Ephesians 5:18-33	Isaiah 60-62	Proverbs 10:23-32
29	Ephesians 6	Isaiah 63-64	Proverbs 11:1-10
30	Philippians 1:1-14	Isaiah 65-66	Proverbs 11:11-20

Daily Bible Reading Schedule

		October	
Day	New Testament	Old Testament (A.M.)	Old Testament (P.M.)
1	Philippians 1:15-30	Jeremiah 1-2	Proverbs 11:21-31
2	Philippians 2:1-16	Jeremiah 3-4	Proverbs 12:1-10
3	Philippians 2:17-30	Jeremiah 5-6	Proverbs 12:11-19
4	Philippians 3	Jeremiah 7-8	Proverbs 12:20-28
5	Philippians 4	Jeremiah 9-10	Proverbs 13:1-8
6	Colossians 1	Jeremiah 11-12	Proverbs 13:9-17
7	Colossians 2	Jeremiah 13-14	Proverbs 13:18-25
8	Colossians 3	Jeremiah 15-16	Proverbs 14:1-11
9	Colossians 4	Jeremiah 17-18	Proverbs 14:12-23
10	I Thessalonians 1	Jeremiah 19-20	Proverbs 14:24-35
11	I Thessalonians 2	Jeremiah 21-22	Proverbs 15:1-11
12	I Thessalonians 3	Jeremiah 23	Proverbs 15:12-22
13	I Thessalonians 4	Jeremiah 24-25	Proverbs 15:23-33
14	I Thessalonians 5	Jeremiah 26-27	Proverbs 16:1-11
15	II Thessalonians 1	Jeremiah 28-29	Proverbs 16:12-22
16	II Thessalonians 2	Jeremiah 30-31	Proverbs 16:23-33
17	II Thessalonians 3	Jeremiah 32	Proverbs 17:1-9
18	I Timothy 1	Jeremiah 33-34	Proverbs 17:10-18
19	I Timothy 2	Jeremiah 35-36	Proverbs 17:19-28
20	I Timothy 3	Jeremiah 37-38	Proverbs 18:1-8
21	I Timothy 4	Jeremiah 39-40	Proverbs 18:9-16
22	I Timothy 5	Jeremiah 41-42	Proverbs 18:17-24
23	I Timothy 6	Jeremiah 43-44	Proverbs 19:1-9
24	II Timothy 1	Jeremiah 45-47	Proverbs 19:10-19
25	II Timothy 2	Jeremiah 48	Proverbs 19:20-29
26	II Timothy 3	Jeremiah 49	Proverbs 20:1-10
27	II Timothy 4	Jeremiah 50	Proverbs 20:11-20
28	Titus 1	Jeremiah 51	Proverbs 20:21-30
29	Titus 2	Jeremiah 52	Proverbs 21:1-10
30	Titus 3	Lamentations 1-2	Proverbs 21:11-20
31	Philemon	Lamentations 3	Proverbs 21:21-31

DAILY BIBLE READING SCHEDULE

DAY	NEW TESTAMENT	OLD TESTAMENT (A.M.)	OLD TESTAMENT (P.M.)
		NOVEMBER	
1	Hebrews 1	Lamentations 4-5	Proverbs 22:1-9
2	Hebrews 2	Ezekiel 1-2	Proverbs 22:10-19
3	Hebrews 3	Ezekiel 3-4	Proverbs 22:20-29
4	Hebrews 4	Ezekiel 5-6	Proverbs 23:1-12
5	Hebrews 5	Ezekiel 7-8	Proverbs 23:13-23
6	Hebrews 6	Ezekiel 9-10	Proverbs 23:24-35
7	Hebrews 7	Ezekiel 11-12	Proverbs 24:1-9
8	Hebrews 8	Ezekiel 13-15	Proverbs 24:10-18
9	Hebrews 9	Ezekiel 16	Proverbs 24:19-26
10	Hebrews 10:1-18	Ezekiel 17-18	Proverbs 24:27-34
11	Hebrews 10:19-39	Ezekiel 19-20	Proverbs 25:1-7
12	Hebrews 11:1-20	Ezekiel 21-22	Proverbs 25:8-14
13	Hebrews 11:21-40	Ezekiel 23	Proverbs 25:15-20
14	Hebrews 12	Ezekiel 24-25	Proverbs 25:21-28
15	Hebrews 13	Ezekiel 26-27	Proverbs 26:1-7
16	James 1	Ezekiel 28-29	Proverbs 26:8-12
17	James 2	Ezekiel 30-31	Proverbs 26:13-19
18	James 3	Ezekiel 32-33	Proverbs 26:20-28
19	James 4	Ezekiel 34-35	Proverbs 27:1-7
20	James 5	Ezekiel 36-37	Proverbs 27:8-14
21	I Peter 1	Ezekiel 38-39	Proverbs 27:15-21
22	I Peter 2	Ezekiel 40	Proverbs 27:22-27
23	I Peter 3	Ezekiel 41-42	Proverbs 28:1-7
24	I Peter 4	Ezekiel 43-44	Proverbs 28:8-14
25	I Peter 5	Ezekiel 45-46	Proverbs 28:15-21
26	II Peter 1	Ezekiel 47-48	Proverbs 28:22-28
27	II Peter 2	Daniel 1	Proverbs 29:1-7
28	II Peter 3	Daniel 2	Proverbs 29:8-14
29	I John 1	Daniel 3	Proverbs 29:15-21
30	I John 2:1-14	Daniel 4	Proverbs 29:22-27

DAILY BIBLE READING SCHEDULE

		DECEMBER	
DAY	NEW TESTAMENT	OLD TESTAMENT (A.M.)	OLD TESTAMENT (P.M.)
1	I John 2:15-29	Daniel 5-6	Proverbs 30:1-9
2	I John 3	Daniel 7-8	Proverbs 30:10-16
3	I John 4	Daniel 9-10	Proverbs 30:17-23
4	I John 5	Daniel 11-12	Proverbs 30:24-33
5	II John	Hosea 1-2	Proverbs 31:1-9
6	III John	Hosea 3-5	Proverbs 31:10-16
7	Jude	Hosea 6-8	Proverbs 31:17-23
8	Revelation 1	Hosea 9-11	Proverbs 31:24-31
9	Revelation 2:1-17	Hosea 12-14	Ecclesiastes 1
10	Revelation 2:18-29	Joel 1-2	Ecclesiastes 2:1-11
11	Revelation 3	Joel 3	Ecclesiastes 2:12-26
12	Revelation 4	Amos 1-3	Ecclesiastes 3:1-11
13	Revelation 5	Amos 4-6	Ecclesiastes 3:12-22
14	Revelation 6	Amos 7-9	Ecclesiastes 4
15	Revelation 7	Obadiah	Ecclesiastes 5
16	Revelation 8	Jonah 1-4	Ecclesiastes 6
17	Revelation 9	Micah 1-3	Ecclesiastes 7:1-15
18	Revelation 10	Micah 4-5	Ecclesiastes 7:16-29
19	Revelation 11	Micah 6-7	Ecclesiastes 8
20	Revelation 12	Nahum 1-3	Ecclesiastes 9
21	Revelation 13	Habakkuk 1-3	Ecclesiastes 10
22	Revelation 14	Zephaniah 1-3	Ecclesiastes 11
23	Revelation 15	Haggai 1-2	Ecclesiastes 12
24	Revelation 16	Zechariah 1-2	Song of Solomon 1
25	Matthew 1, Luke 2	Zechariah 3-5	Song of Solomon 2
26	Revelation 17	Zechariah 6-8	Song of Solomon 3
27	Revelation 18	Zechariah 9-10	Song of Solomon 4
28	Revelation 19	Zechariah 11-12	Song of Solomon 5
29	Revelation 20	Zechariah 13-14	Song of Solomon 6
30	Revelation 21	Malachi 1-2	Song of Solomon 7
31	Revelation 22	Malachi 3-4	Song of Solomon 8

SELECTED BIBLIOGRAPHY

Not all of the opinions and doctrines expressed in the books listed below represent the views of the author of this book.

Barnes, Albert, *Albert Barnes' Commentary on the Bible.* Bronson: Power BibleCD by Online Publishing, Inc., 2010.

Butler, John, *Analytical Bible Expositor: Daniel to Malachi.* Clinton: LBC Publications, 2013.

———. *Daniel: The Man of Loyalty.* Clinton: LBC Publications, 2007.

Henry, Matthew, *Matthew Henry's Commentary on the Whole Bible.* Bronson: Power BibleCD by Online Publishing, Inc., 2010.

Ironside, H. A., *Expository Notes on Ezekiel the Prophet.* Neptune: Loizeaux Brothers, 1949.

———. *Expository Notes on the Prophet Isaiah.* Lexington: Solid Christian Books, 2015.

———. *Notes on the Prophecy and Lamentation of Jeremiah.* Neptune: Loizeaux Brothers, 1906.

———. *Notes on the Minor Prophets.* Neptune: Loizeaux Brothers, 1909.

Jamieson, David, Andrew Fausset, and David Brown, *Jamieson, Fausset, and Brown's Commentary*. Bronson: Power BibleCD by Online Publishing, Inc., 2010.

Sorenson, David, *Understanding the Bible: An Independent Baptist Commentary*. Duluth: Northstar Ministries, 2008.

Strong, James, *Strong's Greek and Hebrew Dictionary*. Bronson: Power BibleCD by Online Publishing, Inc., 2010.

Webster, Noah, *Noah Webster's 1828 Dictionary of American English*. Franklin: e-Sword by Rick Meyers, 2000-2014. Digital Library.

ABOUT THE AUTHOR

Dave Olson became a Baptist preacher in 1993 and has served the Lord in many capacities since that time. After teaching in Bible college, heading up a Christian school, and serving as a pastor, God called Dave into missions. He and his family faithfully served the Lord as missionaries to Zambia, Africa for ten years until a series of ongoing health problems and life-threatening illnesses led to their return in 2012.

In early 2013, the Lord led Dave to focus on a writing ministry, and his books are now used at home and abroad. Dave's experience as an educator and preacher has uniquely equipped him to communicate God's truths to people from every walk of life. In addition to his writing ministry, Dave preaches in revivals, missions conferences, and special meetings across the country.

Visit www.help4Upublications.com for more titles.

Other Titles Available on www.help4Upublications.com

Nobody is exempt from heartaches and hardships. Even great heroes of the faith battled their emotions. Throughout the history of the world, people have battled grief, discouragement, fear, and anxiety. When handled correctly, trials can draw us closer to the Lord and build our faith. Learn how to see your trials as God sees them and react as He has instructed. When you do, you will see brighter days ahead! (188 pages)

Reading the Word of God is the best way to start your day, and *Daily Light* can make it easier! This book can be used for either personal or family devotions to provide practical insight for daily living. It embarks on a journey through the New Testament, including one thought from an assigned daily Scripture reading designed to share either a challenge or a promise for the day. (204 pages)

Trials and temptations take their toll on everyone. Thankfully, we can renew our minds and cleanse our hearts by meditating on the Word of God. Evening Light is a one-year devotional that includes practical thoughts from Job, Psalms, Proverbs, Ecclesiastes, and the Song of Songs. Determine to make Scripture meditation a part of your evening schedule. It will give you something to look forward to after a long day! (208 pages)

Have you ever wondered what God has to say about finances? It's time to learn the proven principles of Scripture concerning money management. Money by the Book provides Biblical solutions for you and your money. Chapters on contentment, giving, saving, getting out of debt, setting up a budget, teaching your children about money, how to reduce spending, and much more! *Money by the Book* is now being used as a textbook in some Bible colleges. (246 pages)

www.ingramcontent.com/pod-product-compliance
Lightning Source LLC
Chambersburg PA
CBHW070639050426
42451CB00008B/222